GOD'S MANY MANSIONS

by Michael Dennis

OZARK MOUNTAIN PUBLISHING

PO Box 754, Huntsville, AR 72740
800-935-0045 or 479-738-2348; fax 479-738-2448

For permission, serialization, condensation, adaptions, or for our catalog of other publications, write to Ozark Mountain Publishing, Inc., P.O. box 754, Huntsville, AR 72740, ATTN: Permissions Department.

Library of Congress Cataloging-in-Publication Data

Dennis, Michael, 1957-
  God's Many Mansions, by Michael Dennis
Michael has regular visits with beings from other worlds and dimensions to understand our purpose for being on this world and in this dimension.

1. Metaphysics   2. Other-worldly Beings   3. Life Issues   4. Channeling
I. Dennis, Michael, 1957-   II. Metaphysics   III. Title

Library of Congress Catalog Card Number: 2011935422

ISBN: 978-1-886940-23-9

Cover Art and Layout: www.noir33.com
Book set in: Times New Roman
Book Design: Julia Degan

Published by:

**OZARK
MOUNTAIN
PUBLISHING**

PO Box 754
Huntsville, AR 72740

WWW.OZARKMT.COM
Printed in the United States of America

CONTENTS

-In my Father's house are many mansions..."

John 14:2

ACKNOWLEDGEMENT

I wish to acknowledge several daring mavericks and metaphysical trailblazers—most of whom I have never met in person but would love to. Your provocative wonderful books contribute to the awakening of the inner wisdom of the soul. They invite us to enter the sacred, mysterious magical caverns of infinite human and spiritual potential wherein sacred knowing, wisdom, and many other gems and treasures lie. Your books have offered me soul-enriching intellectual, mental and spiritual company, and food for my hungry spirit.

Thank you for sharing your bountiful knowledge and life-changing, amazing experiences and for showing us that magic and miracles are as real today as they were thousands of years ago. You have taught in your own ways that the kingdom of heaven/God truly lies within.

By making the journey within, I have glimpsed the cosmic light of illumination, breathed the breath of oneness, and touched the cord of love that connects us all. You beloved trailblazers have taught me the need and value of remaining balanced and grounded on "terra firma," as well as the joyous fulfillment and many rewards that come from exploring near and distant unseen inner and outer realms.

You have boldly gone where only the most daring spiritual seekers venture to go. Namaste! I salute your inner light: Dolores Cannon, Shirley MacLaine, Neale Donald Walsch, Jane Roberts, Carl G. Jung, Shakti Gawain, Jean Houston, Solara, Jane Roberts, J. J. Dewey, Ken Carey, Mary Summer Rain, Lynn Andrews, Ceanne DeRohan, Almine, Richard Bach, Carlos Castenada, and Baba Ram Dass.

DEDICATION

I dedicate *God's Many Mansions* to all seekers on the path of ascension and enlightenment who realize that we have access to infinite knowledge. We also have help from many sources, beings, angels, and guides on many planes, dimensions, and other worlds, as well as from our own soul, higher self, and subconscious mind.

Let us be brave, daring, and bold and go where no one has gone before like the daring crew on the star fleet USS Enterprise on Star Trek! In time we shall all come full circle with our soul evolution and return to our beloved Creator Source. What a grand and glorious day that shall truly be!

PREFACE

Have you ever seen an angel or had an angelic visitation? I did and it changed my life. Have you ever had *other-worldly* visitors, been befriended by *the little people*, or benevolent ETs? I have had many such experiences from these *helpers* as I like to call them. They have shown me that there is more to us than our personality and ego and taught me that we are so much more than our despair, doubts, fears, and limitations.

The cosmos can literally become our playground when we connect with our higher self and make contact with our star family. Everyone has this capability. It is our gift and birthright from Creator Source along with the knowledge deep within our soul that can answer our every question. We can know our purpose for being here and what we have to do. We can be set on the right path and be relieved of our human burdens as light is shed upon life's deeper meanings.

As a matter of fact, one of our reasons for being here on the earth is to accomplish that often very challenging feat. I am very happy to say that these extraordinary, unusual experiences have completely transformed my life and taken away much of the loneliness that plagued me for so many years. I have learned that we are never alone. I invite you to meet some of my friends and teachers from this world, as well as some from other dimensions and worlds.

I am honored to have made their acquaintance and to be able to partake of their love and energy. I thank them one and all for their gifts, the profound knowledge they shared and their messages of hope and truth. They filled me with love and passion. With each contact I experienced profound respect for the sacredness, diversity, uniqueness, and beauty of all people and all life. They taught me to value and appreciate humor, the quest for ancient knowledge, and the seeking of answers for the mysteries that life presents to us. May their stories, lessons and teachings enrich, empower, and fill you with awe, wonder, hope, and a greater sense of purpose as they have me.

INTRODUCTION

I was inspired to share some of my paranormal and *other-worldly* experiences after reading Dolores Cannon's *Convoluted Universe* books. Her books brought me much comfort and companionship because I had had many paranormal and psychic experiences over the years. Unfortunately, I blocked most of them out of my conscious mind because they challenged my *normal* way of thinking and frightened me. Reading Dolores' books filled me with deep soul recognition, inspiration, nostalgia, and a sense of *coming home*.

One day my guide Dresda said, "Michael, there are many wonderful books which are helping people to awaken to their deeper knowing. They are reminding them that they have access to the *all-knowing*. You have access to the *all-knowing* as well. There is much knowledge and information deep inside you that needs to be brought forth to the light of day and shared."

Then I knew what I had to do. I could no longer remain in the metaphysical closet. I had to share my stories and experiences. A few were on tape, and I transcribed the tapes. Others I had written in notebooks. Still others were buried in my subconscious mind.

Hypnosis and regressions verify that the subconscious mind has access to most, if not, all knowledge. I have been hypnotized, as well as regressed, several times. Some of those experiences are included in this book. I was also trained by my teacher, Mary, many years ago to put myself into a type of trance where I can step through time and relive and retrieve my experiences that are not recorded or written down. This thought filled me with so much joy. It was like I had been a *half person* for so many years. Now, I was going to become a whole person again as I reacquainted myself with my subconscious. So many new doors would be opened to deeper and heightened levels of perception. During these times of heightened perceptions, portals would manifest in and outside of dream time, creating gateways to other dimensions and worlds. This would allow many advanced wise beings to come to me, as well as take me on spirit journeys for profound teachings and adventures.

After becoming a professional psychic in 1985, I was to learn that my guides were not done with me. I spent alot of time in meditation, and soon my perceptions began to stretch even more. I began receiving visits from a number of *other-worldly* beings from other dimensions and parallel universes. I had an encounter with a future self. One day I channeled some ancient beings who called themselves the *serpent people*. They spoke in deep guttural tones and said that they were pre-Egyptian. Channelings of other ETs followed. I confess that for a time I thought I was losing my mind. I did not speak of these experiences with my psychic friends, for none of them were involved with anything like that. They would have thought that these new endeavors were just too far out for them.

My psychic work now seemed normal and mundane compared to the new experiences and information coming in. Finally, it all became too overwhelming. I did have one person to confide in who also acted as my battery when I channeled. I wasn't sure what all was going on or what I was really tapping into. I had no framework into which I could place these unusual experiences, and I did not understand how I could be receptive to so many different energies and beings from so many places. It was like I had a direct hotline to the cosmos and could virtually contact endless beings. Unless it was a prearranged channeling, I never knew who would be coming to talk or what they would be talking about. Many beings would come for one visit, never to return. Others would return or show up if requested. They all came in the *white light* and expressed love, compassion, and a desire to be of service. I was always deeply impressed and moved after such encounters, and I came away with answers to questions and much beneficial enlightening information. I was very empowered by their showering of light, love, and blessings. After channeling these loving wise beings, I would be energized for days or weeks at a time.

Many channels are content to channel one entity or being. Jane Roberts channeled Seth and wrote the Seth books. Jach Pursel channeled Lazaris. J.Z. Knight channeled Ramtha. Lee Carroll channeled the Kryon books. One entity would provide enough information to fill several books. How was it that I could hear from so many beings? What is the purpose? I had considered being hypnotized and having my subconscious answer those questions, but I think I was afraid of what I might be told.

I wonder how many people are having their own profound spiritual experiences, visions, and dreams in the daytime without the need to be put under by a hypnotherapist or regressionist? I wonder how many people who are opening up to other realms and dimensions then become confused or frightened and close the door to further experiences? And how many more are coming out of the metaphysical closet and embracing metaphysics and the paranormal as we move into the new era? The numbers are growing, and more stories are coming forth. What a delight it is to hear and to share stories with our soul family.

My spiritual teacher, Mary, told me many years ago, "Michael, I am going to teach you how to achieve altered states via a type of conscious trance you can enter at will. This will enable you to access information not available to the ordinary conscious mind. You will be able to recall your early psychic experiences and much more."

We accomplished this by meditation and various psychic mind-expanding and perceptual-shifting exercises.

I am no longer frightened or haunted by all of the visitors I have had over the years. They imparted so much wisdom and knowledge to me. They taught me that we are never alone and that the call for help always compels the response. My life is a living testimony that almost anyone can overcome childhood abuse and achieve happiness and success. My visitors and teachers showed me that there is so much more to us than we can begin to fathom or scarcely imagine. There is so much more to the soul and psyche and so much information inside us that we can tap to learn more about who we truly are and our marvelous potential. There are many ways to access that unlimited information: hypnosis, channeling, creative and automatic writing, art, music, meditation, dream interpretation, etc.

We are connected to all life, to each other, to our space brothers and sisters, and to beings on countless realms, universes, and dimensions. Not only is such contact possible, it is taking place more frequently as we ascend to higher consciousness and move to a new age. May the sense of being *alone* that accounts for so much loneliness and alienation be replaced by a sense of *all-one,* for that is truly who we are. We are each part of the *All One—the Great All That Is*.

Most of my life I have been aware and attuned to the *other world* as I refer to the realm of the psychic and the paranormal. A psychologist or psychiatrist might say that due to a troubled childhood and my need to escape the terrible goings on at home that I retreated into my inner world and fabricated all of the beings and spirits that I made contact with. I admit that my hostile and dysfunctional *outer world* living circumstances could contribute to my seeking inner relief and solace, but it was not imaginary realms that I began to explore. Instead, I believe that I came into this lifetime with an innate ability to step through portals to other realms. It is just how I'm built. I've done it most of my life. Not having an easy home life just made it easier and gave me more motivation to tap into the spiritual and other-worldly realms.

During those lonely years of my childhood and many of my adult years, my other-worldly friends proved to me that we are never alone. No matter how dark the night of the soul may be or how lost, abandoned, or desperate we may feel, there are angels and many other celestial and other-worldly beings always watching over us. Our call compels their loving response. Without my faith in God, angels, my guides and the precious other-worldly *visitors*, I could not have survived all the terrible things going on around me. They have befriended me for many years and have promised to continue to do so for the duration of this lifetime.

Why do I speak these words confidently? Because I know that things are never as they appear. There is meaning and purpose to our lives even when we are not aware of it. Obstacles often occur in order to wake us and shake us up so that we may enter the vast and grand domains of the soul, spirit, our subconscious, and even the universal collective unconscious mind that Jung speaks of which connects us to everyone and everything. Within our soul and being exist the knowledge, wisdom, strength and resources to liberate us.

At the age of thirteen, I was blessed with an angelic visitation in the back yard. A beautiful radiant angel predicted that I would get away from the horrible life at home. I would attend college and help many people with my gifts and knowledge. That angelic visitation story is told in the introduction of my book *Halfway to Heaven*. I weep tears of joy every time I think about the precious angel who visited me so many years ago, and I weep tears of sorrow for every soul who feels abandoned and alone.

I pray that the sorrowful ones will discover the ray of hope that glimmers in their soul. For as the gospel song "Pass It On" goes, "It only takes a spark to get a fire a going." Reaching out for help will begin the healing process, for the call truly compels the response. Beloved Jesus the Christ (Lord Sananda) stated that "In my Father's house are many mansions." The *other-worldly* beings inhabit some of these mansions.

As the old saying goes, "The sky is the limit."

Let us remember this and constantly reach out more and dream bigger. My motto is *Dare to dream because dreams come true*. It is time to share my *other stories*. If one person can relate to and derive some satisfaction and comfort from my book, then I have served my purpose in writing it.

CHAPTER ONE

A PROPHECY FROM A SEER

I believe that we are all psychic to some degree. Most people have memories and stories whether they have shared them or not. For example, we think of someone, and the phone rings. As a matter of fact, just a few minutes ago I was thinking about my friend Arielle in Indianapolis, IN. I was about to pick up the phone and call her when my computer bell announced incoming mail. The email was from Arielle. I believe that this kind of telepathic communication happens far more frequently than we may realize.

I have been psychic most of my life and able to tune into the spirit realms. I recall the words of my spiritual teacher Mary many years ago: "Michael, you are extremely sensitive and receptive to psychic energy and the spiritual realms. With your experience with hypnosis, you are an excellent subject who is able to enter deep levels of trance. You can meditate and put yourself in altered states to retrieve any information that you want to access. I can coach you to get you started."

I found the idea intriguing and fondly recalled a stage hypnosis demonstration I witnessed in high school. I recalled being put under by the mentalist, The Amazing Kreskin, the summer of my freshman year of college. My music teacher put us under in a music therapy class, and so did my girlfriend Martina a few times after the class.

I can enter hypnotic and altered states of mind where I can recall vivid childhood, as well as past life memories. One strong memory I cherish is when I was learning to talk. Some of the first words that came from my lips were not mama or dadda, but "feny faces." It took a while for me to catch on to accurately pronouncing words, but what I was trying to say was "friendly faces." I would look up and see different faces and spirits smiling and waving to me. I'd laugh and point my fingers in the air and repeat "Feny faces. Feny faces."

"Who are you talking to?" my mother would ask, laughing. "Do you have an imaginary friend?" She thought it was amusing although she never figured out that her little boy was seeing and trying to talk to spirits that nobody else could see.

Those early carefree times were short-lived. My father would make fun of me and tell me to stop acting stupid. For a long time my "feny faces" disappeared, and I did not talk about them anymore. I would think about them sometimes and miss them but they had left. On a soul level I may have asked them to leave, being fearful of what my father might say or do. He was extremely volatile and had a temper.

My father had his first nervous breakdown when I was three. I recall Mom running out the door screaming, "He is going to kill me! He is going to kill me!"

He flipped out and had a pistol and was screaming and threatening to kill her. He spent the next six weeks at Our Lady of Peace mental hospital in Louisville, Kentucky. Dad flipped out many more times over the years and would spend more time in the "loony house," as my younger brother refers to mental hospitals. I never told anybody about my "feny faces," but I never forgot them.

To get away from the turmoil and constant drinking and fighting at home, I got involved with a local Baptist church when I was eleven years old. I had a hunger and insatiable curiosity for spiritual knowledge even back then. About a year later, an eccentric woman began coming to the Sunday morning services. Her name was Pansy Parker. She had greasy straggly gray hair, and her clothes were tattered. She always gave a testimonial, and sometimes her head and body shook. It was hard to make out her words.

Some of the church ladies would whisper amongst themselves and several times I heard this or that one say,

"There goes that Pansy Parker again. She's just a strange, crazy old woman who babbles on about nothing."

Pansy ignored them, and she always made it a point to gaze in my direction. I would get goose bumps and shivers—then look away, embarrassed.

When we participated in the *hand shaking* ritual, Pansy always made it a point to hold my hand a little longer than usual, and she looked deeply into my eyes. My heart would quiver. My knees shook and my face turned red as a beet.

One Sunday, a lady shouted, "Praise the Lord!" and began speaking in tongues. The people were spellbound because this seldom happened at our church. Pansy took my hand and motioned for me to step back. She reached into her pocket and took out something. Then she moved closer to my face.

"Michael, God has given you many talents." She pointed to my head. "Voices speak to you, and you see spirit faces. You must never be afraid or ashamed of this gift. Be very careful who you speak to, for most people will not understand you. They will think you funny in the head like Pansy," she said, smiling.

"You need to know that God and his angels will always watch over you in hard times ahead. God has children all over the cosmos, and they not all look like we humans do. Some are much more advanced and spiritual than people down here. I know you look at stars a lot. This is because you are a star child. Jesus said, 'In my father's house are many mansions.' Your true origin is far from here as is mine and some other people you will meet later on. Michael, you are going to meet some *sky people* in the future. God and Spirit are going to give you visions and show you things about people—good things to help them feel close to God and the angels. Your words will comfort and give assurance that they are not alone, and there is help for them. You are going to help a lot of people with your gifts."

Then Pansy let go of my hand. She had placed a ten dollar bill in it. I nodded and tried to give it back, but she whispered, "Michael, this money is a token sign that God and the angels will always take care of you. You think of Pansy Parker when you hear from *sky people*," she said, giving me a wink.

Needless to say, I was quite taken aback and flabbergasted. What made me sad is that I knew there was no one who would understand what Pansy had said. I was not even sure that I did. And how did she know that I had seen spirit faces? I had blocked that out and forgotten those early memories. That experience in church sent my mind reeling, and I had questions I wanted to ask Pansy. I wrote them down and hid my notebook in my dresser drawer. I tried to figure out a way to have a few moments with Pansy without arousing suspicion. It never became an issue because Pansy Parker never returned to my church after that little talk with me. I kept the ten dollar bill for a long time to remind me that I was not losing my mind nor making up the experience with Pansy.

Looking back so many years later, I wonder if Pansy Parker might have been an earth angel who came to my church those few times. Had she come there specifically to deliver that message of hope to me? Because once she delivered her message she never returned. Perhaps I shall never know. One thing is for certain: I shall always remember Pansy Parker fondly. I often give gratitude for the gift of hope that she gave me. That remembrance and her comforting, encouraging words would help get me through some very challenging and difficult times.

CHAPTER TWO

MY SECOND ANGELIC VISITATION

I believe that our beloved Creator, Great Spirit/All That Is/God has many messengers, and some of them are angels. We've all read or heard stories of angelic visitations and been inspired by them. Have you ever wondered if angels can and do make contact with people in the modern era of the 21st century? Have you ever had any angelic visitations or known anyone who has?

In light of this, I am not surprised that an angel visited me in the back yard when I was thirteen years old. Well, I certainly was surprised when it happened—and then to have a second angelic visitation two years later. That may seem incredulous, but it happened. Looking back over the years, I know that it was all part of my life plan. Now I would like to share the story of that second, magical life-changing angelic visitation when I was fifteen years old.

The year was 1973, and it was during the summer season when the angel came to me. I was living in my third foster home in Big Clifty, Kentucky, a small town about twenty miles south of Elizabethtown. I was a sophomore at Clarkson High School. On Saturdays when the weather permitted, I'd roam the fields behind the house. When it was warm, I'd find a spot with soft thick grass and lie down and stare at the sky and clouds. One day I had a spontaneous urge to move my arms like we do when we make snow angels. I have always been drawn to angels and have quite a collection of angel pictures and figurines. I closed my eyes and drifted into a reverie.

A few minutes later I woke up, startled by some kind of flapping noise. I thought that a buzzard or a big bird had landed next to me. I rubbed my eyes several times and then looked a few feet in front of me. Standing there encased in a golden glow was a very beautiful woman. My heart started racing, and my knees began to shake. I gulped and when I tried to speak, all that came out was a tiny whimper.

The golden glow slowly dimmed until it was gone, but there was still a radiance about the woman. She was petite, and her eyes were the most beautiful blue I had ever seen. They seemed to be a hue I had never seen before. Her shimmering hair was long and golden. She wore a violet robe, and a tiara of what looked to be glittering, sparkling diamonds rested on her head. Speechless, I sat frozen and stared at her. All I could do was marvel in her regal and majestic beauty and presence.

Finally, in a shaky voice I said, "Am I dreaming?"

She nodded her head and whispered the word. "No."

I stammered the words, "Are you an angel?"

"Yes, Michael, I am," she said softly. "I know that you have been having a hard time, so I was sent to pay you a visit. You are a deep, spiritual, and open-minded person which makes it easier for an occurrence such as this to take place. You have always believed in angels, and secretly in your heart you have been asking to see one—or *another* one, shall I say? I am aware of the angel who visited you two years ago. She and I are very close. We are somewhat like sisters to put it in terms that you can understand although we were not given birth like humans are. Before I share my messages with you I want to listen to you. Please tell me what has been happening in your life."

I was so moved by her smile and compassionate gentle nature that I almost cried.

"When you go back to heaven, could you please give the sweet angel who came to me two years ago my greetings?"

"I shall be very happy to do that for you."

"I have thought about her often since the visit. I am embarrassed to admit it, but there were times when I tried to forget about her. To think about her made me want to see her again. I missed her and wanted to go where she lived. The sadness was so overwhelming at times that I tried to block her out of my mind. I had nobody to talk to about her. Still, I never forgot her. To behold such a beautiful creation of God and to be blessed with messages from her is something I am eternally grateful for. I will never forget her."

The angel reached for my hand. "Michael, I understand. If you accomplish everything you set out to do in this life, one of your rewards is that you will see her again. This should motivate you and give you something to look forward to."

"Thank you. The angel gave me so much hope when she said I would get away from my horrible home life, and I'd go to college and help many people. She also said that I had a lot of challenges to overcome, but they would serve to make me stronger. Sometimes her prophecy was all that kept me going and not falling into despair."

"I am very happy to be away from my cruel father, but I have learned that getting away from him does not keep my problems away. Our problems go with us wherever we are. We have to deal with them and try to somehow work them out. This is my third foster home. I have so many emotional problems. Sometimes I find it difficult to be on the earth. I don't feel like I belong here, and I sometimes have suicide fantasies. I came close to jumping out of a two story window at my first foster home."

"I think my other two foster families sensed how troubled I am. They felt like they couldn't do anything to help me. They thought I spent too much time alone and stayed in my room too much. I fight the depression, but sometimes it just takes over and seems to choke the very life out of me. I guess my foster families concluded that I was one screwed up, troubled boy, and they decided to send me on my way so they could foster another child whom they could help. I have been trying so hard to make things work out here with the Samuels."

"I try so hard to fit in and belong. My foster brother Ron and I are the same age. He seems so together. Everyone at school and church likes him. He is my hero. He and his younger brother Gary are very involved with sports. I play basketball, football, and baseball with them even though I am not very good at any of them. Ron tries to coach and help me."

"I buy baseball cards and have memorized the baseball players of the Cincinnati Reds because that is Ron's favorite ball team. When my foster mother bought me a ball glove for my fifteenth birthday, I wrote Dennis Samuels on it instead of my last name because that was their last name."

"I imagine myself as Dennis Samuels, and I feel good for a while, but it never lasts. When the cousins and relatives come around, I always feel awkward and out of place. They try to include me in activities and I try to participate, but I always know that I can never be a Dennis Samuels or a Dennis anybody else. I feel like the misfit, Hermie, the elf, in *Rudolph the Red-Nosed Reindeer*. I fear I will never fit in anywhere."

The angel looked at me intently, her eyes full of love and compassion. I even thought I saw a tear trickle down her cheek.

"Michael, you have had a hard way to go, and I am sorry for that. Part of the reason for your feeling out of place and like a misfit is that you are more of an artist at heart instead of an athlete. And yes, part of it is from living with people and families you have never known before. I know that you like to write poetry, stories, and songs. You much prefer artistic pursuits to playing ball. I am aware that your father berated and discouraged you from reading books. He'd make fun of you and say you needed to play sports with other boys instead of keeping your nose stuck in a book all of the time."

"Those were his exact words."

"Your father's cruel words hurt you deeply and made you afraid of sharing your poems and songs because you didn't want to risk ridicule and being made fun of again."

"It is like I lead a double life. I keep up with my class work and make good grades. I play sports with Ron, Gary, and some of their cousins and friends. Then there is the spiritual and religious aspect of living with the Samuels. My foster mother, Melinda, is very religious. We go to church every

Sunday, and she can get real emotional in her testimonials. Sometimes she cries, shouts, carries on, and gets hysterical in expressing her jubilation and love for her savior, Jesus Christ, as she puts it. I am not offended or bothered by her behavior."

"To each his/her own is my motto. I derive some comfort from the church services, but something is missing. I can never talk to anyone about some of the, how shall I say, more personal and spiritual experiences I have had. They would not believe me. They might even accuse me of witchcraft or something if I talk about visions I have had or my psychic impressions, precognition, dreams and other experiences."

"I see why you feel the need to keep quiet. Michael, there is another reason for the deep loneliness and the feeling that you are a misfit, and by the way, it has nothing to do with being in foster homes."

I looked up at her in surprise.

"Really? What do you mean?"

"Michael, I know about an unusual and special experience you had in church a couple of years ago. You have even tried to convince yourself that it never happened although you know in your heart and soul that it did. A special woman gave you some wonderful messages. She also told you that you will see some *sky people* in the future, and these visits will change your life and give you some much needed direction."

"*Sky people*," I repeated. "That rings a bell and sounds familiar. Yes, I recall. An unusual woman named Pansy Parker told me one day at church that I would meet some sky people. I have wondered for years if she might have been an earth angel. 'Is this possible?' I would ask myself sometimes. Other times I would try to deny that anything happened."

"Not only is it possible, it happens far more frequently than you might imagine. Certain evolved souls are capable of taking on angelic or human form when it enables them to accomplish a certain task and mission."

I so much wanted to ask her if she were Pansy Parker, but something kept me from it, and to my disappointment, she did not offer any information. I may never have the answer to that question and perhaps I am not meant to.

We were quiet a few moments. Then she continued. "Michael, the special lady was correct in telling you that you would meet some *sky people* in the future, but she left something out because you were not yet ready to hear it. There are many beings who are well-aware of a deep aching loneliness that has been haunting you and others like you for a very long time. You have always been a star gazer, and you become wistful and lonely when you look at the stars. Michael, I am here to inform you that part of your loneliness is because *you* are a *sky person*. Yes, Michael, *you* are a star child. Your origins are far away on distant realms. You have spent many lifetimes on those distant realms, and parts of your soul essence dwells on those realms. You visit many of them in dream time and on spirit and star journeys, but you forget the visits when you awake. This is one reason why your depressions are worse in the mornings and why mornings are the hardest time of the day for you. It also explains how you sometimes use sleep to escape your unhappy life. You are literally 'getting away' as your soul takes flight to many places."

"No one is ever alone. There are many angels and helpers you can call upon. There are many beings from other dimensions who will pay you a visit. You will write of your visits and journeys. One day you will share your experiences which will form the base for spiritual books. These books will help a lot of people who also feel this deep loneliness that you experience. You must learn not to deny or try to avoid your deeper spiritual experiences but to embrace and accept them. You are a very old soul with much to offer the world. You also have a lot of healing to undergo. Like the other angel assured you, I promise you that although it may not seem or feel like it, your problems and challenges are going to make you stronger. They are not going to break you. You will be a much more powerful healer and counselor due to all that you have endured and will continue to go through."

"You are going to heal and come to experience and know love and joy that few people ever do. For every tear that you shed and every song of sorrow and sadness that you play on your little record player as you yearn for something you cannot quite name, you will sing and write poems, songs, and stories of joy. You will perform before groups, and people will be moved by your voice and the passion that comes out in your performing."

I smiled. "I do love to sing. People tell me I have a good voice."

"You have a glorious future ahead of you."

"I do believe that I am here to help people, but sometimes I doubt. If I can't even get my own life together then how can I help anybody else?"

"You will overcome your obstacles—all of them. This I promise you, Michael. I have seen it. It is your destiny. I know you are having a hard time, but please take my words on faith and believe me. Think of these words when the despair and suicidal thoughts enter your mind."

"Your *sky friends* and the beings you will encounter are your friends. They love and care for you. They can help you not to feel so alone and like a misfit. Many of them are waiting to pay you a visit when the time is right. You will have many stories to tell. I already know the title of the book, but your destiny must unfold and things will happen when the time is right. For now, take things one day at a time. Perform your earth duties and deal with the people in your life. Make time for recreation and for your writing. Writing is a strong skill that you possess from many lifetimes. I encourage you to write more in your journals. This will hone and refine your writing skills that you will need in the years ahead."

"I was compelled to take up typing when I was in the eighth grade. It's like part of me knew that I would be writing."

"That is true. Along with making time for your studies and your writing, always continue to star-gaze and spend time in nature. You just never know what new friends will show up. I must take my leave now. Michael, please do not forget me or the words that I have spoken to you today. I suggest that you go back to your room and take some notes while our visit is still fresh in your mind. It will give you comfort in the days ahead."

"May I ask what your name is?"

"I have many names, but for you I shall be Morielle. Goodbye, Michael. You are a very special soul. Everybody is, but there is a tenderness and innocence about you that endears many to you and will continue to do so all of your life. I am happy to tell you that not only are you going to meet some fascinating beings and *sky friends*, you are also going to meet some wonderful, passionate, and brilliant spiritual seekers and teachers from all walks of life. You will teach them things, and they will teach you things and help you get established in your work and mission. Do not try to force any encounters. Just follow your intuition and inner guidance and know that you will meet them when the time is right."

Morielle stepped closer. I could have sworn that her feet were several inches off the ground. She gently touched my face with her left hand. The golden glow suddenly returned and warmth emanated from her hand. It felt like tiny electrical impulses were surging through my entire body. The energy was so intense that I almost fell backwards. Every cell in my body seemed to vibrate. It was such an ecstatic sensation that it was a struggle not to cry. It felt like my body was rising in the air. My soul wanted to soar to the heavens. I wanted to go with Morielle. I wanted to leave this earth and never come back.

I know that she read my thoughts because she nodded her head and softly said, "It is not time. After you make your transition, you can visit me and the other angels. Goodbye for now," she said. Then she disappeared.

I have thought about Morielle from time to time over the years, but never have I relived her visit with such vivid recall until I decided to include her angelic visitation in this book. When I feel the despair and depression coming on, I read my notes and I pray, knowing that it will pass. I remind myself of my duties and responsibilities on the earth and my mission and soul contracts to be of service to humanity. This and the promise of my rewards when I complete my duties are what keep me going.

CHAPTER THREE

MYSTERIOUS NIGHT

In 1974 when I was a senior at Bullitt Central High School in Shepherdsville, Kentucky, and living in my fourth foster home near Brooks, Kentucky, we had a very eccentric neighbor. Her name was Miss Howard, and I felt very drawn to her and yet uneasy around her. In this chapter, I will share a story about an amazing experience and encounter I had with this remarkable, unusual woman one summer evening before I left for college.

The means by which this story is told is based on my journal notes and my memories. With my notes and memories I wrote this story for an English class assignment my freshman year at Berea College in Berea, Kentucky. After I went to college, I still found myself frequently thinking about Miss Howard, our connection, and the powerful way she affected me. This later culminated in one of the most intriguing paranormal encounters I have ever experienced.

The freshman English class assignment was the perfect push I needed to share my story, which I had been wanting to write but could never seem to get around to actually doing it. I think that part of me was still rather blown away by what had taken place that mysterious night, and looking back, perhaps I was even a little afraid to allow myself to relive it. I sometimes wondered if maybe the experience needed to simply remain a cherished personal memory. Besides, who would believe it anyhow when there were times I even doubted that it happened?

As open-minded, insatiably curious, and drawn to unusual psychic phenomena as I am, there are still times when I can be overwhelmed, and I sometimes doubt what my heart and soul know to be true. I have come to accept that sometimes I have to pull back and assimilate and integrate what I experience. I think that ultimately things happen in their own time and when we are ready. That evening with Miss Howard was a lot for me to take in and absorb. Yet another part of me accepted and resonated to everything she told and taught me. I think that we are all complex beings to some extent, and it's common to have different sides that may be completely contradictory. I believe that part of the *individuation* process or integrating the subconscious and conscious elements of our being, as the Jungians refer to it, is learning to accept all our different sides. To illustrate this point, I will share a personal story. I recall telling a friend one day that human love is just too much for me to handle.

"I have known so much disappointment and hurt that I pretty much think that I am done with *human* love—at least for this lifetime."

"Michael, I believe that you need to keep an open mind and heart. I feel that you are far from being 'done with human love' as you put it."

A few days later in the bathroom, of all places, I heard the words, "The old me is dying. The new me is being born. You are such a gift to me—dawn's kiss to the morn."

I was so shocked that I went to my computer and wrote an entire poem. Then another. More followed. Soon I had enough new poems for a book of nearly two hundred love poems. *Dawn's Kiss* was published in May of 2009.

In view of the fact that we have different sides and sub-personalities, which can be completely at odds with each other almost as if we were completely different people at times, it is not surprising that I would fear and be fascinated by my neighbor, Miss Howard. I have heard that fear can be a mighty teacher for us. One thing about me is that I am not a person to allow fear or hesitation to keep me in the grips of procrastination for too long. I have learned that when something pushes our buttons and unsettles us, there is usually something for us to learn from it. Otherwise, why would we be bothered or uncomfortable?

Looking back, I see that everything happened in divine timing just as it was meant to when it came to telling this story. In my freshman English composition class, the assistant professor wanted to find out how skillful we were expressing the English language, as well as how we handled punctuation, grammar, and sentence and paragraph structuring. The means to do so was to have us write. I recall that first day in class as though it were yesterday. Written on the chalkboard was our first assignment: In your own words write a story of someone who has strongly influenced you and made a positive difference in your life. The minimum page count is three. There is no maximum page count. Feel free to let your muse write away! Little did my professor know how I was about to take her up on her offer. Looking back, I snicker, thinking that my story may have caused her to create a maximum page limit to the stories she assigned. My story, *Mysterious Night*, turned out to be some twenty-five pages long!

Although many of my stories and journals have managed to disappear over the years, *Mysterious Night* has not. I believe it was meant to be included in this book just as I believe that people enter and exit our lives for reasons. We give and teach each other whatever we agreed upon when we created and signed our karmic contracts before we are born.

Some of our deepest and most powerful connections and teachers are people who we initially may not like or people we may find ourselves uncomfortable and uneasy around. This is often because they mirror some part of us we are not consciously aware of or willing to accept. Sometimes such people can shed insight and help us come to accept and understand these other parts of our self. Such was to happen to me as a result of meeting Miss Howard. As open-minded as I am to the paranormal, psychic, and spiritual realms, my experience with this unusual woman proved that there were even more mind-expanding experiences waiting to stretch my belief system and to broaden my horizon.

This seems to be the story of my life. It is probably the story of all of our lives. Our soul, higher self, and guides want to continually expand and stretch our being so we can take in more of Creator Source's light and move forward in our evolution and ascension. Now on with *Mysterious Night*.

Something about the old woman perturbed me. She had a way of staring at me that made me feel she wanted something. I had no idea what and no intention of finding out. I kept as far away from her as I could, which wasn't easy since she was our neighbor. In spite of the nuclear family age of the 21st century, Veronica's (my foster mother) philosophy was that neighbors were like an extended family. That meant she expected me to be nice to our neighbors, which in her book meant checking up on them and offering help from time to time, especially the ones who lived alone. In our case, we only had one neighbor who lived alone: Miss Howard.

I don't think Miss Howard ever blinked. Her black eyes seemed to pierce right through my soul, and I felt that she could read my thoughts. She lived three houses down from ours. The strange thing is how she seemed to know when I would be going for a walk. It's not like I had a usual time. On weekends I pretty much took off whenever I pleased. Veronica knew that I was a loner. She had no fear of me getting into trouble. I preferred being outside in nature and roaming the fields to being around people.

Shortly after I moved into the home of my new foster family, the Blivens, some of the neighbors commented on a woman in the neighborhood. They said she was strange and was a witch. My foster mother, Veronica Blivens, denied their outrageous claims, insisting that Miss Howard was one of the nicest old ladies one could ever know.

One day while listening to a couple of the boys badger Miss Howard, I interrupted their rambling insults. "Maybe Miss Howard is a witch but so what? Aren't there good witches?"

When I walked past her house, she was often standing in front of a second story window, looking at me as though expecting me. When I looked at her, she'd burst into a big smile and wave at me. Chills would go all through me, and I'd get that strange feeling again that she knew what I was thinking.

I knew that unusual things went on in Miss Howard's house. I could just feel it. I feel lots of things that turn out to be right. To make things more difficult, she was always nice to my foster family. She was constantly giving treats and making dinner for my foster brothers, Jim and Mark. I admit that I was fascinated by her, but I was scared of her as well. It was not that I thought she was evil or practiced voodoo black magic or anything like that, there was just something very mysterious about Miss Howard. I could not pinpoint it but I sensed it the way I sense a lot of things.

Spring and summer were the very worst because Veronica insisted that I cut Miss Howard's grass. I liked her grass being tall and overgrown. At least it served to cover part of her house some of the year. I'd put off cutting it as long as I could, feigning having to stay after school for extracurricular activities. That would sometimes tide me over for a couple weeks, depending on how busy Veronica was.

Then one day, unexpectedly, Veronica would say, "Michael, you've got to cut Miss Howard's grass soon before it grows so tall it covers her entire house."

Little did she know that's exactly what I wanted. At least Miss Howard never pressured me to do it. She never said anything other than an occasional hello. She would wave more often and give me that long stare which I was convinced could see right through to my very soul. When I'd cut her grass, she'd leave me alone—not even bringing me soft-drinks. I broke her from that the first time with my "No, thank you," and icy stare. It didn't seem to faze her but she left me alone. I could always tell when Miss Howard was sizing me up. She would look in my direction, and a mischievous smile formed on her slightly curved lips. The big twinkle in her eyes always made me feel anxious and uncomfortable.

How could Veronica stand to be around her? Her scraggly hair looked like snakes were curled in it. Her wrinkled old clothes never matched, and they were usually torn. Veronica said that I exaggerated and should be a little friendlier to her.

"You never know when you might need to call upon her," Veronica would insist. "One must always be nice to neighbors. That's how I was raised, and that is what I am passing on to you."

"I know," I'd say, repeating her little tirade. "You've told me this a hundred times."

"And I'll tell you a hundred more," she'd reply, pointing at me with a grin on her face. "Michael, why not go over for dinner just once with the boys? They rave about Miss Howard's cooking, and I, too, can personally attest to how delicious her meals are."

"That woman is spooky. The day I carried her groceries inside was the spookiest day of my life. I tell you that woman is in cahoots with somebody or something. There is someone who stares at you from one of the paintings on the wall."

"Your imagination works overtime, Michael. Miss Howard is a harmless old woman. You should be ashamed of yourself."

I'd frown and walk away. My friend Tommy Bailey told me that I must feel something for the old woman; otherwise, I wouldn't talk about her so much.

"I don't feel anything for her," I'd reply, smirking.

Nonetheless, the woman reeked of mystery, and I was the kind of person who had to unravel it. Maybe I'd sneak into her house one day when Veronica took her shopping. Lord knows what I might find.

And why didn't she take better care of her house? Rumor had it that Miss Howard had a lot of money. She could afford to have a new paint job and to replace that God-forsaken porch I feared Mark or Jim were going to fall through one day. The big oak tree in the front yard with so many broken branches from storms should have been cut down years ago. None of the other trees in our neighborhood were a third that size.

Who would listen to me? Sam, my foster father, said he liked her place. He felt that it was nice to preserve history and the past whenever possible. Mark wouldn't care if it was haunted by a hundred ghosts. He'd walk into a dragon's lair if there was food inside.

A few days before Thanksgiving, the mystery was finally resolved. Veronica and Sam were away for the weekend. Mark and Jim were visiting their foster grandparents. Sam said that he trusted me to take care of the place. I didn't have much choice since my English term paper on the paranormal was due on Monday, and I was behind on it. I desperately needed an "A" in English class.

After several hours of steady work on my research paper, I was ready for a break. I stepped barefoot onto the porch to check out the weather. The night was calm with moonlight filtering through the trees. The crisp air was conducive for an evening stroll. I went back inside, grabbed my blue sweater, put on my sneakers, and headed out the front door.

The smell of rain was in the air, and although the weatherman had forecasted rain that night, I knew it wouldn't rain until the next day. How did I know? The same way I knew Miss Howard was unusual and mysterious. I felt it. (Sometimes I can tell who is calling before picking up the phone. I never talk about this to anyone for fear they'll think I'm possessed or something.)

I had a sudden unexpected urge to walk towards Miss Howard's house. When I was about fifty feet away, I stopped dead in my tracks. Shivers ran up my spine when I looked into her living room. A dark figure with a bluish glow around him was dancing with a beautiful young woman to the sound of waltz music. I had to get a close up view of this. I wished I had brought a camera. I wondered if the bluish glow would photograph. Walking considerably slower than before, I headed toward the big oak tree in her front yard. It would shield my presence. I knew that I could not easily be seen from a lighted room.

As I approached closer, the sound of the window opening caught my attention. The beautiful young woman looked out the window. She tilted her head to the left, then to the right before looking straight at the tree where I was hiding. I rigidly arched my body, standing erect to be sure I was well hidden. She held her gaze in my direction for several moments. Did she know I was there? How could she? Then why was my stomach tingling and my heart racing? Why did I have a strange feeling that she actually expected my arrival?

"Stop over reacting," I told myself. "This is probably just your imagination working overtime."

The sound of the waltz music playing in the background faded, and she began whistling softly. A black bird that was perched high on a tree branch fluttered about and then flew away, causing me to jerk. The woman looked up and then moved away from the window, pulling the black velvet drapes halfway shut. The music began playing once more. The drapes swayed in a swirling dance-like rhythm, which made me wonder whether it was the breeze or the woman that was causing the movement.

A few moments later the dancing resumed. I was captivated by the scene. Although the partially closed drapes blocked some of the view, I could still see part of the man's face and the bluish glow which emanated from it. I had to move closer for a better look. Considering whether to walk to the porch, I began feeling drowsy. My mind started feeling fuzzy and confused. The drowsiness grew heavier.

The next thing I knew, the young woman returned to the window. I should have been alarmed, but I wasn't. My fear vanished, and before I realized what was happening, I was walking towards the porch. It felt like the young woman was somehow luring me there. Part of me wanted to run back home, lock the doors, close the curtains, shut off the lights, and hide under my bed, but another part of me was fascinated by the woman and man. I had to find out who they were. A dozen questions ran through my mind. My body felt as light as a feather. It seemed as though I was being carried by an invisible force to Miss Howard's porch.

"Where is Miss Howard?" I wondered. "Who are these people? What is the glow around the man's face? Before I could begin to hypothesize about the situation, the front door opened—at exactly the precise moment I stepped onto the porch.

The beautiful woman I had seen in the window slowly walked towards me, all the while staring at me with black piercing eyes which never blinked. She somehow reminded me of Miss Howard. I felt so strange. It was like every cell in my body was dancing. Her gaze sent electrical impulses through me. Was she aware of her effect on me? I sensed that she was. I forced myself to look away. I took a few deep breaths which calmed me a little. Since the young woman didn't live in Miss Howard's house—or if so, I had never seen her—I was counting on her not recognizing me. I was mystified that her eyes were so similar to Miss Howard's. Maybe she was her daughter visiting from out of town or something?

As my thoughts raced through my mind, the lovely young woman continued looking at me. *Why did she feel so familiar, and why was I such a nervous wreck?* I found it difficult to move. *Perhaps anxiety is paralyzing my body*, I thought.

Several minutes passed before a word was spoken. I had never been looked at by anyone that long before nor felt so under someone else's influence or scrutiny. Feeling totally helpless like I was stalled and frozen in time, finally the woman smiled and greeted me.

"Good evening, Michael. What made you decide to pay me a visit?"

"Excuse me," I said, my voice quaking. "Do I know you?"

She ignored my question and posed one of her own. "How is your term paper coming along?"

"How do you know I'm writing a term paper?"

"Veronica told me," she said, moving closer. I took a closer look at her, and for the first time, her black eyes sent a shocking recognition up my spine. Now my suspicion was confirmed. I could never mistake those eyes, not even a mile away.

"Miss Howard," I exclaimed, my mouth gaping.

"At your service," she answered, offering a curtsy.

"But you look so different."

"Michael, lots of things in this world are not as they appear, including people. I've been waiting a long time for this meeting, but you had to make the effort. Come in, won't you? We can have some tea and a chat. I've made some delicious almond chocolate fudge just for this occasion."

I was torn between fear and fascination, but I chose to join Miss Howard for tea. Her house was surprisingly neat and in order. That was not the way I remembered it the time I brought her groceries in. It was as though she had cleaned and prepared for guests. The furniture which was covered in dust before shone with a lemon fragrance. Wilted flowers had been replaced by fresh roses. The large painting behind the wall near the mantle, which had been lopsided, was straight. I moved towards it for closer inspection while she prepared the tea. The first thing that caught my attention was the dark piercing eyes. They looked exactly like Miss Howard's eyes. The longer I looked at the painting of the tall impeccably dressed gentleman, the more real those eyes became. At one point they moved.

"Could my eyes be playing tricks on me?" I asked, moving away. The eyes followed me just like they had the time when I delivered her groceries a few months ago.

I refused to look back at the painting, no matter how strongly it compelled me. Sitting back in the thick dark plush chair, I began examining other areas of the huge room. My reverie was interrupted by Miss Howard a few minutes later. She brought a tray with a pot of tea, cups, and a saucer with fudge on it.

"What do you think of the painting, Michael?" she asked, pouring steaming cinnamon tea.

"It's very interesting," I commented, hoping she would change the subject.

"Does it look familiar?"

"Now that you mention it, it does," I said, taking a piece of fudge. "The aquiline-shaped nose and dark long hair resemble the man with the glow I saw dancing with a woman earlier near the window."

She looked at me and then smiled. "Is the fudge good?" she asked a few moments later, grinning.

"Yes," I replied, still seeing the image of the man in the painting and the one dancing with her earlier. I was ready to go look at it again but came out of my trance like stupor when she tapped me on the knee.

"Are you alright, Michael?"

"I'm fine," I stammered, my head slightly spinning. She either didn't notice or chose to ignore it. For a moment I felt terrorized, thinking that I had been drugged. When I tried to move my legs, they would not budge. I also noted that my breathing had increased. *Keep calm and don't make a fool out of yourself,* I told myself mentally.

Miss Howard looked at me again. She seemed to really like direct eye contact. Coolness slowly enveloped me and the dizziness subsided. Miss Howard resumed her small talk. It seemed that she could continue forever. For a moment I had the feeling I was dreaming. I looked at her again. Her piercing gaze was so intense that I actually flinched. We continued talking about superficial topics a few minutes until I could take it no more.

"Miss Howard, I can't stand the suspense anymore," I said, interrupting her talk about flowers. "I need some answers. Please!"

"What would you like to know, Michael?" she asked nonchalantly.

"For starters how can you be Miss Howard and yet look like a completely different woman except for the eyes?"

"Michael, isn't there something you're not asking that you really want to know? Sometimes the questions we hold back are the ones we most want answers for."

"You're right. Who is that man you were dancing with? I saw you through the window while I was walking down the street."

"You saw us from behind the oak tree," she added in a nonjudgmental tone. "I don't mind that you were snooping. I was the one who put you up to it."

"Oh," I gasped, covering my mouth with my hand. "That doesn't make sense to me but maybe it helps explain why I'm here."

"How to begin?" she said, pouring more tea. "Would you like more fudge?"

"Sure."

"Michael, you and I have a lot in common," she said, blowing her tea gently before sipping it. "You may not realize it, but you will later. I know that you have had some unusual experiences just as you sense that about me. Since you are tired of speaking of superficial things, why don't you tell me a little bit about some of your past paranormal experiences? I know they go way back with you."

I took a sip of tea and a bite of the fudge. "This fudge is really good, Miss Howard. Thank you."

"You are very welcome. Cooking and baking are two of my hobbies. Now where were you, Michael?"

"Let me see now. When I was about two years old, I saw spirits. I called them 'feny faces' because I could not say friendly faces. Later I would have dreams, some of which came true. Sometimes I know things about people without having to say a word to them or even knowing who they are. I keep this pretty much to myself. One day a lady in church gave me a prophecy. She said I had a lot of talents and that God and the angels would watch over me, and I'd help a lot of people. She said I would have visions and be shown things. She also said that I would meet some *sky people*. About a year later, an angel visited me in our back yard and predicted my future. Two years later, another angel paid me a visit."

Miss Howard's eyes twinkled like stars. She took both my hands in hers. "Michael, we are both fascinated by the unknown, and we possess abilities many people don't believe in or accept. We sometimes see and know things before they happen. We often sense things about people, and we can sometimes portend and see into the future."

I nodded in agreement, my knees shaking and heart pounding.

"Try to relax," she said, moving a long strand of blond hair over her shoulder. "You're in the company of a kindred spirit," she said, emphasizing the word spirit as she looked at me intently. "We all have many different sides, Michael. Sometimes they can clash. If there's a part of us we don't like, accept, or are even scared of, we often try to deny or repress it.

Sooner or later we run into people who mirror those qualities we don't like about ourselves."

"Is that why I've been afraid of you, Miss Howard?" I asked, still finding it hard to believe this young woman was Miss Howard.

"Yes. You always knew when you looked into my eyes that things were not as they appeared, or let me say your intuition knew just like it knows lots of things your mind can't figure out. Instead of trying to reconcile your thoughts with your intuition and learning the truth about me, you chose to maintain intrigue and fascination without trying to solve the mystery you have always sensed about me. Michael, I've always known that we have a lot in common and that we have a very strong connection."

"Why didn't you tell me that?"

"You wouldn't have listened because you were not ready."

"You should have made me listen."

"I'm not a witch," she said, giving me a lovely smile.

I noticed the full round curve of her lips and how beautiful she really was.

"I don't make people do anything. I knew you'd eventually come around and simply waited. Tonight is the perfect time. Things happen when they are supposed to. It's not by chance that your family took off for a couple of days, and you need to complete your term paper this weekend. With your family away, there will be no distractions or interruptions."

"Do you read minds, and did you use your mind to convince me to come over here?"

"Influence, yes, but not convince. I just told you I'm not a witch who casts evil spells. I'm not a witch at all. I mentally sent you the thought and because you are receptive, you received my thought and responded, not knowing whether it was your thought or mine. That is why you felt confused. I knew you were sensing what was going on over here, which

I'll talk about soon. I choose to hide my real appearance from most people so they won't bother me with constant annoying questions."

"Like why isn't a young beautiful woman like yourself married? How can a young woman live in a big house all alone? Things like that?"

"'Beauty is in the eye of the beholder,' as the saying goes, but you have got the basic idea. Since you have the ability to see past appearances, my old woman disguise never convinced you. I encouraged you to come over tonight so you could learn who I really am, as well as learn more about yourself. In a way I am a mysterious person but only in the sense that people tend to be afraid of the unknown and what they don't understand. Some people cringe if you speak words like the occult, esoteric, paranormal, fortune telling, psychic, or divination. Sure, I'm interested in all of the above. The word occult simply comes from the Latin word 'occultus,' meaning that which is concealed or hidden. Just because something is hidden from normal view does not make it evil. People like to see things the way they expect them to be. They don't want their tidy neatly packaged belief systems challenged or invalidated. As long as I play the role of the eccentric old maid, people leave me alone. It makes my life a lot easier and doesn't threaten them."

"This is my home, Michael. I had five wonderful years with my husband Jacob. When he died, I knew I'd never move away. I fabricated a story of selling the house to my grandmother, Caroline Howard. When someone occasionally asks about the young beautiful woman who lived here, I simply say that after the death of her husband, she moved to California. Two years later she met a nice gentleman and is currently happily married. That seems to satisfy them."

I wanted to ask her how her husband died but figured that she would tell me if she wanted to reveal that information.

"There are other reasons why I stayed, which I'll explain later when I tell you who I was dancing with." She looked at me without speaking as though expecting me to figure out the answer to my questions.

"Michael, sometimes we can answer our own questions through symbols, pictures, and images in our minds that we see. Some call this a type of dreaming in the daytime."

"There is so much more to dreams than people realize, Michael. There are also many types of dreams. Dreams can serve different purposes and have meanings that most people do not understand. In the future you are going to discover that some of your dreams will serve as gateways or portals to take you to dimensions far beyond this world. You are going to learn that dreams can open many doors for you, Michael, both literally and figuratively—to add some humor. That is all I will say and all you need to know about this for now. I am planting a seed. In the future you will come to understand exactly what I am talking about."

"Dreams as a portal to other worlds. That is intense, Miss Howard. I have been told that I will meet *sky people*. I guess I will have to find some way to get to them."

She grinned. "Oh, you'll figure it out with a little help from your new friends, I might add. Now back to dreams. Our dreams are our teachers, but few take the time to get acquainted with them and learn what their symbols and messages mean. Just as we see symbols and images in our dreams at night, so can we learn to see them in the daytime. It just takes some practice to learn how. Don't you daydream?"

"Yes, but doesn't everyone?"

"Not as well as you. You've had several which came true. This is called precognition. You are very psychic and clairvoyant, Michael. I hope you realize that this gift of yours is not evil and that it can be used to help you and other people."

"Who would want to listen or believe me?"

"People often listen to us when we are sincere and honest, no matter how strange what we say may seem."

"Perhaps."

"These wonderful psychic gifts you possess are a blessing. We all possess them, but most people never awaken them. Your intuition is strong, but your error is that you usually doubt your original intuitive feelings and then react against them. That is when you are wrong. Do you regret coming over here tonight?"

"No."

"What made you come over? I thought you were afraid of me."

"I *was* afraid of you. Now I don't feel that way. I guess I have changed."

"Thank goodness for change."

"Looking back, I see that I have always been fascinated and intrigued by you. My friend Tommy said I had to feel something for you, or I wouldn't be so obsessed and constantly talking about you. You are the subject of half of our conversations."

"At least that goes to show how much I affect you. Michael, you are here tonight to learn who you really are, who I really am, and who we really are to each other. Part of what made you come over was curiosity, another quality we *seers* possess inordinate amounts of. We have to know and become familiar with things. We need to check them out to get answers. Our minds go over them until at some point, we reconcile our intuition with our reason and come to conclusions that satisfy our mind and heart. It's part of our makeup. We are willing to take risks. We step beyond the perimeters of conventional beliefs and thinking to satiate our need to know. We're simply built like that. It can be no other way. Without your curiosity you would not have been nearly as receptive to my mental suggestion to come over. Seers are extremely receptive to suggestions. We often sense the intention of the sender. If it's in accord with our own, we are compelled to follow the suggestion."

"My suggestion activated your subconscious, which wanted to know more about me. Your body was guided by those unconscious impulses. It was your will that brought you here, Michael. I only prompted and awakened it, so to speak. It did seem as though an invisible force was leading you here, but that force came from you, not me. Did you notice that as you approached my house, the closer you came, the more your fear vanished?"

"Yes, and that surprised me. I expected to become terrified. I truly felt you were luring me to the front porch. It was so bizarre for me to feel more at ease the closer I came to your house since I have always kept a distance from you before."

"Had you come within arm's reach, I might have grabbed you, locked you up, fattened you up, and eaten you for dinner," she laughed. "When an undeveloped seer approaches another one, a psychic connection sometimes can be made. The closer they are in physical proximity, the stronger the connection. This is why you never delivered groceries again after that day. Being physically near me—although we only spoke a few words—caused you to see lots of things, didn't it?"

"Yes. Images and pictures were flashing in my mind so fast it was like watching a movie. Oh, my," I exclaimed. "I remember seeing images of you as you appear now. That image felt so familiar, but since I had never seen you like this before, I became confused and overwhelmed. It's strange recalling this. I can recall that day as though it were yesterday."

"That is because seers can see through time. The past and future all exist in the present for seers. That is why you sometimes have premonitions of the future. Seeing through time gives us amazing memories and an uncanny ability for detail."

"I was surprised how easily I recalled the way this house looked the last time I was here many months ago. While you were preparing the tea, as I looked around, I could see this place just as it was then, as well as the way it is now."

"Yes, you are a seer, dear Michael. You have also 'seen' or known that I am not a mean old hag underneath appearances. That is why you could not forget me or stop thinking about or talking about me. You are going to learn that as you develop more, you won't need to physically be close to someone to connect psychically and pass information on to each other. This is called telepathic linking, and you already do it to some degree. Your ability to use telepathy will become stronger in the future. Now that you've been here tonight, you'll be able to communicate with me much easier henceforth from your house, school, or when you are out walking. It will no longer be mostly one way with me sending you messages. Note, that I said 'mostly.' Actually, you've sent me messages before. There are also a lot of people like us—more than you might think. Mark is also a seer, but he won't know it for a few more years. Your foster parents and James are not, so I don't advise you to tell them about our meeting tonight. They might think I am a bad influence out to corrupt you," she said, grinning.

"Couldn't I tell them I was doing some chores for you or sampling your renowned cuisine?"

"Would Veronica believe that?"

"Sure. She's been telling me for months to be friendlier to you. If she only knew how young you really are, I don't think she'd want me coming over. Some things are best kept secret, aren't they?"

"I agree and now it's time for a break. Are you hungry?"

"I'm starved."

"I just happened to have put a turkey into the oven a few hours ago," she said, grinning. "It pays to be a seer," she said, winking at me. "Give me about a half hour. Make yourself at home. Feel free to look through Jacob's library down the hall on the far left. There are some nice paintings in there as well; some he painted himself as painting was one of his hobbies. I always told him he had talent and should develop it. Or you can watch TV or rest. Are you thirsty? I have Coke, orange juice, and chocolate milk," she laughed. "I keep the chocolate milk for Mark."

"He'll keep you running to the store. I keep saying I'm going to buy him a chocolate cow for Christmas. I'll have a Coke, please."

Miss Howard whisked away so fast I thought for a moment she did a disappearing act on me. A few moments later she returned with a big glass full of ice and a liter of Coke."

"You must think that guzzling drinks runs in our family."

"Not at all. I just want there to be plenty for you. I don't allow anyone in the kitchen when I'm preparing food. I want to surprise you."

"I love surprises," I said, filling the glass with Coke. "Ring the bell when it's dinner time," I teased.

"Over dinner I'll tell you more about Jacob, my dance partner, and those piercing eyes in the painting which stare at you."

A chill ran through me as I recalled looking at the painting earlier. It was so real; the eyes seemed to be looking into the very depths of my soul.

"Thanks, I can't wait to sample your renowned cuisine."

I returned to the painting first thing. Those dark piercing eyes were staring at me as though they had never left me, but this time there seemed to be a slight curvature of the lips, giving the face a slight grin. I looked at it awhile and a sense of warmth came over me. *They must have really been in love*, I thought, feeling a tinge of sadness. I thumbed through a few of Jacob's books and was surprised that many of the subjects were topics I had read about such as ESP, the paranormal, spirits, and psychic abilities. Why was I interested in such things when nobody in my family was? I walked over to the fireplace mantel and admired a collection of mythological figurines and some small African wood carvings.

I found it amazing that a house I had been so afraid of suddenly was very welcoming. I felt so at home now. In some strange way it was almost as if I belonged here. That was a weird feeling I felt sure I'd learn the answer to before the night was over. I thought about my term paper I had left behind and the necessity to return to it. Actually, I could incorporate some of the ideas Miss Howard talked about since I was writing about the supernatural. I could even ask her permission to interview her. Live interviews are always welcomed in term papers. That is how I justified not returning home immediately and getting back to work. In a sense I was at work on the paper. I was conducting an interview with a supernatural unusual woman. After tonight maybe I would even have the nerve to share some of my experiences. I no longer felt so uneasy about the unknown. How can a person change so fast? I wondered. Am I under some spell?

I was looking at the painting again when Miss Howard summoned that dinner was ready. Nine o'clock at night seemed late for dinner, but I didn't say anything. I was as hungry as though I hadn't eaten for days. I wondered if Miss Howard usually had dinner so late. Maybe she was on a different schedule and had her meals later in the day. She would not let me help her serve the meal.

"You are my guest, and it is my pleasure to serve you," she insisted, placing the steaming mashed potatoes in front of me. Then she placed the turkey to my right, telling me to eat all that I wanted. She also served green beans mixed with corn, dressing, and cranberry sauce.

"Jacob was a hearty eater. Help yourself to as much as you want," she said, covering the wooden table with still more culinary delights.

Her turkey and dressing were the best I had ever eaten. I tried to figure out the spices she had in the dressing and gravy but couldn't and decided not to inquire. The vegetables and soufflé were equally delicious. I felt like Louis XIV indulging in a feast.

"Now, I know who the man you were dancing with is," I said. "He is Jacob come back for your sumptuous cuisine. I couldn't much blame him. I think I could put heaven off awhile for these heavenly delights. Now I know why James and Mark come to your house so much."

"You are right," she said, but she wasn't smiling. "This is a good time to unravel some of the mysteries you are wondering about. That man you saw dancing with me is my beloved Jacob. He became my dance partner and later my husband. He swore he would never leave me. Actually, he declared his undying love for me after our third date. I laughed, but there was something about the way he said it that haunted me, never letting me forget it. Now I've come to witness first hand that a love as undying as his for me is more powerful than death itself. Through our paranormal studies we learned how to detach our soul from our body. We often used to take trips around the world in our spirit bodies. When Jacob died, instead of choosing to go on to what is known as *heaven or the spirit world*, he (or at least part of him) stays here with me. He says that he protects me and will stay with me until I meet a new husband. He is so sweet and considerate," she said, wiping away tears.

"It's nice that he approves of you having a new husband," I replied, fighting away my own tears. "I'm sure a jealous spook would not be one to upset. I bet he could make a haunted house look like a toy factory."

She let out a laugh. "I like your sense of humor, Michael, but the truth is that Jacob would not hurt anyone unless they tried to harm me. The glow around his face is his soul radiance which he projects to the top part of his body. This enables him to interact more with me than just as a ghost or spook as you put it. He's sort of in between a person and a ghost."

"The best of both worlds," I teased.

"Something like that. Jacob never wanted to miss out on anything. He always had his foot in both worlds. It took about a month before he returned. For a few hours at a time, Jacob can materialize into an etheric type of physical body. That's the times we dance. At other times he's still here, but no one can see him but me. You could see his eyes through the painting because of your sensitivity and because he wanted you to see him."

"Why are your eyes identical to his?"

"Because we are twin spirits. Sometimes I don't know whether it's me or him looking out."

"That must feel strange."

"Not at all. It's like being double-sighted like some people are double-jointed. Two are better than one," she said, grinning.

"Does a seer have a spirit looking through his/her eyes?"

"Not necessarily. More don't than do. You don't and I don't always. When my new husband comes to me, my double vision will cease although I will always be able to see Jacob and vice-versa."

I wondered who her new husband would be but didn't dare ask. "I hope that Jacob likes me. I am, after all, in his house, talking to his wife."

"I assure you, Michael, that if Jacob didn't like you, he would have made it known."

"I wouldn't want to imagine the ways he could do that."

"Was he smiling at me from the painting a few minutes ago?"

"What do you think?"

"I think so."

"You are right. Jacob likes you. There is no need to fear anything. He was the one who told me to be patient—that you'd eventually come around," she said, reaching for my hand and stroking my fingers gently.

"Is he here now?" I asked, looking around.

"Look into my eyes and tell me," she whispered, moving closer.

"I can't tell. I'm too nervous."

"I'll tell you," she said, kissing me on the cheek. My head spun so fast I thought I'd fall over. She held my hand tighter. Without that contact I think I'd have fainted. We looked at each other for several moments in the silence. I could feel cool energy entering my head. It had a calming effect and helped restore my equilibrium.

"How does it feel to visit an old hag who is in cahoots with the devil?"

"I am bedeviled and beguiled," I said, softly. "You are always saying things that I am thinking."

"That's because your thoughts are so easily sensed."

"Oh, really?"

"Sure. Anytime a thought is backed up by strong emotions, it can easily be sensed by a seer," she whispered, touching my cheek lightly. "Now, Michael dear, I must send you back home to work on your research paper. You have a lot to write about, and of course, you may use anything we talked about or even construct it as an interview. I would be very honored."

"Will I ever see you again?"

"I am your friendly neighbor, Michael," she teased.

"You mean I'll never see you again as you are now?"

"How you see me depends on when you visit," she laughed. "I'm Miss Howard in the day, and at night I become Marie Juliette. You are the first person in this town to meet Marie Juliette."

"What a beautiful name. Marie Juliette," I repeated several times. "Do I really have to go?"

"Once seers get past superficialities, they really like being together. Marie Juliette is so pleased to know you, Michael. I have waited long for this moment as has my beloved Jacob," she said, extending a graceful curtsy. "You have a lot of work to do, but tomorrow you are invited to return—that is, if you are productive and write all day. I wouldn't want to be responsible for you not getting that "A" your heart is set upon. I know how much it means to you."

"You know lots of things about me, don't you?"

"Some things—and I look forward to learning more about you. How about arriving at 8:00 p.m. tomorrow night? Is that a good time? That will give you plenty of time to get a lot of work done."

"Perfect, but won't you be dancing with Jacob then?"

"Not if you are here. He's the perfect gentleman. He knows when to take a back seat. He knows that we have things to learn from each other."

"Could I have one more look at the painting before I leave?"

"Certainly."

Marie Juliette took me by the hand and led me to the painting. We stood quietly for several moments in front of it. Tears trickled down her face. I squeezed her hand gently. The eyes did not move. *Is he still here?*" I thought.

"No," she said, responding to my thoughts. "He's not here. Well, you need to be going now. Thank you for coming over. I've had a wonderful time. I hope that you have too."

"It's been an incredible evening, Marie Juliette. That's all I can say. I should say wonderfully incredible."

"I take that as a gracious compliment from a gentleman. You will make someone very happy one day. I'll walk you to the front door, Michael."

I looked back at the house long after Marie Juliette shut the big front door. She turned off all of the lights except the living room lamp. She looked outside for several minutes. I thought I detected her looking my way as I stood by the oak tree.

After a few minutes, I pulled myself up from the ground, realizing I must have fallen asleep. I glanced at the window.

The man with the blue glow around him was there, but they were not dancing.

"Marie Juliette," I said aloud, wondering if this had all been a dream. "It must be," I repeated, beginning to head towards the porch.

I was surprised that I was no longer afraid or anxious. The precise moment that I stepped on the porch the front door opened and the beautiful woman, who was even more beautiful than I thought, stepped on the porch and greeted me warmly.

"Good evening, sir," she said. "May I help you?"

"Yes," I replied calmly, feeling a strange sense of deja vu, unable to take my eyes from the dark piercing eyes. They were the same ones I had seen in the painting so many months ago—the day I brought Miss Howard's groceries in. I'd never forget those eyes.

"Are you alright, sir?" she asked, softly, making no attempt to avoid my stare.

"I'm fine. It's just that you remind me of someone," I stuttered, struggling to conceal my agitation which quickly overtook the calm I had been feeling.

"Perhaps Miss Howard," she said, smiling. "We do have the same kind of eyes. You could say we are related."

I wondered how but did not ask.

"Now what can I do for you, sir?"

"I'm from out of town," I continued. "Can you tell me how to find the Carter place? My friend Michael lives there."

"You look like a Michael, too," she chuckled. "Wait a few moments. I'll go get Miss Howard."

"Oh, please don't bother."

"No bother at all. She needs to get up now anyhow."

A few minutes later, the Miss Howard I could recognize a mile away came to the door. She was wearing an old black torn skirt and a blouse that didn't match. Her scraggly hair seemed more disheveled than usual. If I didn't know better, I'd think she was wearing a wig. She was also wearing a very nice smelling perfume. It smelled so familiar. *Miss Howard wearing perfume? I'm imagining things*, I thought.

She looked at me intensely. I assumed she was waiting for me to speak first. I even felt some strange attraction to her. We looked into each other's eyes for what seemed several minutes. I was light-headed. I noticed a slight smile on her lips. Miss Howard moved a little closer. I could keep silent no more.

"Marie Juliette," I blurted out and then put my hand over my mouth.

"What a pretty name," she said softly. "Is she a new lady friend of yours?"

"To be honest, I don't know."

"Tell me, why are you here? Do you want to interview me for your term paper? Veronica told me about your topic. It's on the supernatural."

"Yes, I would like that."

"Okay, but not tonight. I'm tired, but if you come back tomorrow night, I'll be more than happy to see you. I will explain lots of mysteries you've been wondering about. I'm not really the mean old hag that you think I am. I could even make you some dinner. People say I'm a good cook in spite of some who think the contrary," she said, pointing her little finger at me, smiling.

"Make sure that you work on your paper all day. You have lots of things to write about. How about discussing some of your own experiences, for I know that you have had some," she said, touching my cheek gently.

"I will," I replied, taking a small bow and slowly walking away from the porch. I whistled all the way home.

I interviewed Miss Howard and got an "A" for my term paper on the supernatural. My English teacher thought I had made the story up or dreamed it. I just nodded and smiled. Yes, I had dreamed it, but what I had done and did not tell her was to *dream into the future. The next day everything that I had dreamed came true.*

I have always been good at recalling my dreams in detail, even the long ones. I recall Miss Howard telling me that my dreams would become stronger and more precognitive. She had also said that some dreams will serve as gateways or portals to take me to dimensions far beyond this one and that I would learn that dreams serve many purposes. They can open so many doors, both literally and metaphorically. I would spend many hours pondering such possibilities.

I left for college at the end of August. Miss Howard threw a big party for me and invited Veronica, James, and Mark. She prepared a sumptuous meal, and we later played some word games. Around 9:00 p.m. a singer from some singing telegram agency came over dressed as a Playgirl bunny in a low cut sexy outfit. She flirted with me and sang a funny song, warning me about the snares and temptations that come along with going to college and being on one's own for the first time. I about fell over I laughed so hard. Even Veronica burst into hearty laughter which she does not often do. When we exchanged our goodbyes, Miss Howard gave me a big hug and told me to remember that time does not exist for seers, and she assured me that we would always have a strong connection and that we would see each other again.

"Michael, not only will you learn many things in college in your academic classes and studies, you will also have more psychic and paranormal experiences. Furthermore, you have some needed lessons to learn about human love. Your sad and lonely childhood has wounded your soul and heart. You have a very deep capacity to love, but the mighty Goddess of Love has some important lessons to teach you. I have total faith that you will pass them all although the tests of human love can be emotionally straining and challenging at times to say the least. Give Love your all, my friend. Don't hold back. Learn each and every lesson no matter how much it requires of you. For that learning will help bring you into the fullness of even more creative and psychic abilities."

Miss Howard gave me another big hug. She then hugged Veronica and the boys who thanked her profusely for such a wonderful party and the treats she gave them to take home.

"Until we meet again, Michael," she said, blowing me a kiss. Then she shut the door behind her.

"Until we meet again, Michael?" Veronica asked with a big smile on her face. "Is there something I should know?"

"Miss Howard let me interview her for my term paper. She expressed some interest in the supernatural and told me some stories. She gave me permission to include what we talked about and made me dinner, which I have to admit was delicious."

"I'm so happy, Michael. I knew you would come around. Miss Howard truly is a wonderful lady."

"And then some," I said with a grin on my face.

"Maybe you can visit her on your college breaks when you come home. She can adopt you as her foster grandson. Would you like that?"

"I would like that," I said, fighting back tears. Veronica and I had never discussed my plans once I went to college. I would be of legal age and no longer a foster child and ward of the state. I would be free to do what I wanted. Other chapters of my life were soon to begin.

I did visit Miss Howard (Marie Juliette) a few times over the next few years during college breaks and vacations. There were other amazing experiences, which I will include in a future book.

CHAPTER FOUR

SOUL-MATE CONNECTIONS

During my senior year in high school, I was accepted at Berea College in Berea, Kentucky, where I started a new chapter of my life. The second semester I signed up for a musical theatre class and auditioned for the musical *South Pacific*. I took an instant liking to the teacher, Janette. One day after rehearsals I noticed that she was standing alone in a corner on the stage crying. I asked her what was wrong. She said that her father had died the week before. We talked for awhile, and she offered to drop me off at my dorm. Chatting and enjoying her company on the way to my dorm gave me a strong feeling of deja vu that I could not explain. It felt like I had known Janette forever.

I also knew in that moment that we would be not only teacher and student but we would also become good friends. My intuition turned out to be accurate because Janette became a dear friend, mentor, and a second mother to me. She constantly encouraged me to study and work hard. She took me to cultural events and helped me with foreign languages.

After I graduated from Berea in 1980, I visited Janette in Bloomington, Indiana, for six weeks where she was taking a year sabbatical. After she returned to Berea, I remained in Bloomington where I wound up living for the next six years. During that time I completed my graduate work in education at Indiana University. I also took classes in French, German, and Spanish while working. Some thirty years later, Janette and I are still in touch. She is truly like a second mother to me. Many years ago a psychic told me that there was a woman in my life who was a talented musician. She said that this woman had been my mother in a past life in Italy when we were both involved with opera. That was no surprise as Janette was my voice teacher in this life, and she sort of adopted me. Shortly after I met her, I was calling her mom, and she would call me her baby boy. I believe it was soul recognition that drew us to each other from the beginning. During my time at Berea, I spent many weekends at her home. I cut her grass and did chores for which she always insisted on paying me and still does to this very day.

Janette would listen to my sad childhood stories and encourage me to move on with my life. I studied voice with her for three years and for a year had aspired for a career as an opera singer. My deep friendship with Janette reminds me that two souls need not believe or be involved in the psychic metaphysical realm for their souls to recognize each other. I believe it is soul recognition that attracts us to certain people. Soul bonds and karmic connections are the basis for forming new relationships in this lifetime.

Unconscious memories and unfulfilled karma determine what connections are to be made with the people who enter our lives. Although this applies to all types of relationships, it especially applies to the people we fall in love with. I am constantly reminding clients of the magic, wonder, and karma that bring souls together to work out relationships—romantic and otherwise. Since I've become more involved with metaphysics, phrases spoken like "I feel like I've known you or we have met before" or "this is a case of love at first sight" have taken on more meaning. One of my metaphysical teachers used to say that karma has a way of creating those love at first sight scenarios we so often see enacted.

I am not saying or implying that every case of *I get the feeling that I've met you somewhere before or love at first sight* spells a past life soul-mate connection. But sometimes it does. I checked out the current Earth population on the Wikipedia website on the Internet, and it said as of January 4, 2010, the census of the current earth population is estimated at

6,794,200,000 people. There are nearly seven billion souls incarnated on the planet at this time.

What are the chances of two souls meeting and falling in love and the myriad of other relationships that are formed? I realize that some of those meetings can appear to be nothing more than coincidence or happenstance, but we metaphysical folks know better. A compelling attraction to someone often exists because we have known him/her before. We may have met that person in order to work off accumulated karma and to experience some needed lessons. If the lessons are learned and experienced and no additional karma is created, the strength of the soul-tie may diminish. The relationship may end, or the involved parties may develop other aspects of the relationship and further deepen the connection.

In some cases, we are working out karma from several past lifetimes. This can account for some very complicated relationships. I frequently remind clients that the opposite of love is not hate—it is indifference. Anytime people hate others, they are bound to them and are destined to meet in a future lifetime to transmute the hatred to love. I tell people that if they walk down the street and run into their ex-boyfriend, husband, wife, etc., and feel strong emotions of anger, hatred, etc., then they are usually not done with this person. When the energy has truly been balanced, there is peace of mind and feelings of goodwill instead of antagonism towards the other person.

This is not to say there is not a place for allowing the hatred and hurtful emotions to be felt and expressed in an appropriate manner. There is a place for healthy fighting and disagreements. It can be very much part of the healing process of moving the energy and working out the karma. If the hatred is not transmuted, it may be even stronger in the next lifetime. Sometimes past life abuses and hatred will account for the intense energy that creates the attraction that two people feel upon meeting. Such past life abuses account for many difficult relationships. The romantic and soul-mate connections can be some of the most challenging and complicated of all relationships.

As the saying goes, "Rome was not built in a day." Neither are most problematic relationships healed in a day. Yes, unresolved childhood issues can account for some of the psychological problems that plague and haunt many dysfunctional relationships. I can certainly vouch for that. But we metaphysical folks know that the soul has chosen to overcome these challenges and obstacles so we can heal and move on to greener pastures or bigger and better things.

I recall a poem that I wrote many years ago called "The Great Price." It is included in chapter seven of this book. One day I was reading the Bible and thinking about beloved ascended master, Jesus the Christ, Lord Sananda. I asked him how he did what he did. His response was that if I were different and holy, it would only be because I was willing to pay the great price. I knew from the bottom of my heart that I wanted peace of mind. I yearned to be free of all the inner turmoil, confusion, conflict, hatred, and anger that had been with me for so many years—and life times, I was later to learn. Rage is perhaps the word I should have replaced for anger.

After I wrote "The Great Price" I was filled with tears. I remember praying aloud.

> Beloved, Jesus, I know that I can never be like you, but perhaps I can become more like you. I want to release the anger and hatred that eats away at my soul. I want to one day be evolved to the point that I can say, like you did, 'Father, forgive them for they know not what they do' for anybody wishing ill will upon me or inflicting harm upon me in any way. Like you, I want to be able to turn the other cheek if someone slaps me. I know I am not there yet, but before I die, that is where I desire to be.

"Then so be it," I heard in my mind as clearly as if beloved Jesus had stepped through time into my world and spoken to me. I could feel his holy radiance and the great outpouring of love that emanated from his presence. That was a day I was never to forget. I intuitively knew that part of my healing and forgiveness would involve owning the hatred I held for my father. The way to healing and moving beyond the anger and hatred is to admit, look at, explore, experience, and then, and only then, can we heal and move through it. It is amazing how so many people deny hating someone when their very looks, gestures, and even words often dictate otherwise.

I, too, have been in the denial mode and have learned how futile being in denial is. How can we heal if we can't or won't admit what is ailing and messing up our lives? I think of a story I once heard about a psychiatrist who was counseling a woman who was married to an abusive man.

When he asked her if she hated her husband, she said, "No, I don't hate him." He asked her again. "No, I don't hate my husband," she said a bit louder. This went on for a few times. Then she screamed, "No, I don't hate the rotten, no good SOB!"

Admitting that part of me hated my father was not easy, but it was a necessary step in my long journey of healing. This insight and realization intrigued me, ignited my interest, and fired my determination, but I knew that this healing journey would be a monumental task to accomplish. I also knew that it was one that I was determined to get through—come hell or high water, as the saying goes.

What does this have to do with soul-mate connections, you may ask? It has everything to do with them. Our soul-mates are not just our partners, lovers, or spouses. They can be our father, brother, sister, mother, cousin, the teacher at school, a neighbor, or even some poor bloke in prison. Our connections to these souls do not originate in this lifetime and often do not end with this one. We often incarnate over and over to meet up and love our soul-mates in different ways. We do not have to have so-called bad karma with every soul-mate. There is good karma as well. Thank goodness for that! When I do readings for people who have little if any conflict with their partners, I tell them that it is their good karma they have earned. I encourage the ones who constantly fight to hang in there and to not run out prematurely. Otherwise, they will most likely meet up with the person again to resolve unfinished business.

Some of our closest allies and soul-mates can be our so-called enemies or nemeses. My fellow writer, Sherri Cortland, in her wonderful book, *Windows of Opportunity,* goes into this frequently and adds poignant insight on the topic. My father is one such nemesis and soul-mate. Although he was basically a heartless, cruel tyrant in this lifetime, fortunately, for my growth and benefit, I learned that behind all of the rage and hatred that we have a deep soul love for each other. Need I repeat this sentence? Yes, I know it's a mouth full and perhaps a bit hard to chew on or swallow. Try telling me that when I was eleven years old, and he was beating my mother and telling me he'd just as soon kill me as look at me—or when he'd tell me that I was a loser who would never amount to anything because I was a low down piece of s_ _t. Such words were sharper than a two-edged sword and wounded me more than physical blows could have.

Being bound, sworn, and determined to work through my hatred for my father and to heal and move on, I believe, is what opened many doors. Like they say, let us watch what we ask for because we do get it. Ultimately, forgiveness and love are choices that we make. Giving up hatred is also a choice, and, no, I do not mean to imply that it will not involve a lot of soul searching and challenges. I do not mean to imply that it is impossible and cannot be achieved. It most certainly can happen if we are willing, persistent enough, and toss in some daring, risk-taking, restless nights, tears, and the whole gamut of emotions to be experienced.

An experience I had over twenty years ago proved to me that our higher self is always active and available to guide us. I have learned that when we reach out for help to our higher self and soul and are ready to make changes and heal, then help is forthcoming. I always knew that in time I would be ready to make a legal name change as part of severing my link with my father and claiming my own identity and freedom.

Finally, after years of using various names, at the age of thirty-three my guide told me that I had made enough progress that I was now ready to make a legal name change. The following week I went to the court house, filled out the forms, and completed the name change procedure.

Around 9:00 p.m. that night I was sitting in my big, soft, plush chair and had drifted off to sleep. I woke up seeing my father's name in big green neon lights on a marquee in New York City.

"Oh, the big apple," I said aloud. "What is that about?"

"You are seeing an image of the big apple because you want it all in this lifetime," I heard in my head. "You are a very big soul and the big apple is a metaphor. It is also to remind you to not forget your dream of singing a concert at Carnegie Hall in New York for your fortieth birthday."

"I recall that dream. That big dream never came true."

"It's never too late for big dreams to come true. You can sing in Carnegie Hall on a parallel dimension or even a future time, so keep plugging away at your dream fulfillment."

"Who are you?" I asked.

"I will tell you in a *writing*. Are you up for it?"

"Sure, why not since sleep is a million miles away."

I rubbed my eyes. I had to get up early in the morning and meet the man at the courthouse to complete the name changing procedure. I was not the least bit sleepy, so I decided to hear what the voice, whoever it was, had to say. I searched for pencil and pen and, of all things, I thought I'd never do, I channeled the higher self of my father. If I had not had the five pages in front of me when I was done, I'd have concluded that I dreamt or imagined that very unusual encounter.

My father's higher self basically told me was that he was very sorry for all that my father had put me through. He went on to say that it was the very putting me through *hell* that made me strong and bound and determined to heal and to make something out of myself. He said that although I appeared weaker than my six siblings, I was actually the strongest one. I would turn my adversities into assets and would go places and achieve things that no one in my family would ever accomplish. He said that my father and I had set up this agreement before I was even born. Yes, we had been rivals in past lives, but it was all part of a game we had chosen to play and learn from. He reminded me that I am the only child to be left-handed like my father was and resembled him more than most of my brothers.

"Go ahead and change your name," he continued. "You have earned that right at this point in time, having accomplished with many years of therapy and hard work what your father's deeply wounded ego and inner child never has been able to do, but be not fooled! This formal and external gesture will not and can never sever the soul connection and deep love that exist between you and your father. You will meet again. Your rivalry will then be transmuted to love, and you shall be as brothers and comrades in other lifetimes."

"You carry as much hatred and rage as your father did, and that is something that you have in common and share although the origins of some of your hatred and rage have nothing to do with each other. Rage and hatred offer many gifts, and both can lead you to the light and to love. I am very saddened to see that your father will not accomplish this task at the ego level in this lifetime, but you will, Michael. You and your father share a very ancient and deep soul love that no amount of hatred or rage can ever sever. You will come to forgive your father and be set free. You will also, by living example, help set him free although much of this will take place after he makes his transition. As your father's higher self, I know that Joe really does love you, Michael. You must never forget this during difficult times. I must take my leave now. Goodbye."

Needless to say, I was floored and flabbergasted. I was filled with a volcanic rage for a few moments and wanted to scream and curse my father to the top of my lungs. I wanted to transmute and shape-shift into an awesome dragon so powerful that I could burn the very shreds of the paper I had written these words upon and any memory that might dwell in my heart and soul. Basically, I wanted to curse my father and his higher self and hope they would both drop dead for all the abuse and horrible things my father had put me through.

Fortunately, that surge of passionate rage was short-lived. I allowed my inner child to cry and to recall many cruel things my father said and did to me. Like I said before, the way to heal the anger, rage, and hurt is to allow the old pain to be felt and relived. My inner child carried on, recalling lots of sad memories. I felt old feelings from many years as if they were recent. My therapists used to tell me it's vitally important for our inner child to feel the old hurts as a part of the release and healing process. If we just talk, that is not enough. We have to feel the old emotions, so I let my inner child, Little Michael, go at it. He even threw a few pillows across the room. When I was done, I was sweating profusely and totally exhausted. I took a shower. When I put on my pj's, it was as though the water had cleansed me. The anger was gone. I managed to calm my shaking hands and trembling knees enough so that I could reread what I had just written via a type of automatic writing.

This time the tears spilled as I read the words spoken from my father's higher self. Without being able to explain how I knew, I knew that I had *truly* channeled my father's higher self. There was no way to deny it and also no way that my conscious ego could have ever written such words. I studied the words and even took the papers with me to the courthouse the next day. This is not to say that I was completely healed. There would be times when I would forget the automatic writing and fall back into the clutches of the ego and inner child part of me that hated my father. But my higher self would remind me from time to time that our enemies can turn out to be our greatest assets and friends.

In time, I was able to move through the hatred and anger. When my father had triple by-pass heart surgery in December of 1997 on Christmas Eve night, then developed a case of Parkinson's disease, and wound up in the hospital for three months, I visited him every weekend. Sometimes I just sat in his room while he slept. Other times I helped him get up and let him lean on me so he could walk up and down the hall to exercise his legs and muscles. When he wound up in a nursing home from 1999 to 2004, the year he died, I visited as often as I could.

Nothing was spoken of about my visit with his higher self. Not a word was spoken about my childhood or the cruel man my father had been. What was spoken about were some of the few happy memories I hold from childhood, such as Dad always making sure we had a good Christmas, taking us to movies, to visit our grandparents, and to various parks and the Great Smoky Mountains camping trip he took us on one summer.

As the tears fell down my cheeks at his funeral, I said to myself, *Beloved, Jesus, I know I am still not as evolved as you, but do you think maybe I have made some progress?*

I then saw an image of beloved Jesus in my mind and then the image transformed into an image of my father. I heard the words from a poem I had written many years ago:

I am a part of all that is.
All that has been and all to be born.
When the spark of life takes me from this earth,
I shall be greeted by the new morn!

I have learned that our soul-mates come in all shapes, sizes, and people. Years ago I would have never imagined in a million years that I would be saying what I am about to say in the next few sentences. I am also known to remind my clients and friends of the very same thing when they say they will never forgive someone or be able to give up their hatred for wrongs done to them. Now I frequently say that if we possess the least modicum of wisdom, we never say *never* because we never know when we are going to have to eat those very words.

What I would have never thought I'd be saying is this, "My father is one of my most beloved and cherished soul-mates, as is my beloved teacher and friend Janette. Although he was a mean and ruthless tyrant, he taught me many things. He forced me to go within to discover reservoirs of inner strength. I might never have been able to find this inner power and strength had my father not constantly engaged me in emotional mental battles and mind games. Janette has been a far gentler, more loving teacher and friend, but we need to remember there is much to learn from the darkness, as well as the light. May we all be strong, bold, and daring, and do whatever it takes to transmute our darkness to radiant light."

CHAPTER FIVE

AN OUT-OF-BODY EXPERIENCE

Since two of my most beloved soul-mates are my father and Janette, I would like to begin this chapter with a little paranormal story of Janette's. I feel that it will also serve as a means to lead into the out-of-body experience that I recount in this chapter.

Although Janette did not embrace or express any interest in the psychic or metaphysical realms, one day she surprised me after listening to me talk about some metaphysical topics.

"Michael, I really don't believe in all this spiritual stuff like you do," she said, "but I did have an experience many years ago that I think you might find to be interesting."

"Please tell me more," I exclaimed.

In her typical, wonderful story-telling fashion, Janette proceeded to tell me about the time when she was in the hospital to have her tonsils taken out when she was around ten years old. The anesthesiologist gave her too much anesthesia.

"I was totally on my way out of here," she told me. "I saw myself going through this tunnel and at the end of the tunnel was the most brilliant white light. I wanted to go towards that light more than anything in the world. I was trying to make myself go when suddenly I heard my father's voice. He was telling the doctors that he could bring me back. Although they gave him a look of surprise and incredulity, they did not interfere because they truly thought I was gone. My father stepped closer and sat right on the edge of my bed. He gently held my hand and began speaking softly.

"My little Janette, you come back to us now," he said softly. "You know you have to go to school, and you have so much to do. Come back," he kept repeating.

"He was driving me nuts because I just wanted to go to the bright white light. He kept repeating himself in his soft tone of voice. That was what made it so difficult. If he had yelled or chastised me, I might have just gone into the tunnel to the white light, but he did not. He was so gentle and determined to bring me back. Finally something happened and *whoosh*! I was back in my body in the hospital room. I haven't thought of that story in many years, but evidently I never forgot it or how could I be telling it to you?"

"Thanks for sharing this story, Janette. I have read many similar accounts in Dr. Raymond Moody's book on near-death experiences, *Life After life*, but hearing your personal story is even better."

Many of us have read and heard similar stories but this came from my special friend who wanted nothing to do with the paranormal. It is for this reason that I especially cherish it.

My first out-of-body experience took place with, of all people, my music teacher, Janette. It was in January of my sophomore year. I was taking her music therapy class. One day she told the class that she had read that some music therapists were working with hypnosis to reduce stress. Certain music therapists reported some success with their patients. Janette had memorized an induction technique and about midway through the course informed us that we were her first guinea pigs. I was delighted and found the idea fascinating.

She told us to find a place on the carpet and get comfortable. She recommended that we take off our shoes. She began the induction and in a soft calm voice she led us down a stairwell to the ocean. As she did her countdown, she went from our head to our toes telling us how relaxed and peaceful we felt. There was not a care in the world, and all was light, serene, calm and peaceful. She repeated the words softly. She told us that we were to go to a very special peaceful place. It might be beneath a tree in a forest or perhaps in a cave or at the beach. Then she played dreamy ethereal music from Debussy's "Prelude to the Afternoon of a Faun" and left us alone in the silence for about twenty minutes.

What happened in that twenty minutes was phenomenal. My spirit began floating towards the ceiling. Soon I was above the roof and upward until I was floating on a cloud. It was the most wonderful feeling I had ever experienced. I wanted to stay there forever and never come back. I saw colors and all kinds of geometric shapes dancing and floating about. The colors looked brighter with hues that we don't have on the earth. At one point I saw a beautiful rainbow. I somehow had the sensation that I was moving towards the rainbow when Janette gently began speaking. I did not want to come back, but I could feel something happening. With each word that she spoke, I was being drawn back.

Moments later, I was aware of myself lying on the floor. I felt very light-headed. It took several moments before I was fully aware of my surroundings. Janette had us wiggle our toes, move our ankles, bend our knees, and take a few deep breaths to help us slowly come back. When I opened my eyes, everything around me looked hazy and misty. It was like I did not belong in that room. It was like I was in a euphoric bubble of some sort—filled with bliss. All was peaceful. It was as though I had imbibed a love potion and was filled with love. I just wanted to tell everyone how beautiful they were, give them a big hug, and tell them that I loved them.

It took a lot of self-restraint not to do just that. I remember thinking "Is it possible that my soul left my body?" Then I felt awkward because that was not something I was familiar with. The music played a few moments longer. Then Janette told us when we were ready, we could get up, put our shoes back on, and return to our seats. She commented that we might feel a little disoriented for a few minutes, but it would pass. Actually, I did not want these wonderful euphoric feelings to pass. At that moment it was *this* world and my surroundings that felt foreign to me. I did not want to be there in that room.

Janette opened the floor for comments. Most of the students said it was a very relaxing experience. A couple of students had fallen to sleep. I said that I came back with a peaceful feeling of well-being. She said that was a common response, and if for no other reason, music and hypnosis can serve a healing and beneficial purpose.

I had to agree, yet somehow I sensed that much more was going on. I often think about the music therapy hypnosis demonstration and all the bright and beautiful colors, geometric shapes, and images that I saw. My thinking about being up there stirred up strange yearnings for something more than my mundane life on the earth. Looking back, I realize that I had a genuine out-of-body experience (OBE) and that journey would feed my hunger and fuel my passion for other experiences.

Who is to say that we cannot project our soul (or part of our soul) up there and have different experiences? A tool such as hypnosis is but one means to help bring that about. I also believe that some people are more naturally receptive to being hypnotized, and I have been told many times that I am one such person. That would be confirmed in future sessions with different facilitators.

That OBE stuck with me for a very long time. I can actually still recall it as if it just happened yesterday. I will never forget the feelings of peace and ecstasy that overcame me that day—at times and sometimes even when I am not thinking about or reliving the experience, they return to me. I have heard stories of mystical revelations, epiphanies, and visions that people have received while taking mushrooms, LSD, or other mind-altering drugs. That hypnosis session reinforced my inner feeling that this world is not my home; I'm just passing through, as the old gospel song says. That experience caused me to stargaze even more and led to additional hypnosis experiments with my girlfriend, Martina, and many more supernatural, paranormal, and other worldly-experiences.

Winter semester and classes resumed, and I became so busy that I put my interest in hypnosis on the shelf. I did keep the notes I had taken after the session, and each time those notes filled me with a deep yearning for more knowledge. I guess I knew on some level that this period of my life was not the best time to delve deeply into hypnosis because I never asked Martina to conduct anymore sessions. It wasn't that I didn't think about it; I just seemed to always to be doing this or that book report, class assignment, term papers, writing and presenting speeches, auditioning for a play or musical, and/or participating in extra-curricular activities, such as choir and track—and all of that plus maintaining a full load of courses, not to mention trying to have some semblance of a social life.

I recall engaging in a conversation one day with my room-mate about the mind and its wonders, powers, and potential. He was a musician who did some composing. He said he often wondered where his musical ideas and compositions come from. He said they just popped into his head and sometimes in the middle of the night he woke up with ideas for a new composition.

For some reason that led me to recall a stage hypnosis demonstration I had witnessed in high school that made an impression on me. This very quick-witted hypnotist went on about how some people are easy to put under. Others are more difficult, and some people block it entirely. What was fascinating, as well as entertaining, was the things that people can do and say while under hypnosis. So naturally we wanted to see what someone would do or say while under. The stage hypnotist scanned the audience as he asked for volunteers.

When he found three favorable subjects, he called them to the stage and motioned for the audience to give the volunteers a hearty round of applause in advance because his "little bird," as he referred to his intuition, told him they would be good subjects. I forget the exact words he said to the boy, but after a few moments the boy took an onion to the audience, walked up to his girlfriend, and told her that he had a big shiny apple and invited her to take a bite. She laughed and said that she would pass on the invitation.

"Come on, sweety," he insisted. "An apple a day keeps the doctor away." Then he took a bite of it and said, "Uuummm—good."

The audience roared in laughter.

The second subject took a bottle of vinegar and told his girlfriend that it was a nice cool refreshing can of Coca-Cola, the real thing, and invited her to take a drink. She also declined. He then opened the lid, lifted it to his mouth, and took a drink.

The third subject was told that he was five years old. He soon began speaking in a little boy's voice and started to print his ABC'S on a big chalkboard that the hypnotist's assistant brought on stage. When someone in the audience yelled out, "Come on Darin, write your name. You know you can do it. This is all fake."

Darin just looked into space and kept talking like a little boy. He curved his hand and with chalk slowly spelled out the letters much like a child will do upon first learning the alphabet.

I know these early accounts are not metaphysically complex, but they were mind-expanding for me, and they served to help introduce me to the wonderful world of the mind, hypnosis, and other altered states which became so easy for me to enter later down the road. Such experiences were the *seed planting times,* as I like to refer to them.

Was the hypnotist a fake? Did he meet with those three boys before the demonstration and set things up to pretend they would be real? Although I have no proof, I personally do not believe so because the boy who tasted the onion and the one who took a drink of the vinegar did not flinch, choke, or show the slightest negative reaction.

As far as they were concerned, it was the apple and Coca-Cola that were real and not the onion and vinegar. I take apple cider vinegar every day, and I know from experience that I still cough and form these funny grimaces on my face because vinegar is sour. The boy did not give the slightest indication that he was tasting an onion and not an apple. I believe the hypnotist must have told them only to take a small amount because neither took in much as it no doubt could have made them sick. When the hypnotist snapped his fingers and brought them back, they did not recall anything.

That demonstration blew me away. That people can respond so easily to suggestion while hypnotized and do and say things they do not recall later, unless told to, fascinated me. It spurred my interest in hypnosis and the desire to understand and explore the mind with its access to infinite realms of information. I knew that exploring the inner world would take on more meaning and become an equal priority in my life along with my daily involvement in the outer world. The journey was just beginning. I knew I could never go back!

I went to Chautauqua, New York, the summer of 1977 to study opera. I was fortunate to meet a retired high school teacher who gave me French lessons.

Even back then I was starting to ask deeper questions because when Miss Lawson would teach me phrases, I would say, "French feels so familiar and natural to me."

She complimented me and said that I had a natural flair for foreign languages. She encouraged me to take up French when I returned to college in Kentucky. I followed her advice and learned French fluently in two years; along with becoming semi-fluent in Spanish and German, I taught myself some Italian.

One highlight of that summer at Chautauqua was that I got to meet the renowned *mentalist,* The Amazing Kreskin and become his subject at a public demonstration at the big outdoor amphitheater. Kreskin invited about ten participants to sit in a row of chairs. He had another five of us stand aside and watch.

First, he did some stage demonstrations, utilizing hypnotic suggestions, such as telling the audience participants that they were riding a camel on sizzling steamy desert sand. I noted that a few of them began breathing harder, and they started sweating. I could actually see drops of sweat trickling down their necks. Next, Kreskin told them they were on a snowmobile in the freezing Antarctica. Their teeth clattered, and they started hugging themselves for warmth. It didn't feel fake to me. The temperature outside was very mild—in the mid-70's, and there was a breeze. It was not warm or cold enough to cause them to sweat or to get the freezing chills.

Kreskin came to those of us who were standing and started speaking softly. At one point he told us to pretend we were ducks and to move our fingers and thumb back and forth like a duck bill. I recall how I closed my eyes and did as he requested, not feeling anything other than that I was humoring him. The others did likewise.

A few moments later he stood next to me and whispered something. My left hand stopped the motions, but then my right hand started the motions. The audience loved it because I was jumping about pointing my left forefinger at my right hand which would not stop the motion. It truly seemed to have a mind of its own. I started yelling loudly.

"Stop, hand. Stop! Stop! What is wrong with you!?" I exclaimed as I jumped about in big strides. The audience found it very amusing and entertaining and applauded, but I was not pretending. My right hand literally would not stop moving. A few moments later, Kreskin moved closer and whispered something else in my ear. The movement stopped. He motioned for me to take a bow, and the audience applauded once more.

His assistant brought out more chairs, and we all sat next to the others. He said something to the effect "Now for the mystical moments. I am going to lead you in a meditation. Just relax and go with it. Try not to let your mind get in the way."

He began his induction. My head started feeling light like it did when Janette put us under. The next thing I knew I was slowly bending forward until my head was completely drooped over.

Kreskin came over to me and said, "Young man, you are extremely susceptible to hypnosis. This is something you ought to check out."

I bought his book *The Amazing Kreskin* and was thrilled that he autographed it "ESP-ecially, Kreskin."

Kreskin was also purported to do such *mentalistic* feats as have individuals concentrate on their telephone or driver's license numbers and then be able to *read* their thoughts and repeat the numbers they concentrated upon. There is a story of him having done something of this sort with some famous people. One may have been Carol Burnett if I recall correctly.

Kreskin was so adamant about not being *psychic* or possessing psychic abilities. I never really understood it because mentalism and hypnosis seem to me to belong to the domain of the paranormal, especially when the hypnotized subject goes back to past lives. Perhaps Kreskin and other mentalists or hypnotists avoid delving into past lives.

My interest in mentalism and hypnosis returned after college when I quit full-time teaching and had more time for my psychic pursuits and writing. I even considered becoming a stage hypnotist and was wondering how I would get certified for that, or was it just pure entertainment? I wondered if I needed to have subjects sign a form that said "For entertainment purposes only" or some such thing. I wanted to delve deeper and explore other layers and domains of the mind because I already had several experiences which led me to believe there was far more to us than our conscious awareness.

I do believe that things happen when they are supposed to. It's as though our higher self and guides help to manifest and bring to us those circumstances and situations that will be conducive to our growth. Often we are consciously aware of what we need to experience and we simply attract it via the law of attraction. Some say we should watch what we ask for because we will get it. I wanted to delve more deeply into the mind and inner world. I was to get far more than I could ever have dreamed of or hoped for.

CHAPTER SIX

AN AUTOMATIC WRITING
SPIRITUAL EPIPHANY

Although I had many paranormal and psychic experiences up to this point, I still had my daily life to deal with and problems like everybody else. I had to deal with the everyday mundane world like all people, and one area that I was not good at was the domain of human/romantic love. I suffered from a deep loneliness and yearning to have a special relationship. It just never seemed to happen. I could attract people but could never sustain or find any lasting satisfaction in my relationships. One advantage to being receptive to spiritual guidance and information is that during a crisis divine spiritual intervention can come to us seemingly out of thin air when we least expect it. Such is what happened to me in the wee hours of one morning back in May of 1984 when I was suffering from the woes and throes of unrequited love.

Now in my early fifties, I have moved beyond the need for so much drama when it comes to human love, but it took a lot of bumpy roads before I arrived where I am today. I think of a verse from Helen Reddy's song "I am Woman," "Yes, I am wise, but it's wisdom born of pain. Yes, I paid the price, but look how much I gained."

That seems to sum me up quite well at this juncture of my life. But to illustrate the power of God, love and the higher self, let's take a little journey back to the time when I was in what I like to call Love Academy 101, for I believe that everything we experience is a lesson for our soul.

To be in love! How grand. How blissful. How painful. How scary. How tempting. How irresistible. How crazy. How wonderful. How long will it last? To many people, the experience of being in love is one of the primary purposes for life on the earth. So many people are sad and lonely because they have not successfully been able to sustain the *in love* feeling and experience. Many of us yearn, hope, and pray that the love of our life will come to us and give us that feeling of completeness that we ache for and hope will last.

"Please love me forever" goes an old Bobby Vinton song.

I read one poem where the Cupid-struck lad promised the lady of his dreams that he would love her forever and a day. That's a pretty long time, don't you think? Songs, poems, movies, and books are filled with stories of star-crossed lovers, and far too often the endings are not like in the fairy tales where the jubilant couple lives happily ever after. Many are lucky if that *in love* feeling lasts a few years, or nowadays a few months, let alone forever. Forever and a day. I wonder how many people really believe in this possibility other than in the realm of fantasy.

Like many people, I have spent more than my share of time dreaming, hoping, and yearning for love. To find the so-called *right person* to love me forever and to spend my life with has been a lifelong hope and aspiration. If we are lucky, or dare I suggest unlucky, we may have even have had the experience of being *madly* in love. This usually involves a certain degree of obsession with our beloved. We can't get him/her out of our head or heart. We think about him/her at least a hundred, if not more, times a day. Some of us have gone so far as to confiscate a personal object or article of clothing of our beloved to help us feel close to him/her when not in his/her presence.

When I knew my beloved was going to spend a year studying in England, I sneaked into the laundry room one day and helped myself to an article of his clothing. I relished that little article of clothing the whole year he was gone. I would even walk two miles just to see the little doughnut shop where he worked, and I would say, "My beloved works there."

The things we do when in love. The relationship was far more one-sided than I liked. Still I dreamed. I hoped. A few crumbs would be tossed my way to keep me hoping, and the proverbial carrot was ever dangling in front of me but never mine to grasp.

Days passed and I grew more wretched, and despair began gnawing at me days and nights. "What is wrong with me?" I asked myself over and over. "Why is my beloved toying with my heart and constantly dangling carrots before me? How come he comes closer to me, allowing certain intimacies, only to pull away the next time? Why? Why? Why?" Many of us have been there, and it's no day in the park, to say the least.

To escape the pain and turmoil, I tried avoiding my beloved. That only made it worse. It was better to live with a few crumbs than none at all. I thought of an Elvis Presley song that said, "I'd rather live with your lies than to be without you at all." Well, my beloved was not a liar but most assuredly was someone who toyed with my heart and constantly manipulated me. And, yes, I know it takes "two to tango," as the saying goes. In time I was to learn that this was all part of my karmic dance with this person.

One night I went to bed agonizing over my beloved. He would toy with my heart, back off to some degree but would never completely pull away. The fact that we were best friends made it much more difficult. I have heard that we should never fall in love with our best friend. I have also heard and come to believe that we do not usually get to choose whom we love. This is chosen and pre-planned on the spirit realm before we are born and is based on our unresolved karma from a past life or lives.

The challenge is that we don't remember our agreement and signing of the karmic contract once we get here. What we do remember is the soul-mate connection (although this is usually unconscious but no less compelling) and our powerful attraction to the person. This can account for many cases of love at first sight. There can be far more to this than people realize. This can help to explain why relationships can be so complex, trying, and challenging. Often times we have loved this soul in more than one past life. In one life or more, there could have been much love expressed and good karma created.

In another lifetime negative karma could have been incurred. In this lifetime a balance and working out of the karma must be achieved, or the two people will come back in a future incarnation to complete the lessons and karma. I was to learn of several past lives I had had with my beloved, but at the time I was not aware of any of them. What I was aware of and what was driving me half-crazy was how madly in love I was with someone who would only give so much and who constantly led me on.

An interesting point is that Christopher had always dated women and although I had been with men, I had not really dated any, excluding the brief love affair I had with a Frenchman in France. Nonetheless, I was to learn that when there is soul recognition and karma to work out, the person's gender bears little upon the karmic dynamics to be worked out. This unrequited love was shredding my heart and soul. I was obsessed with my beloved Chris, and there seemed to be nothing I could do about it. The more I shoved the thoughts away, the more they came back.

I had fantasies of throwing myself over a bridge just to end the pain. Finally, in desperation one night as I tossed and turned in bed, tearful and restless, I begged God to not let me wake up. The pain was too much. I could take it no more. Well, I did not have the good fortune to not wake up. Dying in my sleep was not an option.

I woke up at 5:00 a.m. with the words dancing in front of my eyes, "Your beloved will one day see the light, but there is a price for enlightenment."

"What?" I cried out, thinking I was still asleep and dreaming. I was compelled to get pencil and pen out. I wrote "Messages to my Soul" via automatic writing, and I scribbled the words very fast.

MESSAGES TO MY SOUL

Your beloved will one day see the light,
But there is a price for Enlightenment.
It is alienation from the crowd.

For you who have the courage,
You can see the truth past the illusions.
You may feel alone sometimes,
But deep in your soul you know
That you are not.

You are one!
Whole and complete!
You do not need the crowd.
As soon as you give up your illusions,
You shall come to know God more fully.

You are a part of God.
God is Love and so are you.
God simply is
And you must be.
Thus you struggle on the earth.

You see God in others.
They see God in you.
Too often you refuse to see God within.

God says to you:
My beloved children!
I am incomplete without you.
I am alone.
I need your company.

That is why I created you.
It was for companionship.
That I might know myself through you
And that you might know yourself through me.

This is infinite love.
I am infinite love.
So are you.

When you believe this, you shall come to know me.
You shall never feel alone again.
Your searching shall end.
Your soul shall know peace
But only when you come to know me.

I embrace you with loving, open arms.
You are all my children.
I am your loving father and mother.

I am one!
If I am whole,
How can you not be?

Suffering can lead you to joy.
After the rain comes the rainbow.
Enlightenment comes after much pain.

Your soul is willing to pay the price
For it hungers for its home far beyond.
You know that pain is an illusion.

Jesus knew.
That is why he bore his cross and burdens.
He does not regret it
Nor shall you regret the crosses you bear.

It is only in losing your life that you gain it.
To say this in the words of one of your beloved saints,
St. Francis of Assisi,
It is in dying that we are born to eternal life.

Remember these words and be sad no more.
Know that these difficult times shall pass.
This I promise you.

I am with you always!
That Which Is!

My fingers were tired after scribbling all those words down. Yawning, I looked at the words, many of which were difficult to make out. Admittedly, 5:00 a.m. is not my prime time to be awake, let alone to write or read. *This is too much* I recall thinking. *I am going back to bed and forget I wrote this. Maybe I just imagined those words anyhow.*

To my surprise, when I got up a few hours later, I had a strange exciting feeling. It made no sense to me, but it was better than the despair I felt before going to bed. Something profound and life changing had happened to me all in the span of a few hours. I had experienced via that automatic writing some kind of spiritual awakening. I had had an epiphany. My attention was drawn to my journal lying on the kitchen table. Over breakfast that strange anticipation and excitement became even stronger. I took my journal and turned the pages until I found the new writing I had scribbled a few hours earlier. The title was "Messages to My Soul." This time I took the time to read *the writing* carefully.

Needless to say, I was quite taken aback and astounded. I wasn't sure what to make of parts of it, and I was quite amazed that I could just wake up and write something like that. I had read many books and heard that there are many layers of the mind we seldom tap into. Had I tapped another layer of my own mind or soul? Had the angel who visited me so long ago returned with a new message for me? Could I have actually received messages from God as *the writing* suggested? One thing was for certain, I concluded, *This was not my conscious everyday self communicating. I simply did not think or talk like that.*

I recalled reading somewhere that people sometimes make creative breakthroughs after going through "a dark night of the soul." Well, I certainly had had a dark night of the soul. I truly feared that this unfulfilled, unrequited love was driving me mad. My grip on reality felt very fragile. I had hot flashes and would be overcome with spells of dizziness. To quote a line from a Gilbert and Sullivan operetta, "I was a love sick boy." Actually, I was more than that. This crazy love was killing me, or so I thought back then. Emotional reactions are often exaggerated in our younger years, especially regarding the matters of the heart.

My responses and reactions are much more mellow these days, but this, I realize, offers little if any consolation to those tortured souls enduring their own version of unrequited love. One reason I shared this story is to point out to people undergoing the emotional agony of unrequited love that such dark nights of the soul can lead to epiphanies such as happened to me. Such spiritual awakenings can forever change our lives and alter the course of our destiny in a positive way.

While caught up in the throes of unrequited love, we can be overcome with so many raw, irrational emotions that we become imbalanced. We can even entertain fantasies of suicide; in more extreme cases, very sadly some do take their lives during such desperate moments. I admit there were many days during those times that I did not wish to continue living.

Since this was my first such writing, I naturally tried to figure out where "Messages to My Soul" came from. To believe and entertain the idea that it came from God seemed to be more than I was ready to take on or prepared to handle. To entertain such a concept was too mind-stretching for my already open mind. I see now that the seeds were being planted, and God knew exactly what she/he was doing.

Many years later I was to write a metaphysical book, *Morning Coffee with God*, based on dream visits I had with God where many of my deep questions were answered. Now it's perfectly clear and obvious to me that my despair and desperation had opened the very doors of heaven, and Divinity itself came to my rescue. The *writing* speaks for itself. Other experiences and writings, such as "The Voice Behind Your Voice" in *Morning Coffee with God* would further validate my contact with God.

But like I said, back then I was not ready or prepared for a direct encounter with God, even though as God had pointed out in the book, I had already had several encounters with him/her before. Now I cannot imagine *not having* such contact. I believe from the bottom of my heart that God wishes to have personal contact with everyone. I think of a line God, Mr. Divine, said to me in *Morning Coffee with God.* To quote him/her, "I am as real as your capacity to receive me is, and your capacity to receive me is much greater than you can ever begin to imagine."

My dear friend Leslie, whom I had known for a couple of years before *the writing* came, said she had no idea where "Messages to My Soul" came from. She suggested that I keep an open mind because the messages were clearly positive ones.

"To be truthful, I had no idea where this came from. It was all very new and different for me. I could not get over the idea that I could wake up in the wee hours of the morning and write something so profound in a rapid creative burst of energy. If I had found writing like that in a book, I would have passed over it, concluding that it was too deep and far out for me; however, as was to be the case with other writings, I found that I could not just toss aside and disregard something that came from my own mouth, or rather my own pen. I reminded myself that this was not the first time I had had unusual experiences. I thought of the angel who came to me at age thirteen, and then it dawned upon me that she appeared to me at a very difficult time of my life, as did the second angel two years later. So here I was again—having an unusual spiritual experience during a particularly difficult time.

I read "Messages" several times during the next few days and did feel better. Some of the peaceful energy and excitement remained with me. However, it was not long before the old yearning for my beloved returned. Chris called a few days after I wrote "Messages" and wanted to go jogging, which we often did. Afterwards we exchanged sensual massages. This only served to awaken the desires I was trying so hard to quell. How could Chris be so sensual and yet restrained? There was such tenderness and even passion in his touch, but it was restrained passion.

Trying to figure out what was going on and not being able to openly discuss this up front with Chris was very frustrating.

I had rehearsed lines dozens of time of what I'd say to him. I'd tell myself the next time I saw him I was going to tell him how I felt. For some reason I could never figure out why I could never follow through. Even though I sensed that he knew I was in love with him, Chris never brought the subject up either. Part of me feared I might lose his friendship if I brought anything up, and I could not bear that. We had so much fun together. I loved our jogging, our long deep philosophical talks, speaking French together, sharing dirty jokes. I cherished our friendship. Chris even felt like a brother to me at times. Neither of our fathers were there for us; I believe this is partly what drew us together. Later, I would learn that we had played out many different roles in several past lives. That makes so much sense now because then I knew I had never felt such a connection with a man before Chris and never have since. Instead of confronting him, I continued to hope and dream. Things did not progress the way I wanted, and this put me in a state of utter despair.

Overwhelmed with sorrow and depression, I tossed "Messages" aside in a drawer. I ignored it for days and weeks. Then one day a strange thing happened. I was having dinner with Leslie, and for some reason my attention was diverted to the lady at the next table.

"What will you be having tonight, Annie?" the waiter asked her.

The lady paused a moment then said, "I am ravished, dearie. Hungrier than a bear. Let me see now, for starters I'd like a nice hot bowl of your clam chowder with lots of crackers, and, of course, a salad with extra blue cheese dressing. Then for my entree, let's see—oh yes, I need some sole. Yes, I'll have your filet of sole."

She went on describing exactly how she wanted the sauce and what veggies she wanted. After the word *sole*, I heard little more except the waiter who said, "Yes, Annie sweetie, anything you want." I remember smiling, thinking that his tip jar must grow twice its size after Annie left.

"I need some sole," I kept hearing in my mind, looking in the distance lost in a kind of daze.

"Are you okay?" Leslie asked.

"I'm fine," I replied, smiling, a little embarrassed and wondering how long I had been distracted. "It was the way that lady ordered her meal," I continued, pointing at her nearby table. "See her. She's the big lady with the curly black hair. When she said, "I need some sole." I got goose bumps all over. It reminded me of that strange *writing* I got that morning a few weeks ago."

"Very interesting," Leslie replied, sipping her wine. "Wasn't it called 'Message to My Soul?'"

"Yes," I answered.

"Sole. Soul. O Sole mio I sing you an Italian solo, and he sang so low you could hardly hear him. Do re mi fa SO la ti do. Sew me on a fresh new button if you please. So on and so forth I continued, snickering."

Leslie started laughing. "Stop it, Leslie or you'll have me punning again."

She looked away a moment; then her eyes slowly met mine again. "You know, Michael, kidding aside, the mind can play tricks on us. But hold on a moment here. Maybe this sole/soul thing is some kind of omen or something. You've been really down lately over *you-know-who*. You said that 'Messages' gave you some relief for awhile. Have you read it lately?"

"I'm too depressed to read anything."

"You didn't destroy it, did you? If you did, I'll wring your neck, Michael."

"No. It's' in a drawer."

"Thank goodness," Leslie said, giving a sigh of relief. "I know how you can be sometimes. I think your guides have helped create this little scenario with the lady wanting her filet of sole to get your attention. You know how you love to pun. Well, now that the guides have your attention, I think maybe this is a sign that you ought to dig 'Messages to My Soul' out and reread it. There's probably something in it that you missed before."

"Maybe. What have I got to lose but a little sole?" I said, trying to be funny. "Lots of fishy things going on lately with you-know-who."

Leslie was not smiling. She knew I sometimes reverted to corny puns when I was depressed.

"Well, you started it," I said, mimicking a pout. "So, you don't like *pun*-y men. Okay, I'll stop being *punny*," I said. "Go ahead and *pun*-ish me. To be truthful, I'm so desperate now that I think I'd give my very soul for some relief."

Leslie tapped me lightly on the hand in a gentle reprimand. "Don't you ever say that again, Michael. No one is worth our soul. It is ours and ours alone, given to us by God our beloved Creator Source. It's a very special part of us that we must love, honor, and cherish always. We must never give that much of ourselves to anyone. To do so is like killing yourself and dropping dead on their doorstep. If you give your soul to someone—not that it can even be done since lord knows we may never really understand what the soul is or fully entails—you're as good as dead and at their total mercy."

"You ought to write a book, Leslie. You sure do get going sometimes."

"Hearing things like that really affects me somehow. People say things like that all the time. You even hear it in songs, and it disturbs me. I know what you're going through to some degree and have only love and compassion for you, but please don't think you need to give your soul to *you-know-who*. Not that it would even help one iota if you did."

"Capisco," I said, kissing her on the cheek. "Maybe I should give my soul to you, and we can get married. You'd never hurt me, Leslie."

"You are right. I will never hurt you, Michael. Cross my heart and hope to die," she said, grinning, "but seriously, go home and reread 'Messages.'"

When I got back to my apartment, I took out a diet Pepsi from the fridge and sat on the front porch, enjoying the breeze. A little while later, it was as though I could see Leslie's image in front of me and hear her say. "Read *"Messages"* again." I read it three times as tears trickled down my face. After I put it down, I kept hearing the lines:

Remember these words and be sad no more.

I am with you always.

That Which is!

"'Be sad no more,'" I whispered. "Easy for you to say. Who are you anyway? Surely this cannot be a message from God. 'I am with you always,'" I read and saw this image of Jesus telling his disciples that "Lo, I am with you always, unto the end of the world."

"Well, whoever you are, thanks," I whispered.

When I woke the next morning *"Messages"* was on my mind, so I read it again. My sadness had abated somewhat, and this time I was much more open-minded and receptive to the messages in the *writing* than before.

I called Leslie and said, "I read 'Messages' several times and paid more attention than before. One thing I have to admit is that wherever 'Messages' came from, it makes me feel that somehow I am not alone, and its inspirational messages are quite profound. I guess this is reason enough to keep the *writing*. If it truly is a message from God, so much the better. I used to talk to God as a kid a lot. Maybe he just took a while to get back with me," I said humorously.

In the days ahead I came to accept and be glad and grateful for 'Messages.' I thought more about writing and realized that I have always loved words and writing. Even as a kid I used to say I am going to be a writer. I was always making up stories. I loved to participate in spelling bees. I always had several books going. I got good grades in English, creative writing, and journalism classes. For presents I asked for notebooks, pens, and pencils, instead of guns and GI Jo toys. The fact that my writing was moving into new directions didn't alter the fact that writing is a healing creative outlet for me.

"Messages" helped me to feel that my deep loneliness of so many years might be coming to an end, or at least reducing. I had read and heard that many artists and writers derive great

comfort, fulfillment, and satisfaction from their creations. Some go so far to say that their art is more important and fulfilling to them than personal relationships. I once read about a lady who took to sculpting after her husband died. She fell so in love with her art that she gradually became a recluse. She even stopped attending church. When asked what had come over her, she said that her muse came to her late in life. She had to put an end to most of her social life because her art was her new love and life. There was so much to be done, and she could not afford to indulge in idle chatter at boring parties and social events.

I was certainly not ready to take things that far, but that story always fascinated me. It gave me much comfort to know that some people truly enjoy spending great amounts of time alone being creative and artistic. Artists and creative people usually have something to show for their time alone and solitude.

This new *writing* led me to conclude that we are not alone. Even when I thought despair would engulf me and the pain of my torn heart would shred my soul into bits, the faith and hope of that *writing* kept me going. It would be awhile before the next *writing* came, but in the interim I kept dreaming. I had made first contact. Surely, there would be more.

Later, as I read this and other writings, I was very humbled, to say the least. That such agonizing misery could open the door to heightened levels of awareness and wisdom of cosmic proportions was mind-staggering. It made me start to think of suffering in a completely different light and helped me redefine its purposes, or at least some of them. That such pain could put me into contact with my higher self and God was mind-blowing at first. This experience challenged some of my very core beliefs about life, suffering, and pain. It would stretch my spiritual vision and lead to new insights. The breakthrough made me see that pain is so much more than pain. In the *greater picture,* pain is a most honorable and worthy teacher. It can transport us past our human ego into the very arms and embrace of the divine. It gave new meaning to the axiom, "No pain, no gain."

Thinking about pain and its lessons has surely occupied many hours of my time, especially when I have had so much of it. Learning that pain is a great teacher did not mean that I wanted to become some kind of masochist who couldn't get enough pain to satisfy some abnormal neurotic impulses and fantasies. Rereading "Messages" touched my soul deeply. The words reminded me that I am a child of God/All That Is; I am important and have a place in the grander scheme of things, as everyone does.

I re-read the part where God referred to St. Francis of Assisi's prayer, "It is in dying that we are born to eternal life." I realized that one of the purposes of unrequited love and the tremendous suffering it entails is to deal some death blows to the unhealthy attachments of the ego that is looking outside *self* for love and wholeness. To seek outside self for love and wholeness is futile.

Love begins *within* self. When we love and embrace the wholeness of self, we don't need love from others. The paradox and irony is that when we don't need it from others, then love comes to us from others. We attract others to share in the oneness that we have come to embrace in our self. This sounds like a contradiction but it is not.

To help illustrate my point, I think of the saying, "If you love someone, you must set him/her free. If he/she comes back to you, then it is meant to be. If he/she doesn't, it was never meant to be." By detaching our self from the selfish needs and clutches of our ego and personal attachments, we free ourselves from the burdens and suffering which result from having such attachments.

"Messages to My Soul" emphasized the importance of divine love and the need for us to realize and feel our connection to God and to embrace our inner wholeness. It shamed me to think that I was so torn and incomplete that this led to despair and desperation for love from someone else. It horrified me to think back on how desperate I had become because my beloved did not reciprocate the love I felt so deeply and passionately. That pain and desperation drove me to fantasies of suicide. To have taken my life would have been to commit a disgrace and abomination against *self,* which may have taken several lifetimes to recover and heal from. "Messages" was a profound spiritual epiphany and wake up call for me. To think I had to depend upon someone outside of me to give me that sense of wholeness and feeling of love was scary. And yet that is how I thought and believed for many years.

It reminded me that I had slipped into the embrace of oblivion and illusion. In time I began to realize that to continue to pursue someone who is not reciprocating love is very dysfunctional and unhealthy. It can never satisfy the soul, for the soul knows it is whole and complete in itself. Its love is universal and unconditional. It seeks to share its love which is totally unlimited. I think of my chapter "On Love" in my book, *Morning Coffee with God,* where I say this:

> Love is complete unto herself, remaining invisible to all who refuse to see themselves for who they truly are: whole and complete souls.
> There at the sacred altar your ego and soul will be wed. Then you will no longer search outside yourself for completion.
> It is at this time, and this time only, that Love can make herself visible to you through someone else's eyes.

I wrote/channeled "On Love" in 1990 and see that here again my soul was trying to get me to see that I was looking for love in the wrong places, as the song goes. After all I had read about, written and channeled, I was still not getting it.

I also pray that people will be able to work through their karma, for if they do not, then they will return to repeat it all over again. My metaphysical teachings tell me that the lessons become harder in each future lifetime. As an optimist I hope and keep the faith that readers who find my book and have their own karmic dramas and relationships to work out will arrive at the point where they will also realize the truth of the profound, loving universal messages that God gave to me in "Messages to My Soul." We all need to be reminded that the God spark of light is true essence of our soul.

"Messages" showed me that God wants us to know how special, beautiful and unique we each are. We are all his/her children and like he said, "You are one. Whole and complete!"

As soon as we give up our illusions, we shall come to know God more fully. In another verse he said, "I am one! If I am whole, how can you not be?"

I still cry when I read the *writing*. My favorite line is "God is love and so are you. God simply is and you must be."

I was also touched how he points out that suffering leads to joy. "That after the rain comes the rainbow. Enlightenment comes after much pain."

God honors our soul and points out that the soul is willing to pay the price of enlightenment, for it hungers for its home far beyond.

Then, as if tossing another pearl of hope and truth after acknowledging that pain and suffering lead to joy and enlightenment, he adds, "You know that pain is an illusion." He shows us that we will come to not regret the crosses and burdens we bear and that in losing our life, we gain it. To me this refers to the death of the unhealthy attachments of our ego. And in that dying we are born to eternal life. God invites us to remember the words he speaks, and he promises and assures us that these difficult times will pass.

Then lastly, he promises that he is always with us, "I am with you always! *That Which Is!*"

That really blew me away because God/All That Is/Great Spirit ends the profound *writing* by dismissing the label and term *God* which, we know, can have many negative connotations and arouse anger in some people who have seen some of the abominations and atrocities committed in God's name. He uses the more all-encompassing, all-inclusive name of "*That Which Is*" which is similar to "I am that I am" he referred to himself when Moses asked him his true name.

Like the angel who visited me when I was thirteen, God offered me hope during a horrible painful time of my life. I read *the writing* until I memorized it. This did not take away the emotional pain, but it gave some relief. I do have to confess there were times that I would get angry at God and try to forget "Messages to My Soul." That would be my ego ranting and raving, and that, too, shall pass, as the saying goes, I would tell myself. The ranting and ravings of the ego are part of the clearing of the karmic sludge. The benefit of a writing divinely inspired is that we have the choice and opportunity to step outside our karmic situation and to make contact with our higher self, who is part of God. That is why I think I received the *writing* at the time I did. In a way it was a life saver for me. I also believe that my higher self was completely aware of what was transpiring, and it had a part in shaking me up with that automatic writing.

Looking back, I see that although it can be very comforting to receive an inspirational message in the wee hours of the morn, such comfort can be short-lived while still in the throes of unrequited love. No matter how much information we may read or receive from God, our guides, etc., however profound and enlightened it might be, it does not efface the karma that we have yet to pay off for past life abuse and imbalances of energy in the love department. I was sure to learn that from experience.

I also know that God and our higher self can and often plant seeds whether it be via dreams, revelations, epiphanies, visions, or even a book or movie. This can help us deal with our karma although it cannot take it away in most cases. A mystical direct encounter with God or other angelic divine beings can be so powerful that to recall them when we are caught up in the drama of our karma can offer some relief and comfort. Even a small glimmer of comfort and hope might be all that it takes to keep us from going over the edge.

Sometimes we are lucky enough to get blasted with a Zeus lightning bolt, to insert some humor, or an enlightened *writing*. In other cases, the ailing, suffering person may come upon a book or magazine that says what he/she needs to hear. I read one story of a lady who said that a book literally fell from a bookstore shelf, and it was perfect for what she needed to hear. Pat Mischell, the author of *Beyond Positive Thinking*, says that coming upon Joseph Murphy's book, *The Power of the Subconscious Mind*, is what helped to set her upon a healing path where she healed her physical body. So, as the saying goes, "God works in mysterious ways."

Even though I have moved on from the torturous *unrequited love period* in my mid-twenties, I have never forgotten how heart-felt and wrenching a relationship can be, as well as the joy, bliss, and ecstasy I experienced. It is my hope and wish that readers can take some comfort from "Messages to My Soul" and be encouraged to invoke God and their soul and guides for comfort and answers.

CHAPTER SEVEN

A VISIT WITH JESUS THE CHRIST

The *writing* "Messages to My Soul" was a turning point for me. It connected me to a deeper part of myself and reminded me that we are much more than humans having third-dimensional experiences. We are a soul having divine, as well as human, experiences. Or differently said, we are spirit souls coming to the earth to participate in human experience for our growth and learning. Although seeking, searching, and yearning for human love and that special soul mate would occupy a lot of my time, I now felt connected to a deeper love. I felt like a child of beloved Creator Source who loves everyone and does not wish for any of us to suffer.

After reading the part in "Messages to My Soul" where Jesus was referred to, I began thinking of him a lot. I took out my Bible and read from the New Testament and was very inspired and uplifted. I began to feel Jesus' loving, radiant presence—sometimes in dreams and sometimes during the day time. I wondered how he was able to achieve and accomplish what he did, and I asked him many questions. A month or so later I felt the urge to write. "The Great Price" is what came to me.

The Great Price

You calmed the storms; you stilled the winds.

Clouds vanished at your command.

When turbulent waters rocked boats to and fro,

Tranquility was restored when you waved your hand.

87

You walked on water; you healed the sick.
You asked for bread, and it came from the sky.
You changed water to wine; you raised the dead.
You were also a man who cried.

Tell me your secret, Great One, I humbly ask.
To bring peace to troubled souls is my request.
I want to offer hope to this world.
For weary souls I want to be a haven of rest.

If you are sincere, he replied to me,
And truly desire to relieve suffering on earth,
In many ways can you alleviate pain.
I can teach you the concept of rebirth.

The road that I traveled is traveled by few.
It is steep, rocky, and uphill.
The path to self-mastery is a difficult path.
It is the ultimate test of the will.

Before you help others, you must pass many tests
To be worthy of the work you wish to do.
You must forget about yourself and freely give.
To serve humanity will require much from you.

Many temptations you will face on this path.

Envious souls will want to see you stumble and fall.

You can succeed if you are determined enough.

You can climb over the highest wall.

You must walk many days in deserts below,

But you will never die of hunger or thirst.

You will feel alone and forsaken at times.

By jealous souls you will even be cursed.

Many powers can be yours, dear seeker,

If you succeed in all your tests.

A will of iron you must have and never give up.

For this, you will truly be blessed.

Yes, like me you can be in many ways—

A bright light that shines like a star.

Many souls can you heal; many storms can you calm.

When pure, there will be peace wherever you are.

Know that to master the self takes time.

Through your efforts much progress have you made.

Enlightenment is not achieved overnight.

Remember to call on me when you need aid.

I will send mentors to help you.
They will gladly share what they know.
Work hard and prepare yourself well.
Remember, the seed must slowly grow.

One day you can help people find peace.
For them you can be a haven of rest.
I can share many secrets, dear seeker.
Are you still serious about your request?

Many others make similar requests.
They wish to know the secrets I knew there.
I see through their deception and insincerity.
They put up facades and they really do not care.

I have begun the journey, Great One!
I am willing to walk every road.
I wandered in darkness until I glimpsed the light.
I want to help carry others' heavy load.

You can find peace after much toil.
People may one day seek your holy advice.
If you are different and holy, it will only be
Because you are willing to pay the great price.

I would ask myself many times just how willing am I to pay the great price? Often the spiritual healing journey became so difficult that it seemed I'd never escape all the briers and brambles that life tossed my way. I would read the "The Great Price" over and over until I had it memorized. I may have been one mixed up young man at the age of twenty-five when I wrote "The Great Price," but I was sincere in my desire to heal and to relieve suffering on the earth. I was to learn that we must first heal ourselves before we can help to heal others and relieve their suffering. We must each learn that there is much we cannot do. This is because everyone has his/her lessons to learn. Growth often entails challenges and obstacles that can be monumental.

I thought about Jesus saying that before I can help others, I must pass many tests to be worthy of the work I wish to do. One of the primary tests would be learning to tame and control my ego that can be quite a handful at times, to say the least. It is so easy for the ego to start working overtime as a friend of mine used to say. This is especially true when we start to develop and come into our psychic and spiritual gifts and powers.

I was to be no different from many others who fall into temptation; however, one thing that I had going for me was that I was strong enough to keep a close eye on the workings and doings of my ego. In the past when my ego began working overtime and I started getting a *big head*, I'd shut down and pull away until I had my ego back in check and under control. This can be quite a challenge because the ego will constantly utilize different tactics to get what it wants. It does not like to lose control or to surrender to the higher self or soul. Like a spoiled child, it wants what it wants and when it wants it, I might add.

I think back to the summer of 1986 when I underwent some intense psychic training with my spiritual teacher, Mary. When I'm in the flow and in balance, constant opportunities come my way. People show up out of the woodwork. Clients find me on my website, in the phonebook, and on the internet.

Even the media finds me. Shortly after Mary and I decided that I was ready to begin doing professional psychic readings, a friend of mine put me in contact with a journalist from the local newspaper. A week later he interviewed Mary and me and did a feature story on us. When I give interviews, I ask the media people to give my contact information so people who are interested in my services can reach me. On the day the article came out, I was visiting a friend out of town.

Mary called me and said, "Michael, get back here now. The phone is ringing off the hook."

Mary had booked a long list of clients wanting psychic and past life readings. I was busy enough that my readings paid my bills the rest of the summer, thus allowing me to complete my graduate courses at Indiana University to earn my teaching certificate.

People said the readings were very good and some even said that they blew them away. They were telling their friends and family about me, and my calendar began to fill up more. I was getting names and initials for people, picking up messages from departed loved ones, and I was *spot right on* with the psychic messages.

Then I slowly started getting a *big head*, as the saying goes. I became arrogant and cocky. The compassion and love that so filled me at first was transforming into mindless indifference and detachment, and I became curt at times. Finally, Mary had had enough and called me on it. She always had a way of being critical when she needed to but always in a gentle manner.

I was stunned as she reprimanded me, reminding me that my psychic gifts were to be respected, and everyone was to be treated with kindness, respect, and love. I knew that in my heart, and to be honest, I do not know how I slowly began to change. Mary reminded me that my guides would take my gifts away if I did not change. I was so full of guilt and shame that I shut down for an entire year and did not do a single reading.

I took my first French teaching job in September in a small town in southern Indiana. Along with teaching and becoming involved in some extracurricular events with the students, I did a lot of soul searching, reading, and studying of metaphysical books.

By the end of my 1st year's teaching assignment, I felt I had learned my lesson, and I began taking a few appointments. Slowly my business began to build up again. All these years later, I constantly monitor my ego and the ego of others in the business. I've been known to give a few *Mary talks* of my own to some psychics whose egos have worked overtime.

I think of Jacob in Genesis 32 of the Old Testament who wrestled all night with the angel. He said he would not stop until the angel gave him a blessing. I believe this story can be interpreted on one level as a metaphor to illustrate the ego doing battle with the higher self in its endeavor to be in charge and in control. I also believe that the tests can continue throughout our life. With each test we pass, we climb a rung higher on the ladder of ascension until one day we merge with divinity and return home to creator source. What a grand day that shall be!

CHAPTER EIGHT

MERGING WITH A ROCK

In the fall of 1990, I met a fascinating, unusual young man through a mutual friend. Robert was interested in healing and various forms of energy work. He said that he had always been able to affect people positively with his energy. One of his skills was to help people open up and tune into healing energies and realms beyond this one. He said it was all part of the contract he chose for this lifetime, and like all contracts, it had its benefits as well as its many risks and challenges. Robert called himself a *light wielder*. Not only did he attract those with beautiful, glowing, radiant hearts, but he also attracted dark souls eager to steal his light. This had resulted in some pretty intense battles.

Robert was a delight to listen and talk to. He was a philosopher at heart and well-read in philosophy and occult books. He told me story after story after we did our energy sessions. Then he'd wink at me and say that his energy was so strong because he came from very far away, "as do you, Michael," he'd add, pointing his arm and finger upward. He'd get this twinkle in his eye and take on a look of nostalgia.

One day he said, "Michael, I come from worlds where the big Central Sun is brighter and much more powerful than the Earth sun. I am a type of interstellar, intergalactic traveler and coach. People use the term *life coach*. I, too, am a type of life coach who works with energy. Actually, I have many names. You can call me an activator and awakener if you wish, for that is partly what I do. I help activate people's inner power, so they can become more of their true *god self* or become a superman or super woman, to quote my favorite philosopher,

Frederick Nietzsche, who is also one of my star brothers. He came to shake up the world, but he went overboard. Unlike my star brother, I am not advocating that people become super men and women as to replace God, who Nietzsche proclaimed was dead. My job is to help people to believe, acknowledge, and become one with God and all life. This is my sole mission in this lifetime."

Naturally, I was fascinated and eager to see what would happen, so I invited Robert over. He informed me that nothing extraordinary would occur for the first few visits. He would have to scan my energy and make some needed adjustments. If I was patient, the fireworks would come later. I lit a white candle when Robert came over. We sat in a semi-lotus position and meditated for about a half hour. Then we shared what we had felt and what images and impressions that came to us.

About a month later, Robert said, "Michael, today is going to be very different. You are now much more aligned and stronger than before."

I thanked him for the compliment and waited to see what would happen. A few minutes later in a nonchalant tone of voice as though he were talking about the weather, Robert said, "Michael, I am going to entrust you with something of mine that is as vital to me as my soul—my silver cord. This is something that is rarely done and only an advanced sorcerer knows how to protect an entrusted silver cord. As you know when the silver cord snaps, then death is the result."

I took on a look of sheer terror and horror. "Robert, are you telling me that you are entrusting your very life in my hands?"

Robert's black eyes bore into my soul. He gently rubbed my face as though to wash away my anxiety and trepidation and then in a very calm voice he said, "Yes, my friend, I am."

"Robert, this is crazy. This is madness."

"What is madness is what will happen if you don't do this for me. I will explain everything."

"Robert, I don't want you to explain anything. I think you must have smoked some really good weed before coming here today. Your story beats some of the LSD drug-induced hallucination stories from the sixties era. I think you have totally lost it and gone off the deep end."

"Michael, I know this sounds far-fetched and completely crazy, and you know that I do not do drugs. I assure you that I can understand your concern and fear, but I have dreamt about this many times. You are the person I was shown who is meant to help me."

"Drugs can mess with your dreams, too."

"Michael, I just told you that I do not do drugs. Now try to calm down and hear me out. Please," he said, softly in a pleading tone of voice. "Here is what I need you to do. I need you to shift your perceptions. This will allow part of your soul to enter a large rock and merge with it. This will enable you to be the grounding force and energy for me. It will also protect my soul while allowing part of it to leave my body. I have something very important that I have to do on another plane."

"I have no idea how to do what you are asking of me."

"Your subconscious knows. First, we need to sit so that our knees touch. Then we hold hands firmly. Begin to shift your perceptions and visualize a thick cord going through your entire being. Then shift your consciousness and visualize a large rock. Next will part of your soul to enter into the rock and then merge with it. There, you can protect and hold onto my silver cord while I soar to an astral plane where I will do battle with a certain sorcerer who is bound and determined to capture, assimilate, and steal the remainder of my soul pieces. He already has some of them. With your help and power, I can retrieve them. As long as you hold onto my silver cord and stay inside the rock, he cannot snap my cord which would kill me and give him my soul pieces. No matter what happens, do not open your eyes and do not release me from the rock by letting your attention divert. You must remain very focused. Do not let go of my hands. See only the rock and keep your consciousness focused inside it. You have to do this, or I can be in great danger. I could even die."

"Robert, this is the most bizarre request I've ever had from anyone, and I've had some pretty strange ones. Please, let's just forget this. Can we go for a walk or something? Let me treat you to lunch. You look kind of skinny. Maybe you have not been eating enough, and you are becoming delirious or something."

"Michael, I am fine. I have a very strong feeling and a gut knowing that you can do this. You can hold the energy. I know that you can. You can protect my silver cord while I leave my body to do battle with the sorcerer. Something told me that you have to do this to help me escape the dark sorcerer's soul theft and black magic. I know that you have been a powerful sorcerer in more than one lifetime. You will automatically and instinctively know how and be able to carry this assignment out. Like I said, I have dreamt of you many times and long waited for this moment. That is why you said on the first day we met that I felt familiar to you. You work with dreams, and you know that some dreams can be precognitive visions or psychic revelations."

"Again, remember how familiar you said I felt to you that first day we met at that drumming circle. You insisted that we had met before, and you were correct. We had met, alright, just not yet on the physical plane. We have been meeting in dreams and on spirit realms for a long time, and we are soul brothers from many past lives. In other times and places it was you who soared to other realms and did battle with evil dark lords and sorcerers while I grounded the energy and protected your spirit and silver cord. You are to return the favor in this lifetime."

Robert looked at me a few more moments in the silence. Then he reached for my hand and held it. Tears poured down his face. I don't think I had ever seen such a look of sadness and desperation. His soul seemed to be in agony. I had never seen him like that. Both of our hands got warm and then hot. It felt like I was on fire, except that my hand was not burning nor was there any pain. The burning sensation was replaced by coolness that went from my hand to my toes and throughout my entire body. It felt like liquid light and fire were pouring through every cell and molecule of my being.

I began to tremble and feel light-headed and dizzy. I tried to release Robert's grip on my hand, but he would not let go. He took his other hand and placed it on top of my head. It felt like his hand weighed a ton, but there was no pain. I wanted to force his hand loose and tell him to leave me alone and that he was frightening me, but no words came out. Some kind of force seemed to immobilize me. I was not sure if the force came from Robert or from me.

A few minutes later Robert removed his hands. I felt like I weighed a ton. What had he done to me?

"Please, Michael," he pleaded again. "You have to help me. I have given you a lot of energy and power. As a matter of fact, I even took some energy from the etheric rock you are to enter and infused some of its essence into you."

"It does feel like I weigh a ton now. Perhaps we are both going off the deep end."

I wondered if I was imagining things, but I saw the image of a large black eagle soaring across the sky in full spread-winged flight.

"Go with it," a voice in my head said. "Call me a lunatic, but I will do this, my friend," I said softly in resignation.

I scooted next to Robert so that our knees touched. I grasped his hands and held them firmly. Then I visualized a huge rock and part of my consciousness inside of it. A bright light appeared and encased the rock. As my perceptions began to heighten and shift, another bright light appeared and surrounded Robert and me. A thick silver cord appeared above Robert's head. I instinctively knew that the bright light encasing the rock would protect the silver cord that joined his soul to his body and the one surrounding us would protect our physical bodies.

I had no idea how light could radiate from inside a rock or how it could protect his silver cord, but this was not the time for questioning. I had messed up a telepathic exercise with my teacher Mary back in the mid-eighties by losing focus and diverting my concentration. It had zapped her, and we never engaged in any telepathy exercises again. *Maybe this is my chance to redeem myself,* I thought, *and prove that I can hold the energy by concentrated focus, effort, and determination.*

I kept my eyes closed feeling that this somehow helped to seal and keep the grounding energy intact. We sat in the quiet for what felt like an hour or longer. Robert would make a few grunts and moaning sounds from time to time. He chanted a few deep guttural tones and strange words. Then he would take a series of deep huffy breaths. He would bounce about and shake so hard at times I thought our hands would separate. I held onto him tightly and nothing was going to make me release my grip.

About twenty minutes later he let go of my hands and jerked his head back. His breathing slowly returned to normal, and he opened his eyes. There was sweat on his face, neck, and chest. He took out bottled water from his backpack and guzzled half of it.

"It was one hell of a battle, my friend, but I won, thanks to you. Your concentration did not waver one time. I have my soul pieces back, and the dark sorcerer will never be back."

"Just where was he and where did you go?"

Robert pointed his hand upward. "We met up there on a dark mountain on the astral plane. There I saw many captured soul pieces hiding here and there, in a crevice, nook, and cranny, or in some cavern, beneath this rock, or that log. My heart went out to the souls these pieces belonged to, and I could feel the despair and sense of fragmentation these people felt back on the earth. There is so much more to shattered hopes and dreams than we can begin to imagine. Where there are shattered hopes and dreams, you can bet your bottom dollar that there are shattered soul pieces hiding in various places. This can be caused by stress and trauma or through dark sorcery and soul theft. Often it's a combination of both, but it was not my task to retrieve them, at least not at this time. I will come back to this place another time and retrieve them, but only when the time is right."

"The people I am meant to help will find me. Our lights will beam out a similar frequency which will lead us to each other. That is how it works. You call it the law of attraction. I call it the law of frequency vibration. It's the same thing."

Robert guzzled the rest of his water. He then gave me the biggest bear hug and leaned against me for several moments. I could smell and feel the sweat that was dripping from his neck onto his chest.

"You look wiped out," I said, taking a paper towel and wiping his forehead.

"Yeah, that was one heck of a battle. Some of the most difficult ones are not the earthly battlefields but those on other planes and dimensions. Believe me, you never want to go there unprepared. If you are lucky, you may never have to go at all. I just knew you had to help me. I was told in a dream that it was an old debt that you owed and that you would deliver. Thank you, my friend. I have to get going now. I need a shower and some sleep."

I stared at the white candle. The flame darted back and forth. I sat mesmerized for the longest time. I simply could not get up. I could barely move my legs. I instinctively touched my arm, my hand, and fingers. I was in no rock. Yes, I was back on terra firma. Safe and sound.

But to enter a rock? I heard the words from the Simon and Garfunkle song- "I Am a Rock. I Am an Island." That song would never have the same meaning again. I wondered if I had truly gone off the deep end. I had had many paranormal and psychic experiences, but this one may have topped them all. Robert moved away two weeks later after his college graduation. I never heard from him again.

I find it interesting how people come and go in our lives. Some stay for a time, maybe even a few weeks months or even years. Others remain but a short while. This does not mean that they cannot or do not impact us in ways that transforms our lives forever.

I now believe that everything has happened when it was supposed to in order to make me the person I am today and to prepare me for my psychic and spiritual work and for what lies ahead in the future.

I believe that just as I gave Robert supportive grounding energy when I helped protect his silver cord while in the rock, I was also given energy which opened me up more deeply and contributed to my acquiring more spiritual gifts. My clairvoyant skills heightened, and it became easier to read for people. I began to see auras. Sometimes I could detect holes in them which pinpointed areas in the chakras needing balancing and cleansing lest some health issues ensue. I could enter houses and tell if spirits were there and if they were earthbound, trapped or lost. My shaman friend and therapist Elizabeth, and I did several house clearings and cleansings. Robert helped me open up to more of my latent psychic and paranormal abilities. I think of him often and wonder how his soul retrievals and battles on other planes are faring.

CHAPTER NINE

MIND MELDING AND

THE MUSIC OF THE SPHERES

A few weeks later I met another young man, David, who attended one of my public events where I channeled some Native American medicine ancestor shaman spirits. We struck up a friendship and began hanging out together. One day we were meditating at David's apartment, and he said, "Michael, there is some imbalance in your energies. Your crown chakra needs some aligning and fine-tuning. Then you are really going to be blown away by what you will start to see, hear, and experience. Are you ready for this?"

I told him about Robert, "I was rather blown away by the energy work that this man Robert and I did some time back. He's been gone for several months now. I guess the guides want to give me a fresh tune-up so who knows what might take place? Bring it on."

We listened to a drumming tape while sitting on the floor, leaning against the couch. When the tape stopped, David said, "Lie on the floor so that your head is against my legs."

I did so and David began placing his hands over my head. They were very warm. He cupped and moved them until they were barely touching the top of my head. He chanted very softly and blew air slightly above my head. My head started tingling. It felt like he was tickling the inside of my brain with a feather. It tickled so much that I almost laughed, but I forced myself to refrain. I didn't want to interrupt what David was doing. His hands got hotter and in a short time the tickling sensation was replaced by a prickling sensation. It hurt a little but not enough to let out a cry or to complain. I trusted that David knew what he was doing although I had no idea of what he was doing. I simply had to take his word that he was fine-tuning my crown chakra and giving me energy.

At one point, he placed his fingertips on various parts of my head and applied gentle pressure. "I am sealing some of the holes," he said.

I had no idea what that meant and did not ask for clarity. I have heard that it is best not to speak when energy work is being done unless the one doing the work initiates conversation. David applied various touches and pressures on parts of my head.

Then he tapped me on the chest and said, "All done, Michael. You are good to go."

When I sat up, I was dizzy and almost fell down. David gently lifted my shoulders and helped me up. "You may feel a little bit confused or disoriented for awhile, but you will be okay. It will pass. Your body and chakras have to absorb and integrate the energy that I gave you."

"Thank you. I do feel better—somehow lighter and more balanced."

"From now on you are going to be feeling lots of things," he said with a twinkle in his eyes.

He placed his thumb on my forehead near the third eye and applied light pressure. A tingling went through my chest and made its way to my abdomen and into my groin. I snickered, a little embarrassed.

"Just moving the energy," he said. "It's all about energy. You are going to become an expert energy-mover yourself, Michael."

"How do you do this? How do you know what you are doing?"

"I just do," he replied. "It's natural for me. I've always been able to touch people and affect their energy. They say it makes them feel better or helps to open them up. I can live off of a compliment for a month. It lets me know that in my own small way I can contribute some loving, energy, and healing to people."

"You did a great job. I wish you could have met my friend Robert. This makes me think of him though what we did was completely different."

"It was meant for you to meet Robert, not me. We meet who we are supposed to when it's time."

"I believe that, too. I just think you two would have hit it off."

"You never know. Maybe on another plane we know each other."

"I wouldn't be surprised."

"Well, I got to get going. The ole girlfriend is expecting me."

"Thanks, David."

"You are most welcome. Anytime."

"Anytime" turned out to be just one more time. I visited David two days later. We sat on the couch and listened to some music and watched the candle flame flicker. I closed my eyes and started hearing words in my mind, and then I heard little tunes. I happened to have my tape recorder with me, so I sang what I heard.

"It feels like Russian," I said.

"Well, we can find out about that. As a matter of fact, I happen to have a Russian neighbor down the hall. Let's see if he is home."

Dimitri came over, and we sipped wine and snacked on some cheese and crackers. David told him about me hearing the Russian song and words, leaving out the part about him doing energy work on me.

Dimitri listened to the tape and said, "Wow! That is very interesting. You only speak a few words that are Russian, but they are definitely Russian."

Then he got a little twinkle in his eye and snickered. "A couple of the words you sang were quite romantic and poetic. Other words were less clear. It was like they were part Russian and part English if that makes any sense, but the song itself has a very Russian plaintiveness to it. How did you do that? Have you studied Russian at the university?"

"Never," I replied, sheepishly.

"Wow is all I can say. So what did you do to him, David?" Dimitri asked. "I know you are into some weird stuff."

"Moi," David replied, snickering, with a big grin on his face. "I only put Michael in a little hypnotic trance."

"You ought to try it again soon and let me sit in on it. Maybe we can make a telepathic connection and come up with something interesting."

"We could maybe do that," David said, shrugging.

I yawned and took that as a sign I needed to get back to my apt. I shook hands with Dimitri and gave David a hug. He walked me outside and said, "Come back in a couple days, Michael, and I will do another adjustment. Who knows what you may hear."

I called two days later, and David's phone had been disconnected. I stopped by and nobody answered. His friend Tony said that David and his girlfriend broke up, and he moved back to northern Ohio with his parents. I was sad but I have been told that things happen for a reason. People come and go for various reasons. Still, I was sad. Like Robert, David wound up moving away.

What was this all about? Was it something about me? Was I chasing everybody away? I was beginning to develop a little complex. Could it be that my guides were giving me crash courses in spiritual development, energy adjustment, and lessons on detachment?

I heard other songs in my head. One evening in my apartment I just started singing some strange words in some type of language whose tones were nothing like English. It felt like Chinese or some oriental language. I went on for the longest time.

A few days later, I talked to a Chinese woman who lived down the hall. She wanted to listen to the tape. "That music is very pretty. Where did you hear those songs, Michael?"

"In here," I said, pointing to my head.

"In here," she said, in her heavy accent, mimicking my gesture. "The words are not clear, but you are singing some old Chinese folk songs from about the time of my grandmother. A few words come through but most make no sense. The tunes are definitely old Chinese folk songs."

I thanked her and left feeling very strange. I listened to the tape a few more times and felt a strange comfort at hearing the unfamiliar tones, tunes, and words I was singing. Could I have been accessing my own subconscious mind and contacting another lifetime I may have lived in China many years ago? I did not know, but to this day when I play the tape of those folk songs, I am filled with a silent reverence and a sense of nostalgia and wonder.

I thought about something else. In both instances—with Dimitri and the Chinese woman—someone from the native culture had lived in the same building a few doors down the hall. Was it mere coincidence that I happened to hear words and songs from their native language, or was I somehow experiencing some kind of mind-melding or telepathic connection with them? Could that connection have become stronger if David and I had done more energy work and Dimitri had sat in as well? Dimitri jokingly said we ought to try to make some kind of telepathic connection and see what would happen.

I thought about another experience I had had many years ago. One day, my fiancé and spiritual teacher, Mary, and I were listening to some Russian art songs. We became wistful and melancholy. I finally asked her to turn off the tape because the sadness was starting to get to me.

We lay on the floor next to each other, held hands, and meditated. The next thing I knew I was hearing some strange words in my head. I spoke them in the tape player and tried to phonetically write them down. I invited a friend over who was majoring in Russian. I told her about the experience then played her the tape. She got the biggest grin on her face.

"Michael, those words are very romantic, and although you didn't quite pronounce them correctly, you were close enough that I could tell what you were saying. You really ought to sign up for Russian. I think you'd do great since you are very proficient with languages." She hugged me. "Well, maybe you were Russian in a past life?"

"Actually, I've been told that, and I am very drawn to Russian culture and literature."

Still, I wasn't satisfied. I asked Julie if she would listen to the tape Mary and I had listened to. I wanted to see if I simply unconsciously memorized some of the words and for whatever reason had managed to randomly unconsciously select various ones. Julie was game. Mary poured us a glass of wine, and Julie made a toast in Russian. We repeated the word. Then we listened to the tape. Julie wiped tears from her face.

When the tape finished, she said, "There is no romance in these songs. These are all plaintive songs about people who have lost their land and forced to move from the homeland. Michael, I don't know how you came up with those romantic words."

I shrugged and said, "Beats me," and thanked her for coming over.

We've all had experiences where a certain smell, aroma, image, picture, etc., can stimulate memories from long ago. Perhaps this is what happened to me. It's possible that the memories being activated or reactivated originated from a previous life. I had been to Europe. I studied in France and frequently had deja-vu. I had it in Italy as well. I later had regressions of lives I have had in both countries. One day I will visit Russia and see if I have deja-vu there, or I may treat myself to a past life regression and see what comes up. Who knows? Perhaps nothing will come up. Perhaps I shall never have answers to these questions as there are some things we are just not meant to know. Nonetheless, I found the experience with Mary, David, Dimitri, and the Chinese woman very interesting and I am still hoping to hear other songs.

I could not get the idea of mind-melding and telepathic exchanges out of my mind. I kept remembering other experiences over the years. Back in early 1990, I worked for a few months with a young man named Brian. He was a very talented musician, earning his music degree in performance and composition at Northern Kentucky University. He played keyboards, drums, guitar, and flute. Not only could he read music proficiently, but he also had an ear for music and was excellent at improvisation.

We'd begin our visits with lunch. Brian was a vegetarian. He once lived with the Hare Krishnas as I had. He was a deeply spiritual man who had no interest or patience for superficiality and the mundane. Brian could ask provocative, deep questions, and he could offer some profound insights. I knew from the moment I met him that he was a very old soul.

After our visit, Brian would turn on his keyboard and start *playing around*, as he called it. As he played the notes and just went where the music wanted him to go, lyrics and tunes started popping in my head. I would sing them as Brian played. We bounced back and forth off each other. Brian would make sure to have his taping equipment set up, so we could record the songs. We never finished anything because every week when Brian would play something new, I'd start singing tunes and fill in the words that popped into my head. My favorite song was "Soul Cry."

In "Soul Cry" my voice took off like I have never heard before. I went into a type of falsetto that my opera coach calls "sopranist" where I can sing higher notes than most women. I felt possessed by the muse of music and the goddess of love as I sang that song. It was very intense.

I later played it to another friend, and he strongly encouraged me to polish the song and rehearse it. He said he had connections in the music industry and felt that this song had chart potential, but we had to polish and refine it. He could not believe that we had composed this song in the initial take.

Another time as Brian was playing the lower notes on the keyboards, I sang in a dark baritone and began toning and chanting, going up and down the scale. It felt like I was in a type of trance. In the few months we worked together, we created ten songs, and each one was very different. "My Secret Love" was dreamy and ethereal, and I sang it in a light tenor voice. I belted out other songs in a completely different voice.

It was almost spooky how intensely Brian and I connected. How he would start playing music and the lyrics would just pop into my head out of nowhere was mind-blowing. This was different from my other telepathic exchanges, but it was evident that some kind of mental and soulful transference was taking place.

I enjoy it when my muse gives me poems, stories, and writings, but it is equally fascinating and rewarding when we can collaborate with another artist or musician. I often think about the Vulcan mind-melds on Star Trek. I think there is far more truth in some science fiction than most people are inclined to believe. At times it actually felt like Brian and I were participating in a type of mind-melding. The energy I received in his presence and while creating music with him was boundless. It was like our minds became as one. Brian's music somehow opened doors to my subconscious and higher self and brought out the very creative essence of my soul. If that was not a type of mind-melding, then what is? Needless to say, such melding was powerful, intense, and mind-blowing at times. I felt that the sky was the limit! How I looked forward to more tapping into the music of the spheres!

One day to my utter shock and disappointment, Brian told me that we had to stop making music together. He said that he could not handle the intensity of the energy when we created songs. I was heart-broken. I had thought that, alas, my childhood dream of performing and sharing my heart and soul via music and song would at long last be fulfilled. We seemed to perfectly complement one another.

How could Brian not feel a profound soul connection? I concluded that it was so strong that it scared him away. I still have a tape of the songs that Brian and I created in his little apartment studio after our deep spiritual talks. When I listen to it, I feel sad and wonder what was it about me that scared Brian away? Did he not possess an intensity of his own that matched mine?

When he played music, his eyes would glow and get all glassy; he'd get a faraway look on his face. I am convinced that he channeled much of his music from spheres far beyond this realm. Was he afraid of his own muse and God-given creative abilities and talents? Was I afraid of mine? Did Brian's *dumping me* mirror some part of me that fears my muse and creativity?

The music we created seemed to take me outside myself to transcendental realms beyond this world. What a high and thrill it was! Was it too much of a good thing? How could this be? If Destiny and the Fates blessed us both with a tad of musical genius, could it not be enhanced and magnified when two such souls came together?

Questions. Questions. Questions. They never cease. *Maybe I'm afraid to claim my power*, I told myself one day. *Maybe other people sense it subconsciously, and they back off, just like some part of me might be doing.*

I wondered how many lives I might have had as a musician and what negative karma I might have incurred. It seems that every time I attract a talented musician, we work together awhile and then something ruins things. Is it possible I have already completed my music karma and am done with it? Then, why did I study voice for four years in college? Why was I involved in singing for years, and why did I write many songs before I met Brian? Perhaps the mystery shall never be solved.

Two years before I met Brian, I met another musician who I will call John Jackson. He played guitar and was trying to open up a recording studio. We worked on several songs. A few months before I met him, I had awakened one night hearing music in my head. For the next two hours my entire chapbook of love poems became songs. I'd just turn to a page and hear a tune and sing it into the tape player. John said the songs were good, and he wanted to record them. Not only did I hear the tunes and music, I also would see entire video stage productions being recorded of some of the songs/poems that were longer and written in prose instead of rhyme.

Of all the songs I've written my all-time favorite is "The Clown." It is three pages long and very deep. My very favorite line is the last line that says, "A clown I still am but a different clown; there will be no paint on my face." The song is about accepting our unique individuality and not creating facades, such as a clown will do with make-up, wigs, and a mask.

When my friend Janet first heard it, she cried, saying it described her boyfriend to the tee and touched her very deeply. She even put two dollars in an envelope and posted it on my apt door. She lived a few doors down from the apt and asked me to make her a copy of the song/poem. One day I listened to the recording John and I made in his basement studio, and I saw an entire video being made of "The Clown." I could see the stage, the blue lights in the background, the clown at the vanity table putting on his make-up, with the tears falling down his cheeks. At last, after the mystery visitor gave him permission to be his *true self*, I could see the clown removing the paint on his face.

Another of my favorite poems that John and I recorded is called "Look Not Away." I listened to that tape one day and heard an entire orchestra in my mind performing this song in the form of a cantata. I heard the flutes, the violins, and all the other instruments, and the intervals and movements for the different parts of the cantata. In that moment I knew that the cantata was the perfect musical expression for "Look Not Away" because it was not just a song or poem, it truly was a story.

Destiny or Fate intervened yet another time. John called me a few days later saying that he lost his house and was having to move in with his mother. He had to find some kind of *normal* job because his wife was six months pregnant, and they were broke. He wished me good luck and said he did not know when we could get back together. Needless to say, I was heartbroken. I did not possess the financial capital or resources to bail John out as I was living on a high school teacher's salary and had my own bills and expenses to take care of. So another music dream bit the dust.

I was to pick up the shattered pieces of my broken heart and move on. What else was there to do? I certainly am as human as anybody else and more sensitive than most people, so when things like this happen, I take them very hard. Yet I also know that things happen for a reason. I now know that we attract our life situations and experiences for learning and growth. As I pondered another dream failure, a few thoughts came to mind. Perhaps I was just not ready to embark upon the stage as a performer. Perhaps I was paying off some old karma from having abused and used my musical skills and talents for personal gain and self-aggrandizement in some past lives.

Still, I am fascinated by and love music and cannot wait to get back to it. My love and passion for music, singing, and performing are as strong as they were when I was that thirteen year old boy aspiring to be a gospel singer and recording artist. I know dozens of songs, and I love learning new ones, as well as writing new ones and poems that often become songs. My desire is to make some music CDs and other CDs of sound healing.

I want to make a CD of love ballads and songs from musicals, as well as some pop songs. I want to make some CDs where I go in trance and channel dolphins and whales, for I am fond of their songs and hear them sometimes. I want to channel the songs of the stars—the songs of the Arcturians, Pleadians, Sirians, Andromedans, and other evolved loving ETs. I want to make CDs that awaken soul memories and stimulate the higher chakras, especially the heart chakra, to help open people to love. I am grateful and honored that I have been blessed with a good voice and for being able to study voice in college. I am grateful for my musical sensitivity and receptiveness to the music of the spheres.

I shall always ask questions and be grateful for whatever answers come my way. I suppose my guides will give me the information when I am ready for it and bring me like-minded, sensitive, passionate musicians who are in my soul family. In the meantime, I shall ponder the mystery of mind-melding and telepathy and wonder what all is involved when I am teaming up with other musicians.

Another fond memory is one I have of a day where I was studying Italian in the student lounge at the Indiana University Memorial Union. A young man started playing the baby grand piano that was in a corner. I was very drawn to his playing. I was amazed at his agility and ability to go up down the scales of the keyboard so easily and effortlessly. I took out a notebook and penned the words to a song.

When he was finished, I approached him and told him that his lovely playing inspired me to write a song. He read the words and was very surprised. He thanked me and said the song was beautiful.

"Maybe we could get together sometimes," he said, offering me a hand shake. I have to admit that his offer scared me because all my past collaborations had bombed. Still I wondered what made it so easy for me to connect and collaborate with musicians?

These experiences make me wonder if I might be tuning into a more universal musical vibration that is sometimes referred to as "the music of the spheres." It is said that some composers, such as Mozart and Beethoven, heard this celestial divine music and they captured its divine beauty and sound via the musical notes which became compositions. Anyone who has the least amount of musical sensitivity and appreciation is surely bound to be touched deeply in the soul when they listen to the Mozart Requiem or his many other concertos, operas, symphonies, sonatas, string quartets, choral music, songs, and compositions.

For humanity to be blessed with such a highly evolved prolific musician (one of the most influential of his and perhaps all times) capable of translating the music of the spheres to notes that mortal ears can hear is nothing less than a miracle. How beloved Mozart created or gave expression to the music of the spheres in so many different styles makes my heart sing. How sad that this precocious genius did not even live to the age of forty. Mozart's many accomplishments certainly give us reason to challenge the truism that life begins at age forty.

I believe there is something about the music of the spheres that has a way of taking our breath away. The music of the spheres has a way of surviving time and becoming classic. I certainly do not mean to imply that classical music is the only type of music that can survive time and be labeled as the divine, immortal celestial music of the spheres.

I think that one of the most beautiful songs of all times is an old pop song recorded by Mac Davis, "I Believe in Music," which I have sung publicly several times. My favorite lines are these: "Music is the universal language, and love is the key to brotherhood, peace and understanding, and living in harmony. I believe in music. I believe in love."

I also believe in love and I believe in the music of the spheres.

CHAPTER TEN

AN UNUSUAL SPIRIT MUSE

I used to tell my girlfriend, Mary, that she was my muse. She inspired me to write love poems, and the fact that we also had a psychic and spiritual bond made our relationship even stronger. It was not long after we split up that I made another breakthrough; except this time my new muse was not living on the third-dimension.

One day I was especially feeling lonely and sad and missing Mary. I took a walk in the woods and recalled how we used to spend time in nature. We'd sit on a fallen tree and hold hands for long spans of time without speaking. Sometimes little forest critters would scamper about and stop to look at us. Often they would come right up to Mary, and she would pet and talk to them. Mary had a way with animals.

The next morning I woke up at 6:00 a.m. to the sound of a voice in my head that said, "We have met before. It is time for us to become reacquainted."

Startled, I looked about. Nobody was there.

"I don't live out there," the voice continued, "so stop looking for me out there."

"If you insist," I said, kind of amused and wondering if a new spirit guide was coming to me."

"Oh, I'm a lot more than a spirit guide. You can bet your bottom dollar on that."

"And you can speak the slang and jargon of our English language to boot."

"Of course—because you and I are very connected. Now close your eyes so I can show you my face."

"That sounds like a contradiction if ever I heard one."

"Not at all. I just told you I am not out there."

I closed my eyes and the image of a woman with long dark hair, an oval shaped face, and piercing emerald eyes appeared. I don't think I had ever seen a woman so beautiful.

She laughed. "Well, I suppose that beauty is in the eye of the beholder. With me you are going to see that life and beauty can take on an entirely enriched, new, and more profound meaning. For now I want you to take out a pen and some paper. It is time to for a new writing."

"Sounds good to me. Thank you."

The woman's image faded. I took out my notebook and wrote the following verse:

Bow down before the altar at the feet of love.
Surrender your worries, your fears, your cares.
Let the mistress of your art soothe you.
She will wipe away your tears when life pulls at you
So fiercely, rocking you on stormy seas.

Call out to your spirit muse.
She will rescue you immediately.

Go forth to the sacred altar.
She waits only moments more.
You must make the choice to invite her
Or she closes her heart's door.

She is not your enemy.
She is the granter of hopes and dreams.
Go now and receive her embrace.
Your spirit muse calls to thee!

"That is so beautiful," I said, feeling dreamy as I put my notebook on my nightstand. "The spirit muse," I said out loud a few times.

I wonder who she is? Is she the person who was talking in my head awhile ago? And where does she come from? I pushed the curtain back to look at the full moon. It seemed to be smiling at me.

"The man in the moon," I snickered. "What about the lady in the moon? Whichever one you are, you certainly are a beauty," I said, gazing with wonder.

I went to the mirror and looked into my eyes. *I wonder if the eyes are the window of the soul?*

"Soul," I whispered, moving closer to see my eyes more clearly. *Can I see my soul if I look long enough? How can we see the soul? How can we really tap into the vast reservoirs of our essence? Could that verse have come from my soul or from this being talking in my head?*

"Did you give me this writing?" I asked, wondering if the spirit or whoever she was, was still around. *Enough of this,* I thought as I got dressed.

I had a blueberry pop tart and a glass of milk then headed out. I patted the dash of David, my 1986 Ford Escort, as I turned on the ignition.

"Hello, fellow. How goes it? You've sure been a good car, never breaking down on the road. Wonder if it's because I talk to you and rub your dash?" I laughed. I fastened my seat belt and then looked into the mirror.

The image of a dark haired lady with piercing emerald eyes looked out at me. "What?" I blurted out in astonishment. "Who are you?"

"I am flame. I am fire. I set in motion the heart's desire."

"That's pretty intense. Nonetheless, I could use a little fire to light up my heart's desire since my life is rather boring these days. Who are you? Surely, you have another name-probably something very exotic."

"I am called Dresda, and I am the mistress of your art like you wrote in the poem."

"Mistress of my what?" I said, looking around to make sure none of my neighbors were watching me have a conversation with myself in my car. I moved closer to the mirror.

There she was staring at me. It looked like there were little stars in her eyes. I am the mistress of your art, Michael. Put another way I am your muse. And we have met before."

"Are you the one who woke me up this morning talking in my head, and did you give me that new poem I wrote?"

"Yes, but we also have met before this morning."

"Well, Dresda, I have to admit that you do somehow feel familiar. Can you please tell me where we have met before?"

"We first met two years ago during your psychic training with Mary. While you were meditating one day, I appeared to you and spoke the phrase, 'I am Flame. I am Fire. I set in motion the heart's desire' and I told you who I was."

"I must have forgotten that although I recall that Mary and I had a lot of psychic experiences and we saw a lot of things in our meditations."

"Yes, and you will recall other things when it is time. Nothing is forgotten. It's all stored in that wonderful subconscious mind that Creator has blessed everyone with. After today I don't believe you will ever forget me again."

"What does that mean?" I asked, but Dresda disappeared.

I thought about Dresda and the poem all day. That night I arrived at the art museum ten minutes before eleven where I worked as a part-time night watchman.

"You're early," teased Karen, my co-worker.

"Early bird gets the worm."

"You may get it, but you will never hold it for long," she chuckled. "What's your batting average on being early? About once a month?"

"Something like that."

"It really doesn't matter. You know I'd never report you as long as you don't make it more than fifteen minutes. And you never do. You always make the waiting worth my time."

"Now do I?" I replied, grinning.

"Certainly. Our little talks mean a lot to me even if they are little talks."

I do have to work, don't I? It's fine to be a writer, but manuscripts don't feed you or pay the rent."

"Maybe not, but they sure do feed my soul, and if you stick with it, your writing will one day pay your bills. You are a good writer, Michael, and you are going to make it. Never doubt that. I feel it deep in my soul."

"At least I have one fan, eh," I said, tapping her cheek and winking at her.

"Two. My mother has been reading your stories and poems and loves them. You need to be more aggressive about your marketing. Why don't you find an agent, and let him/her do all the work while you sit back and write, half of which you do here," she laughed.

"It's not that simple. You're supposed to have a book published so agents know that you are good enough for a publisher to take you on. Without an agent many publishers won't even look at your manuscript. Without a published book many agents won't consider you. It's kind of a catch-22 situation. I'm thinking about looking for one nonetheless. If I had an agent, that would give me some time for other things, wouldn't it?"

"Indeed," Karen said, winking at me.

"Behave yourself," I reproached her playfully. "Art is a jealous mistress. She would never let another woman compete with her."

"Well, I would sure like to give her a little competition. Has your muse inspired any new poems lately?"

"Yes," I said, taking out the poem I had written earlier and reading it to her.

"It's beautiful. The words are very enchanting. For me, it conjures up images of pagan goddesses waiting in temples for their men. What do you think about it?"

"I'm not sure. I did have a strange experience after getting in my car which may be related to it."

"A strange experience," Karen laughed. "Since when do you have *a* strange experience, Michael? They come in the plural for you. I'm all ears. Tell me about it. I guess I ought to let you take your rightful place behind the counter, shouldn't I? I wouldn't want to upset the paintings. Those two

Madonnas over there might jump right off that palette and slug me. After all, eight hours is long enough to have to look at anyone's face, even for a painting. Let's trade places."

I placed my backpack behind the counter in the corner, and then I took out a green tie from my coat and slipped it on."

"Naughty. Naughty," Karen chided me.

"Long ties choke me."

"I don't blame you and who's here to see you anyway, except a couple of security guards and maybe another auditor or two. Now tell me about your strange experience."

"It's nothing, really. I think my imagination ran a little wild, that's all. After I wrote the poem, I looked in the mirror, musing about the soul. I forgot about that experience once I realized it was time for work. In my car, before starting it, I looked in the mirror. There was the image of a long dark-haired lady with piercing emerald eyes. She said her name is Dresda and that she is the mistress of my art. 'Mistress of my what?' I asked, taken aback. She said that we had met before (I wasn't about to tell Karen about mine and Mary's psychic work), and then she disappeared. That's all there was to it."

"Humh," said Karen, moving closer to me. "Can I be the mistress of your art?"

"Not tonight dear, though your perfume is really nice," I whispered. "Seriously, do you think I am losing my marbles?"

"Oh, maybe just a couple, Michael. Then again you are always losing things. Fortunately, your sanity is stored away in a nice little corner of your brain, so there's no danger of you losing it. I'd say forget about this Dresda lady."

"You are probably right."

"Maybe, if you'd make a little more effort to go out with real women, your subconscious mind wouldn't have to conjure up imaginary ones. Hint! Hint!"

"You think so? When I finish my novel, I may just take you up on that not so subtle invitation."

"Subtlety was never a virtue of mine," Karen teased. "Okay, it's nearly eleven-thirty. This is our longest little talk ever." She reached for her purse. "Have some fun writing,

Michael. You should be able to finish a few scenes tonight. This place has been dead today. I suppose everyone is away on vacation."

"I love the quiet here at the museum. I wouldn't trade it for anything. Not even if my salary were doubled."

"I envy your free time, but since I'm not a night person, your job would bore me terribly. But someone has to stay here and watch over the paintings at night. Goodnight, Michael. Maybe this mysterious lady will pay you a visit later."

"I doubt it. She probably has better things to do than show up at this art museum."

I took the Snickers bar from my pocket and bit into it while walking to the employee's frig to get a Coke.

"Coke, the real thing," I sang, wondering how many Cokes were consumed in one day around the world. Suddenly, I heard a noise which sounded like footsteps a few feet away.

"What's that?"

Nobody answered.

"Don't tell me there's a rat in here," I said, walking in the direction where the sound came from. "Almost midnight," I said, looking at my watch. "The magical hour for everyone, people and spooks included."

I hummed the words to the old song "I'm Gonna Wait Til the Midnight Hour," as I turned on the light in the area I thought the noise came from. It was the Madonna corner as we refer to it.

"Did you hear anything, ladies?" I asked, looking up at my favorite Madonna painting which had always enchanted and mystified me. There was something about the eyes that reminded me of the image I saw earlier.

"Are you Dresda?" I asked, moving back a few inches. It seemed that the eyes moved.

"Just my imagination," I said, glancing at the adjacent painting. If you look at any painting long enough, it seems to be looking back at you. *Maybe that's why people don't like to be looked at intently. Can it somehow put them in contact with their soul?*

"There I go again about the soul," I said, gazing at the other corners looking for any visible sign to verify the sound I had heard. "I guess whatever it was scurried away. Just the same I'll mention it to Sam. He will want to check it out. The last thing we need is some rodent scaring people away."

I returned to my area, dimmed all the lights except the ones above me, and took out paper and pen, hoping a new scene would come to me. I had written two scenes when Sam, the night custodian, brought me a steaming cup of coffee.

"You look like you could use this, Michael. I noticed your head drooping over. Nobody but me would probably know if you were sleeping on the job. This silence is enough to make you fall asleep. What are you working on?"

"A story about a woman who is pursued by her son's math teacher."

"I hope it's an agreeable pursuit," Sam said, snickering.

"I think it is. It's the principal who's going to be the bad guy in this story."

"You'll have to tell me about it when you finish it. Enjoy the coffee, and try to stay awake," he chuckled. "You just never know who might pay us a visit."

"That would be a welcomed change, wouldn't it? I like working here. I just wish there was something to watch besides those dames in the Madonna corner. By the way, I heard some sounds there earlier—sounded like some rodent was scurrying around."

"I'll check it out. Nice chatting. Funny how you mention the paintings in the Madonna corner. Sometimes when I'm cleaning over there, I get the feeling I'm being watched. I guess it's just art magic which makes those eyes seem to look at you no matter which way you turn. Being here all night is enough to make the imagination wander, isn't it? Got to run now. See you later."

"Thanks for the coffee, Sam."

"You're welcome. Good luck on your story. I know you won't stop until it's finished or the sun comes up, whichever comes first."

"I'm obsessed with writing. I guess it could always be worse. I suppose I could be addicted to sex, drugs, booze, or valium."

"I'd prefer the first one you mentioned," Sam said, snickering as he walked away.

I took a break from my story at 2:00 a.m. and did some paper work. "If my boss, Matthew knew I did the paperwork in less than two hours, he'd probably fire me. He doesn't need to know that my mind goes three times faster than the average person."

I was completing my tally of last month's museum attendance when I heard the soft footsteps and scurrying sound again. My head jerked forward and my heart pounded. This time the sound shifted as though it were coming from the ceiling and the walls. I was going to beam on the bright lights in the Madonna corner, but something made me refrain.

"This is bizarre," I said, moving away from the corner. *Could there be more than one rat or critter in that room?* I took a small flashlight and slowly headed towards the Madonna corner. There was a coolness there that I did not feel up front in my work area.

"What is this? It must be at least ten degrees cooler here," I said, shivering. I better check the thermostat. I walked to the control and looked. Seventy degrees. "Well, it sure doesn't feel like it."

I had the urge to look at my favorite Madonna. I gazed at her a long time.

"Whoever painted you must have really loved the lady of his dreams. I wonder if you were inspired by a real live woman. You look so real."

Suddenly a glowing golden light encircled the painting. I was frozen, unable to move. I turned my head around. No one was here.

"Come on, Sam," I stammered. "Where are you when I need you?" I tried to move my left leg, but it was totally inert.

"What is happening to me?" I cried out, hoping someone would hear. The golden light began encircling me as well. My head felt light-headed, and I thought that I would faint. I remained still, helpless to the invisible force which was keeping me in place.

Staring at the painting, I said in a joking tone, "If I've offended any of the paintings, which I don't think I have as I admire them all, I humbly apologize."

"This is pathetic," I said, frowning. "I'm talking to a ghost or ghosts I've not even seen yet. Maybe heard but not seen. And since when do ghosts hang out in paintings? Seems rather boring even for a ghost."

After a few more moments of silence, I had the urge to take a few deep breaths and visualize myself being free from whatever force field this was. I thought of Luke Skywalker trying to harness *the force* in his Jedi training. I willed the force field to drop, and suddenly I could move again.

"That was spooky," I said aloud. I looked in front of me at the Madonna painting, and instead of seeing the Madonna, I beheld the image I saw earlier in my car.

"It's you," I blurted out, jumping back. The image disappeared. I closed my eyes and still saw her image. This was very strange. She was smiling. Then she disappeared. I opened my eyes and she was not there. I advanced until I was standing inches from the painting. I lightly gripped it with both of my hands.

"What would Sam say if he came in and saw me gripping this painting? Would he think I was trying to remove and steal it?"

I heard a mental whisper in my mind. My thoughts were racing so madly I could barely make out the voice.

"Maybe I'm starting to hear voices in my head and am losing it? What is happening to me?" I said, looking upward and rubbing my sweaty forehead. I removed my hands from the painting and took out my handkerchief to wipe the sweat off my face. The painting looked okay except for a tiny glow I saw in the eyes which resembled the golden glow which had earlier encircled it.

I was tempted to run out of the room, grab my backpack, head out the door, and never come back to the museum. But I knew I could not. Something was going on here, and it was not my imagination. I was not sleeping, and I was not dreaming. What was up? I had to find out.

How could I explain anything like this to Matthew, Sam, or Karen? Not that I wanted to explain anything to anyone. Part of me just wanted to get away, but another part of me wanted to stay. My curiosity was so aroused. I knew that I had to see this through. I put my handkerchief back in my pocket and slowly moved closer to the painting.

"Just chill out," I told myself. "Just because you have no explanation for this unusual experience doesn't mean that one does not exist. You've had lots of psychic and paranormal experiences. What is one more?"

I had the urge to place my hands on the side of the painting again so I did. *What would Karen say? That I am becoming so desperate for female attention that I am resorting to wooing a painting. Would she be right? No, just because I'm twenty-nine and don't date does not mean I am abnormal. I'm dedicated to my writing. There will be time for dating later.*

I looked around again. Everything looked fuzzy. Maybe I've entered a trance or some non-drug induced altered state of consciousness, I wondered. I remembered a psychic telling me once that things are not as they appear and that if people make the effort, they can grasp reality in its more expanded essence. She said that there is more to everything, but most people are not capable or spiritually or psychically opened up enough to perceive it. Miss Howard certainly taught me a lot about that many years ago.

"Expanded essence," I whispered, looking at the painting. "So is it true that what we see is not what all there is to see?" I asked aloud, almost expecting an answer from the Madonna whose wry smile had always mystified and haunted me.

"*Open your mind and heart and see,*" I heard in my mind. I wondered if this was coming from my subconscious or if some spirit could be communicating with me? Perhaps I would never know, but my curiosity was definitely piqued. I even managed to lighten up a bit and find humor in the strange situation.

I looked back at the Madonna painting and said, "I suppose Karen would be jealous if she knew that I was talking to a phantom Madonna. I wondered what Sam would say if he walked in and saw me standing in front of the Madonna painting staring at it. He knows how much I love it. A small golden glow once again emanated from the painting's eyes.

I noticed that the glowing light disappeared when I became preoccupied with my thoughts or when I spoke.

"It's getting late. It seems I've been standing here in front of this painting for at least an hour. There is more work to do before the shift ends, and I want to finish my new story. Relax and chill," I told myself. "It's not every day you have a Madonna painting communicating with you."

I know that sounded crazy, but something very extraordinary was happening and I had to see it through. *What is happening to me? I wondered. A beautiful woman who does not live on this dimension wakes me up this morning and tells me that we have met before and that knowing her will cause beauty and life to take on new and more profound meaning. And now one of the Madonna paintings is coming to life. I think I need a good stiff, and very strong I might add, drink.*

I knew I was procrastinating due to being anxious and nervous. I needed to do what the voice suggested and open my mind and heart—whatever that entailed. I concentrated upon quieting my thoughts and being silent. The glowing light reappeared. I continued to keep quiet and entered a meditative frame of mind. The light slowly brightened and soon enfolded the painting. I stared, not knowing what to expect but feeling very excited nonetheless. Moments later the image of a beautiful woman appeared. It was the same woman I had seen early this morning and in the mirror of my car.

"It is you, Dresda," I stammered. "You are back."

"Hello, Michael. It is I, Dresda."

"Did I really see you this morning and in the mirror of my car?"

"You most certainly did."

"This is a little hard to swallow and take in, Dresda."

"I know and I have infinite patience. What you need to know is that you have been reaching out to me on other planes and dimensions. There is much more to your wonderful being and essence than your everyday mundane realm and what you are consciously aware of. There is so much more to your life experiences than your human mortal self can begin to imagine."

"The truth is that you exist on many realms and dimensions at any given point in time, and in actuality, time does not even exist. Neither does space. That is why I can pass through time and space and pay you a visit. You and I are in the same soul family. We are companions and explorers on many realms and dimensions. Much of your soul is not even present in the ego identity that you know as Michael Dennis. Parts of your soul are active and busily engaged in activities and having wonderful adventures with many other beings on many realms. You are going to start becoming more aware of them on a conscious level. If you were to have a minute glimpse of the vastness of your soul, it would overwhelm you. I come to you as Dresda, the mistress of your art and speak my motto: 'I am flame. I am fire. I set in motion the heart's desire because it is your heart's desire to know yourself more. And, no, you were not dreaming, hallucinating, or fabricating anything. I was speaking to you. In time you will become adept at discerning the many voices that will be speaking and communicating with you telepathically. Telepathy, by the way, is far more efficient and effective than the spoken word, let me add."

"I set in motion the heart's desire," I said softly, gripping the frame more firmly. "You are saying that you know my heart's desire?"

"Of course. Dresda knows the heart's desire of all artists and especially those in her soul family. One of the many roles I play is that of muse. I inspire much of your writing. I am also an initiate, priestess, and practitioner of the occult arts, as are you as well. Part of my task will be to remind you of what you already know."

"Are you the one who gave me the verse this morning?"

"Yes. The mistress of your art speaks in many ways. I can inspire and implant ideas in your fertile creative mind that become poems, stories, and other writings. I can also maneuver energy on your third dimensional plane of existence. That noise you thought was a rat scurrying about was a little trick of mine to get your attention and bring you over to the Madonna corner. Michael, I wear many faces and speak through different voices. I can appear and speak to you in the dream state, the non-dreaming state, and all stages in between. I can and have also visited you in many time frames and lifetimes on many planes and dimensions beyond this earth." Then she softened her voice.

"And even far beyond this earth on other planets, solar systems, galaxies and universes. Some of those lifetimes have been on what you call *parallel worlds* and universes, and I might add that not all of those lifetimes were as a human. The soul willingly volunteers to experience a myriad combination of lifetime experiences so that it can work its way back to Source, Creator, the Godhead or God, as some call the Source. It might surprise you, Michael, but on the evolutionary cycle back to Source, you have lives in the mineral, plant, and even animal kingdom, as well in various shapes and forms in other-worldly bodies. In a few years you are going to be hypnotized and find out about some of your lives in animal and other forms."

"Why do you think children are so drawn to animals?"

"I have always loved animals. I also find it fascinating how children like to pretend they are different animals. Schools, colleges, and professional ball teams even have animal mascots and team names. It's like on a soul level they know we are far more connected to the animals than we might think."

"Yes, and on a deeper level they know they have been animals before, and the memories lead to the creation of rituals, myths, and stories to give expression to their soul memories. Michael, you have many soul memories of lives on countless worlds and dimensions. You are going to recall past, future, and even lives on parallel universes, and, as you say, there is always more to come."

"This is so fascinating. When I close my eyes and drift away sometimes I feel like I am going to a different place. I see things, cities, buildings, and people. Some of the people do not look like humans as we know them. At first I thought I just imagined them, but as I had more experiences, something told me I was not imagining them."

"No, you were not—to quote one of your favorite sayings from the Bible, 'In my Father's house are many mansions.' Michael, you are stretching your psychic and spiritual soul muscles, so to speak. Your soul is expanding which is allowing you to experience more of your total complete essence. We made our initial contact in dream time, but now you are becoming so much better at shifting and stretching your perceptions that I am now able to meet you on your third-dimensional world in the day time."

"Could you be considered a ghost or a discarnate spirit?"

"Although your friends would not see me if they were here, I am far from being a ghost or a discarnate spirit. And just because they would not see me does not mean I am not here. You are looking at and having a conversation with me. This is a totally real and hopefully enjoyable experience for you."

"I am enjoying it very much, Dresda. Thank you."

"Such encounters with friendly other-worldly beings will become more common to you—and to others as well, I might add—because your planet is undergoing a shift of energy. It is being raised to a higher level of vibration and consciousness. You are a part of all that is, all that has been, and all to be born as you wrote in a poem. 'All that is' is seeking to know and experience more of itself in its many expressions and life forms. In a sense, parts of you are coming to visit, teach, share, and learn from you. There are endless possibilities and beings that make up God/All That Is, of which you are a part as is everyone else."

"Well, at least I won't have to feel so alone."

"No, you won't, and you will also help a lot of people whose dreams are, how shall I say, as intriguing and interesting as some of your own. Many guides and beings attempt to make contact in dream time and often do so. People can learn to train their minds to recall these dream visits and encounters. With practice the psyche becomes more agile and flexible, and the soul and psychic abilities begin to blossom. This will allow them to meet with their guides and other-worldly visitors in the daytime when they are not dreaming, such as you are starting to do more frequently."

"This does not mean that you need to resort to these visits as a means to avoid working on yourself and seeking more understanding to help your struggle with depression and the deep loneliness you often feel. You have written some fine poems to express and explore that loneliness. I want you to explore your human side and how you have struggled and dealt with your loneliness over the years. This is all part of your healing and will be helpful to others as well. From your years of study and background in psychology, your time in therapy and your work on yourself, you have a lot of important and useful knowledge and information to offer. From your personal history you have a lot of heartfelt emotional experiences to share which will be helpful to others. You will even write a book about your childhood and your spiritual healing journey."

"Well, my beloved Michael, I am very happy we have made contact once more. There shall be many more occasions. For now I must take my leave, for other duties are calling to me as you would say."

"Will I see you again?"

Dresda smiled and nodded then her image faded and she disappeared. I stared at the painting for a long time. Part of me wondered if this had all been a dream, but I knew in my heart that it was not. I just didn't know if I could convince anyone else of that. To be honest, I felt that I had no need to convince anyone of anything. The experience spoke for itself.

I thought of the time many years ago when I went to a spiritualist center and my grandfather on my mother's side came through in a personal seance. The spirit guide of the medium gave me my Papaw's first and middle name, which was William Robert. I had to think about that for a moment as he was always just Papaw to me. Then I recalled that my older brother is named William Bernard (we call him Bernie) after our grandfathers. Mom's father was William Robert, and my dad's father was James Bernard. When Papaw came through the medium's voice, he said, "Hello, boy!"

I was astonished because when Papaw knew we were coming to visit, he would always be standing on the hill next to the big hickory tree waiting for us. They lived on a big hill about a mile away from the highway. We had to walk on the bumpy old dirt road to get to the house. Papaw would be wearing his overalls, a white tee-shirt with holes in it, a cap, and have a hoe in his hand since he was a gardener. "Hello, boy," were the exact words he would say in greeting me. The messages he gave me were all relevant.

Do I have proof that this séance truly transpired? Yes. I went. Do I have proof that Papaw came through? Yes, I know what happened. Can I prove this to others? No, and I have no need or wish to. I have also had readings from other psychics where names of people I knew came up and the messages were spot on. Yes, I have some tapes of the readings; however, you could walk on water, and the disbelievers still will not believe you. I think of one of the final scenes in the movie, *Oh God*, where George Burns plays God. God does perform a miracle for the panel. Then when he leaves, the panel agrees that *this just did not happen.*

I have always respected other people's beliefs. Some people are content to live their entire life and not explore the deeper spiritual metaphysical realities. Perhaps they did not come into this lifetime for such experiences. Others seem to be born with an interest in the paranormal and psychic realms. Still others find themselves opening up after something unusual and out of the ordinary happens to them.

Sometimes, losing a loved one can open the door to the spiritual realms. As a matter of fact, it was after the death of my Papaw that my Mamaw began telling us that she saw Papaw outside the house. In the séance Papaw told me that she was correct. He was appearing to her, and in her grief-stricken state of mind, her third eye or psychic vision somehow opened up. Nobody would have believed me if I told them about talking to Papaw at the séance, so I took comfort and simply told Mamaw that I was sure Papaw was looking out for her.

If truth is relative as some philosophers claim, then perhaps truth is in the eye of the beholder as is beauty. I thank spirit every day for Dresda, my wonderful guides, and my other-worldly friends and visitors. Their company and companionship are priceless. Equally important are the messages, information and teachings that I am given. They are each as real to me as the image I see when I look in the mirror. Sometimes I believe they are even more real!

CHAPTER ELEVEN

A SHAPE-SHIFTING HEALING

I know that sadness and pain have much to teach us. I also know that the lessons can be difficult and even excruciating. Past life regressions and psychic readings can shed some light and understanding on where our soul has been in past lives and what it has experienced with the people in our soul family. I have had my share of regressions and readings. They can also reveal what mistakes have to be corrected in this lifetime. Knowledge is power, as the saying goes, but it does not take away the dynamics of the actual learning and working through and paying off the karmic debts that have been incurred.

I have learned that just as we are creatures of habit in this lifetime, likewise do we bring back past life behaviors, ingrained beliefs, perceptions, and ways of relating and dealing with people. When we have developed negative qualities, such as manipulation, selfishness, possessiveness, and other dysfunctional patterns, they become more ingrained and likewise are harder to break. What we don't learn in one lifetime, we carry over into the next or a future one. I learned that I have experienced several lifetimes where *human love* was not brought into balance and harmony. Having failed to achieve that balance, I brought back what I call several bucket loads of karmic gook and sludge to clear out. Many times the task of dealing with human love has seemed as colossal as Hercules clearing out the dung in the Augean stables. There were times that I felt I would never clear out enough of my karmic baggage to make one iota of progress when it came to dealing with human love.

After the breakup with Mary in 1986, I fell into a major depression. I was tortured by regret, guilt, loneliness, and a host of other negative *poor me* emotions. I had written several poems in an attempt to ease this heart-wrenching, aching pain that was tearing at my soul. I would often speak the last line of my poem, "Sadness:" "Tomorrow I shall live again, but sadness I shall not know."

"Well, what tomorrow is that going to be?" I would ask, full of rage and pain.

Each day grew worse, and my depressions became so severe that it became a major chore to get out of bed. However, being the fighter that I am, I fought the fantasies of suicide and the desire to just give up and call it quits. In my desperation (just as I had prayed to God at the age of thirteen and told him I had to go to college, and he had to help me), I made another appeal to the powers that be.

"I need help," I cried in soul anguish. "My heart is ripping apart. I am not sleeping, and when I do sleep, I am haunted by nightmares. Please help."

As the saying goes, God and the powers that be work in mysterious ways. I received a card from Mary a few days later.

Michael,

I know you are in a lot of pain, and my heart goes out to you.

Please know that I shall always care for and love you, but we are not compatible. I know that breakup recovery is difficult. When I was having marital difficulties before I met you, I derived a lot of comfort and help in talking to a psychologist named Briana Smith who came highly recommended from a friend.

*Briana is a very compassionate woman who cuts right to the chase. She does not sugar coat, and she will not stroke your ego and allow you to play any **poor me** games. I suggest you give her a call. As a matter of fact, I have told her that you will be giving her a call. You once said that you would do anything to heal. The healing process is time-consuming, but it is worth it. If you really want help, please give Briana a call. She has told me she is willing to work with you even though you have limited financial resources.*

Michael, I wish you recovery and healing, and I send you much love.

Mary

I wiped the tears from my face and took a Kleenex and tried to dry the ones that had spilled onto the card. I cried more as I looked at Mary's handwriting, recalling love letters and cards and poems she used to write me.

"I am one f_ _ _ed up dude," I said and thought about getting drunk.

Instead, I picked up the telephone and called Briana Smith's office. A perky lady answered, saying that Briana was in session with a client, but she would be happy to schedule an appointment for me. We set it for the following Monday at 11:00 a.m.

I managed to get through the rest of the week, and by Monday on the way over I was a nervous wreck. I had thought so many times to call and cancel the appointment, but something would not let me. I had decided to get through it. I could always walk out or finish the session and never return.

137

Briana was a pretty lady with long dark hair and blue eyes. She had a nice figure and showed some cleavage. She had me fill out a questionnaire, and then she said, "Michael, what do you want to work on?"

I felt a tug of resistance and said, "I don't know if I want to work on anything. To be blunt and honest, I don't know if I even want to live another day."

Briana gave me a look of sincere concern.

"Well, you are here, Michael, so that leads me to believe that part of you wishes to continue living."

I looked at her, full of despair; then a few moments later I said, "I don't know if I can live another day. This dark pit is about to engulf me." I cried, fighting back tears. "I can't deal with this agony anymore. It's like there is this big black hole deep in my soul, and it gets bigger every day. It's like a big black demon tearing at my soul. The darkness actually seems to be alive. Sometimes I just pull the covers over my head and hope I will disappear into nothingness. Do you know what I mean? Have you ever felt this way," I said, looking at her desperately.

"Actually, I have," Briana replied softly, gently touching my hand. "In time I will share a personal story with you—one that might change your life and help steer you on the road of healing and recovery. But first we have to work on some things. Okay?"

I reluctantly agreed. I wondered if she were just flattering me, but her offering to share a personal story intrigued me. I could see no reason why a psychologist would make something like that up. I wondered why she would offer to share a personal story. It seemed inappropriate and unprofessional to me. Nonetheless, I decided to continue seeing her. We plugged away for three months. Then on the first day of July, Briana kept her promise.

"Now, I feel that it is time to share a personal story with you, Michael. Ordinarily, I don't divulge my personal life to my clients, but it feels right to tell you this now."

Briana was quiet a few moments. She ran her hands through her long hair and stared dreamily into space. I lifted my head up and looked her squarely in the eyes. I was surprised she didn't acknowledge me. She was far away in her own thoughts. My hands fidgeted on my lap. I didn't know what to do or say. I noticed tears dripping down her face. I wanted to take a Kleenex out of the box for her but refrained.

"Why is she crying?" I wondered. *She's the psychologist,* I thought. I had never seen this side of Briana before. She had always been a sensitive listener but had maintained a professional detachment. Nonetheless, I sensed that she cared about me. Although I didn't think she helped me much, I always came back. I sensed that there was more to her than she let on, and I sensed that there was something she had to offer me.

Moments later Briana broke the silence. She took a drink of her Diet Coke and then moved a little closer to me. "Pardon me for spacing out like that, Michael. It is still difficult dealing with that memory sometimes."

"What memory if I may ask?"

"The memory of my mother who committed suicide when I was fourteen. She said some similar things that you said today. She just couldn't get out of her black pit. She used to wake up in the middle of the night screaming that shadow monsters were eating her soul. Her doctor said that she suffered from delusions and wanted to put her in a mental hospital. She killed herself the day before my father was to take her to the hospital. So you see, Michael, I am familiar with what you are dealing with although the dynamics are different for other people."

There was silence for several moments. I looked at the clock. It was time for the session to end. I reached for my coat.

"Don't you want to hear the rest of my story? You are my last client today. I'm not concerned about time."

There was much sadness in her eyes. It seemed that Briana actually needed me to hear her story. I had never seen her look vulnerable. As she looked at me, she wiped more tears away.

"I'm so embarrassed. Please pardon me, Michael. I'm being totally unprofessional."

"It's okay, Briana. Psychologists are people, too. I've often wondered who they go to when they need to talk."

"Cats are great listeners," she said, snickering.

I wondered how old she was. She didn't look over thirty. I also wondered if she was married. She wore no wedding ring. The comment about the cat made me think that she might be single. I did not have the nerve to ask her.

"Back to my story. I was devastated by my mother's suicide. For awhile I considered it myself. I talked to my counselor at school. She recommended that I see a friend of her mother's. The woman was quite eccentric, and my counselor said that some people called her crazy. In spite of the tall tales, the woman was known to help people haunted by death wishes and the dark. She was part Native American Indian of the Navajo tribe. My counselor told me that the woman was a medicine woman and shaman known as Shadow Chaser. I saw her for several months, and she changed my life. I truly don't think I could have continued living without some extraordinary help. Shadow Chaser gave me a completely different perspective about death, darkness, and life."

"What do you mean?" I asked, becoming more interested in Briana's tale.

"Shadow Chaser was a shaman and a witch. She talked to spirits and said that we all have spirits we can call upon to help us. She said there were many levels of reality interspersed within our own and that there was so much more out there and in there—referring to our minds and souls or spirits—than most people were aware of. She talked about perceptual maneuvering as a means to contact other levels of reality. She talked about other worlds and other beings who live on other planets, galaxies, and universes. She talked about many things."

"Very interesting," I replied. I also believe in other realities and life on other worlds. So tell me, did you talk to any spirits?"

"That and much more. More on this later. Shadow Chaser also believed in magic power. She gave me a black oval stone the last day I saw her. She said that anytime I felt darkness enveloping me, to put the stone in my hand and to rub it. She said the power in the stone would help the darkness to befriend me instead of torturing me. I was very scared of the dark in those days. She also said that the stone could help make a person a shadow chaser."

"What does that mean?"

"It means that you chase your shadows and fears instead of letting them chase you. She would say that your shadows and fears have been chasing you. The way you chase them is by calling them towards you. You stop running from your fears. Instead of shunning and running from the darkness, you walk into it. According to her, anyone brave enough to face and chase his/her own darkness is ready to receive its power, which can be imparted through certain stones that have been blessed and given power by a shaman. The stone bridges the spirit realm or world where shadows and darkness dwell and the realm of matter. The stone is very powerful."

"How so? This sounds crazy, Briana, with all due respect. Are you trying to humor me?"

"Not at all," she said, looking at me seriously. "I wouldn't do that. I know that you believe there is more to reality than most people perceive." She tilted her head a little closer to me. "And I also know that part of you has always believed there is more to life and reality than what we see and perceive with our physical senses. I've wanted to talk to you about the other world, as Shadow Chaser referred to it, for some time, but I didn't feel you were ready. Today you are. Desperation has opened the door to magic and healing many times. After all, what do you have to lose when you're that depressed?"

"I want to know about the power."

"It's different for everyone. Anyhow, if you like, you may borrow my black oval stone," she said, opening the drawer and taking out a small black velvet pouch. She untied the string and handed me the stone.

"It looks so ordinary," I said, taking it.

"Looks can be deceiving."

I rubbed the stone gently a few moments and then moved my hand near my chest. I opened and closed my eyes and began shaking violently. Briana gently rubbed my forehead with her left hand. The spasmodic jerking ceased. I slowly opened my eyes and looked at her intently.

"Wow, that was awesome, Briana. It felt like my soul was trying to exit my body."

"No. It was your spirit sensing the presence of your shadow or darkness. The stone heightens your vision and senses, allowing you to see what is normally invisible. You will meet your darkness soon. It will identify itself and can take on any form. I suggest you hold the stone when you feel the darkness about to engulf you. It is time to meet your shadow and let it guide you. Take this stone if you'd like. Let me know next week how things go."

"This sounds like something from a fantasy book. I've always felt that things are not as they appear; there is more to reality than we normally perceive. I'm impressed that you already knew that about me as we have not discussed this before. I thought you would just think me deluded or hallucinating."

"Michael, you are now ready to make contact with the other world, and I don't mean via death, at least physically. You are ready to know more of yourself and to discover the vast reservoirs of power that dwell within you."

"I will take the stone home, Briana. My friends would say you have lost your marbles if I told them about today's session, but I have no intention of telling anybody anything. Besides, I've had lots of psychic and paranormal experiences so I'm not surprised that I've met you nor do I believe it is a coincidence. I believe that people cross paths for reasons, and I also believe there are different realities. I have experienced some. My heart just seems to be stuck in this one at the current time."

"It takes time to learn to discern reality from appearances, or different realities I should say. Nonetheless, the invisible realities are very interconnected and influence the everyday visible reality where most people live and exist."

"Briana, you are not the first person to tell me such things, and I somehow believe you, especially after this experience with the stone. I might not if that stone hadn't made me feel so alive. Who knows? Maybe you did something to me—gave me some energy or something. Maybe I did hallucinate, and you're telling me this to amuse me. If so, I don't care."

"I've been dead inside since my eighth grade teacher, Mr. Peters, killed himself. He shot himself in the head in a barn. Everybody loved him. No one could figure out why he took his life. He seemed to be stable and happy man. I have never been able to let that go. Mr. Peters was like a father to me."

"The stone will help you face and deal with that old hurt."

"Maybe," I said softly.

"I want to do a little exercise with you, Michael, with your permission, of course. I want you to place the black stone in your hand, and I will put my hand over yours. Are you game?"

"Sure."

Briana scooted next to me on the couch. I couldn't help but smell the perfume she was wearing. My heart missed a few beats. She looked at me with a genuine smile on her face. I made myself come back to the moment and took the stone from my pocket and placed it in my hand. Briana gently placed her hand over mine.

"Close your eyes, Michael, and let the stone attune to you."

I closed my eyes. Immediately I saw so many lights I feared I'd go blind even though my eyes were completely closed. I also saw the sun, but it didn't hurt my eyes, my soul, or whatever I was seeing with. I saw shadowy forms dancing about, jumping in and out of the sun. I thought I even saw a face. I saw dancing flickering sparks of light which merged and disappeared into the sun. I felt like they were known as *the sun people*, and I wanted to visit them.

Then as quickly as the images appeared, they faded. Briana must have sensed it because she gently removed her hand and spoke softly.

"Michael, what was it like?   Tell me what you experienced."

"I saw all of these bright lights and faces and I wanted to go and visit the sun people. I know this sounds crazy."

"It is not crazy.   You were just experiencing a different kind of reality—a more expanded reality, let us say. The stone, with a little help and energy from me, awakened you to what shamans call non-ordinary levels of awareness. In those states all is more expansive.   No one need take drugs to expand his/her mind.   Power also expands it, but it requires a confrontation with the darkness first. It is time to end our talk now. See you next week. Will you be okay?"

"Yes, and thank you for lending me the stone. I'll take good care of it."

"I know that you will. Good bye now, Michael," she said giving me an affectionate pat on the shoulder.

"Goodbye to you, too, and to think this beautiful gift and information on power would be coming from a psychologist of all people," I said, smiling.

Briana returned the smile as she got up to lead me to the door.

"Remember what I said before, things are seldom as they appear; that goes for people as well."

I felt elated the next couple of days. I had put the stone in my drawer and let it be. By the fourth day my new enthusiasm had begun to wane, and the old depression started gnawing at me again. I suffered in silence, smiling at everyone around me and forcing myself to keep up appearances.

The day before my session with Briana was almost unbearable. I had visions of black demons gorging on my body then spitting out my soul, which was then engulfed by a frightening abyss which had come to life. I wanted to find a cliff and jump into a chasm.

That night I knew that something was about to happen. I could feel it, but what?

"Power," I whispered.

The picture of Mr. Peters seemed to stare right at me. I picked it up and held it a long time.

"Why did you have to die?" I cried out. "It was not your time. You left me all alone. You had me. You could have fought the darkness, whatever it was, but you wouldn't. You could have told me what was bothering you. You just gave up and quit. I hate you for it," I screamed, throwing the picture across the room. "You are a coward. A big coward. I live with this god-awful darkness every day of my life. I haven't killed myself yet."

I wiped tears from my eyes and then picked up the picture. The small frame was cracked down the middle. I carried it to my bed and sat down on the edge.

Memories of times with Mr. Peters flooded my mind: how he spent the entire day with me at the science fair exhibition, the times he took several of us boys camping and caving, and how he had shown us a few karate moves. Then I talked to him as though he were there.

"I was not aware of how depressed you had become the year before your suicide. If you had only talked to me, Mr. Peters, maybe I could have helped," I muttered in a tearful voice. "We shared so much. We students were like your family. You once told me I was like the son you never had. Why wouldn't you tell me about the darkness and what was bothering you?"

"If something ever happens to me, you have to promise me that you'll take care of yourself," I recalled him saying a month before his suicide.

"If what happens, Mr. Peters?"

"Oh, I don't know. Life is never guaranteed. We could all be dead tomorrow. A house could fall from the sky on our head like in *The Wizard of Oz*," he had said, trying to insert some humor.

"*The Wizard of Oz* is just a movie. Nothing bad is going to happen. We don't die before our time, and it's not time for any of us to die."

"You're probably right," Mr. Peters said, putting his arm around me.

"What caused the darkness?" I asked, looking up at the photo. "What took his love of life away?"

Suddenly I felt panicky. Invisible claws clutched at my throat. I fell back on the bed gasping for breath. "Take the black oval stone out of the drawer and hold it," I heard in my mind. It took every ounce of strength in me to get off the bed. Some dark force was holding me down. For a moment I wanted to surrender to the force and die. It would be good to go wherever Mr. Peters was. Life was meaningless since his suicide.

The phone rang. I jerked, and my face was deathly white. Trembling, I picked up the receiver.

"Michael, this is Briana Smith. I am aware of your struggle. As difficult as it is, you must not give up like your teacher did. If you do, the darkness will win. You must stand up to the darkness once and for all. Do battle with it, and you will free yourself from its clutches. Your teacher will be freed, too. Go get the stone! Now!" she said so loudly that I felt my head would burst.

My breathing became uneasy. I looked up and saw a big shadow hovering a few feet away.

"Get the stone while you can and let its power help you," Briana commanded. "If you don't, the darkness will win, and you will become its slave when it is meant to serve you."

"I don't know what you mean," I said, trembling, wondering if I was losing my mind.

"The darkness is a personification of your fears and your inner darkness. You are so powerful on subconscious levels that you are unaware that you have given your darkness outer form so that you may do battle and then merge with it. Think of this experience as a sort of waking nightmare if you will. However, it is much more than that. There is no time now to get into all of that. I will save that for later. Now hurry and get the stone before it is too late."

I jumped off the bed and opened the drawer. The stone was not there.

"It's too late," I yelled. "It's gone."

"No, it isn't," Briana countered. "The darkness is veiling the stone. Feel for it. With your eyes closed, you will draw it to you. Will it to release itself from the shadow's grip. You can do it."

Mr. Peter's image appeared in front of me. Phantom hands were grabbing for him, but a small glowing light would not let the shadow touch him.

"Mr. Peters," I cried out. "What is happening?" I shouted, hanging up the phone.

Then I heard his voice in my mind. *The darkness has come for you, Michael. It wants your soul just like it wanted mine. It has not been able to reach me because of you. Your love is what sustains the white light between me and the shadow. It is time to end this battle. You must name this shadow and look into its black eyes.*

"What is its name?"

In your case its name is Death, but don't call on its name until you are holding the stone. Hurry now! Time is almost over.

"This all sounds so crazy. It can't be real," I pleaded.

The image of Mr. Peters disappeared. Frantically, I reached desperately for the stone. I could not feel it. Everything was fuzzy and blurred. I wondered if I was losing my mind. My teeth chattered. I was freezing cold.

"I can't find the stone," I whimpered, moving away. "I'm so cold." I closed my eyes and headed back to my bed. I drew the covers over my body, but the freezing air still permeated my bones, making me shake and shiver all over.

"I can't fight Death. It is too powerful. I just want to sleep," I whispered. "I need to sleep."

Moments later the phone rang again. Startled by its loud ringing, I picked up the phone. It was Briana again.

"Michael, Shadow Chaser told me that your darkness almost has you in its grip. You can't give up. You can fight Death and your darkness and win. You must. I did and I won. Now my mother is free, and you and your teacher can be free as well. Get the power object stone. Let it do its work."

"What work?" I muttered, incoherently.

"I don't know. It's different for everyone. But do it. I know that your teacher came to you. I saw him in a vision."

"You mean he really was there? I wasn't imagining it?"

"No. He was there alright. The stone brought him to you."

"I thought I was hallucinating. You once said that deep depression can lead to hallucinations."

"Yes, but this was no hallucination. You have to trust me. Get the stone."

"I tried. The stone is not there."

"Yes it is. The shadow's anger has veiled it. You have the power to remove the veil. Love is stronger than anger and hatred. Your love for your teacher can unveil it. Do it for him."

"Why should I? He deserted me. Abandoned me. He just gave up. Why should I help him?"

"Because you are stronger than he was. We must stop talking. The shadow is filling you with its rage and hate. It is delaying you. It is making you question. It is draining your energy and life force. It is numbing your reason. Don't let it freeze your instincts. It has been torturing you ever since your beloved teacher died. You can't let it take you. If you don't act soon, you'll be depleted and then won't be able to do anything, and the shadow will only be stronger. Your depressions will increase to the point you could have a mental collapse. The shadow wants your love to melt into hatred. Can't you feel this? It's already happening. The light that protects your teacher is almost out. Your anger is growing by the second while the light dims more and more."

"How do I know if I can believe you? Maybe this is all a dream, or I am going insane."

"I promise you this is not a dream. Now get the stone before it's too late, Michael," she shouted and then hung up. The shadow hovered over the drawer. I opened the drawer with all my might and willed the stone to manifest. "Disappear, darkness. Stone, show yourself to me. Come back to me," I commanded. "You have to come to me now. In the name of love, come back." I saw Mr. Peter's faint image. "In the name of love, come to me. Come back to me," I shouted over and over.

Finally I felt the shadow lift. I opened my eyes and saw the stone. I grabbed it and then fell onto my bed.

"Show me your face, Darkness," I commanded. Then I blacked out.

"Where am I?" I asked. I looked up. It was pitch dark. An old man, whose face I could not see, appeared. He was carrying my weary body up a mountain.

"Where are we going?" I asked the old man. "Please tell me who you are, and why won't you show me your face?"

"I am Death," the old man said softly. "You are willing to look at and face your darkness and fears. In your case, another name for them is death. You have a deep fear of the death or dissolution of your soul into nothingness. You have a fear of madness and insanity. You are not destined for madness or insanity. Facing and merging with your darkness will give you the strength and power to overcome your fears. It will lead you to the light and to liberation. Most people fear something. These fears create and give form to their darkness. The form or forms it takes depends on the creative resources of the soul and the subconscious mind."

"You are extremely creative and resourceful and highly attuned to and in touch with your subconscious mind. You will not lose yourself in its many mazes and labyrinths, or you *could* wind up insane in a mental institution. Your guides and higher self will not let you go too deeply into the subliminal and unconscious realms. Its terrains are vast. All must eventually make these journeys and, like you are presently doing, they must face their inner darkness and do battle with it. They must be willing to look into the face of their deepest fears and darkness. Yours is the dissolution of your soul, not your corporeal essence. Many people fear the death of their mortal human self. They are attached to their humanity."

"On the contrary, you and others like yourself struggle with your humanity, for you know that you are so much more than a mortal being. The origins of fears are different for everyone and depend upon many variables and experiences of the souls. In time you will learn the origins of your fears which you actually create just as you create your own nightmares in an attempt to understand and deal with your fears. Learning the origins of your fears will take place at a given point after your fears are faced—all fears must be faced."

"It is not time for you to see my face yet. I have not come to claim you but to lead you up the mountain where life awaits you. You are destined to fully experience life and all that it entails. You and others like you are destined to merge with your divinity as all mortals are at some point. This is a very monumental task, I might add. Taking the inner journeys to the shadow lands of your psyche is part of the process of self-realization, actualization, and empowerment. Your darkness can lead you into the light."

"I'm reminded of a poem I wrote that said, "Seekers retreat to hidden caves to find the light. The last line says, "The answers are there where the darkness shines, and the voice that speaks softly is your own."

"Those profound words are full of wisdom. They demonstrate that you have some understanding of the interrelationship of the darkness and the light."

"Perhaps. So you say that you are Death. Is that who you are? I thought you were the enemy," I said in a whisper with barely enough strength to speak.

"So people say, but such is not true. It is people's fear of me that can destroy them, not I. Death can be your friend. I am your friend. I can teach you many things. I can teach you about life and becoming fully human and fully alive."

"Death is my friend," I repeated.

When I woke up, I spent two hours writing down the experience that seemed as real as any waking moment has to offer. The next day I arrived at my appointment an hour early, hoping that Briana had no appointments before mine. She came in the lobby and greeted me.

"Hello, Michael. You're early. Make yourself comfortable," she said, shaking my hand. She had never shaken my hand before, except for our first meeting. "I'll be with you in a half hour. This is my last appointment before you. We will have plenty of time to talk. There are many magazines to read."

"Thanks," I said, looking at her. I noticed that her eyes were different. There was an amber glow I had never seen before. I wondered if I imagined the glow.

"Briana will probably want to put me away when she hears about last night," I said aloud.

But she called me last night, didn't she? She told me to fight the shadow, or did I make all of this up? Could it all have been just a dream?"

The wait seemed like eternity.

"At last," I muttered when Briana came for me.

When she closed the door, I spontaneously threw my arms around her. Neither of us spoke. We held each other tightly a long time. When we sat down, we looked at each other deeply. I wanted to speak but was unable. Briana finally broke the silence.

"You won, Michael. You won," she said softly. "The darkness came for you, and you named it and faced it. Death befriended you and revealed to you who he truly is. You can also thank your teacher for his help."

"So, Mr. Peters really was there? I didn't just imagine or make it up?"

"You know that it was very real, and yes, he was there in spirit form. Your teacher is free now, and so are you. You will never have a desire to commit suicide again. Your courage was stronger than your fear. The darkness cannot touch you in the absence of fear."

"What is the absence of fear?"

"Love."

"Did the power of the stone lead me to Death who took the form of the old man who would not show me his face?"

"Yes."

"Was what I saw in the dream real?"

"Yes, but there is more to it."

"The old man told me so many interesting things about facing our inner darkness and fears and how the darkness and light are interconnected. He said that unlike most people who fear the death of the mortal human self, I have a fear of the dissolution of my soul, as well as a fear of madness. He assured me that neither will ever take place. He said that I will one day know the origins of all of my fears, and in time everyone will. Taking inner journeys to the shadow lands of our psyche is all part of the process of self-realization, actualization, and empowerment. I recall quoting a poem I wrote years ago which stated something very similar. I spent two hours writing everything down. It's so strange how I have such dream recall."

"Michael, you are a time walker and a shaman at heart like me. We walk upon many different realms at any given point of time because we know that in reality time is an illusion, albeit a somewhat useful tool. It is as easy for us to journey to and access the terrains of our subconscious psyche as it is to recite our ABC'S. Perhaps easier," she added, laughing.

"Did Death really did carry me up to the mountain to hand me over to life?"

"Yes, but what you experienced was no dream. It was a spirit journey that just happened to take place while you slept. And you are not yet at the summit. Death will continue to carry you up the mountain. Death is your friend now, your guide. For you it takes the form of an old man. For others it takes other forms. Death will appear to you in the daytime henceforth, as well as at night. Your journey with Death last night was much more than a dream. Your journey with Death was real on other levels of reality."

"What seems like a dream is often real on other levels of reality, just as what seems real is often but a dream on other levels of reality. Most people fear Death, but Death is nothing more than Life in disguise. It is also our deepest fears and old hurts that we must confront in order to become free of them. Your deep hurt and pain over the death of Mr. Peters has been eating away at your soul for many years. You had to deal with and come to terms with that. We all need to see *past* or beyond appearances to what is real."

"I like that statement, Briana. I want to see *past* appearances."

Briana approached me and placed her hands upon my head. She blew out several deep breaths, and her fingers applied light pressure on various places on my head. Moments later standing in front of me, Briana had transformed into an old Indian Woman.

"Who are you? What have you done to me?" I asked, feeling a bit disoriented and frightened.

"There is no reason to fear," she said softly. "I have just shifted your perceptual awareness and am helping you to see with your soul vision. Shamans do this all of the time. You asked to see past appearances. I am granting your wish."

That made me feel better.

"You are Shadow Chaser, aren't you?"

"Yes. I am also Briana Smith."

"This seems crazy, but I feel like I'm someone else, too."

"You are. Rub the stone and ask it to show you to yourself."

I took out the stone and gently rubbed it. I could feel myself changing. Shadow Chaser led me to the mirror. Standing in front of the mirror was the perfect image of Mr. Peters.

"Mr. Peters," I cried out.

"No, it is you in another form that you can shape shift into with a shift in your perceptions. You have always wanted to be like your teacher. The stone has granted you that wish. I, likewise, always wanted to be like Shadow Chaser. The stone granted me my wish. I told her after a few sessions that I'd like to be like her. She said that could be arranged. She also told me that her time was nearly through on the earth."

"So now you carry on her work? Is that how it goes?"

"Our work. Briana helps people who would not understand Shadow Chaser, the healer shaman. As Shadow Chaser I help people who need more help than traditional psychology can offer. I don't reveal my Shadow Chaser self to many people. You are the third person to meet her."

"Why is that?"

"Most people are not physically, psychologically, or spiritually prepared to handle such knowledge. When you spoke of the darkness as though it was a living being, then I knew that you were ready for deeper knowing."

"Will I be able to become Mr. Peters at will?"

"You won't literally become your teacher. With practice and training, you will be able to take in some of his energy and essence and merge it with your own. You will have some of his strengths and qualities to draw upon. In time, as you become an adept shaman, you will be able to project his image. Those who can benefit from his knowledge will see that projected image. But you will not be ready to do that for some time. Knowledge and power must be assimilated and integrated slowly. I can teach you some things if you are interested. Now that your teacher's spirit is free, there is much work for you to do. You no longer will feel his fears because there is no more fear. Your love, courage, and power freed him."

"I wonder how this will all impact me."

"You will help many people, Michael. People who have survived encountering the darkness like we have, make good counselors. We can empathize with people, and we understand suffering and soul agony because we have been in the pit and abyss. We came back, and it is our suffering and pain that led us to our inner reservoirs of power. We are in a position to help others do likewise. We are able to journey to spirit and dream realms to get help from many healing spirits."

"You will never be the same again, Michael. Your perceptions are expanding, and you will be having many more experiences of what are considered to be paranormal. Your soul is expanding, and this will allow you to make many contacts from people in the spirit realm and also people and beings from many dimensions and other worlds. The boredom you have felt will not be around much anymore. You will enjoy your new visitors and learn much from them, and you will impart your knowledge and help others. There are many books for you to write that will touch many lives."

"That makes sense. I am going to be a spiritual counselor, as well as writer, Briana. I do want to help people. Will I ever have my own stone?"

"In time. You have more to learn first. Are you interested in becoming my student instead of my patient?"

"Yes," I exclaimed. "No one will have to know."

"Between you and me, I'm not charging you anymore. This will be our little secret, Michael."

"How kind of you. I can't believe all of this is happening."

Briana patted me on the shoulder. "The fun is just beginning. Okay, it is time to be Dr. Briana Smith," she said, rubbing the stone with one hand and my forehead with the other. We both returned to our normal self.

"What will my other shaman self be called?"

"You think about that and see if something comes up. You can tell me next week."

"Maybe that old man will tell me in a dream tonight."

"He just might," she said, kissing me on the cheek. "I will show you out."

I was fascinated by that last visit with Briana Smith, and I still think about it sometimes. I know that it was a valid, intense healing experience even if some of it occurred via perceptual shifting and on spirit and other realms. This made it no less powerful or healing to me. I have never since desired to commit suicide, and I incorporate shamanistic healing techniques in some of my spiritual work.

Now I can deal with the hum drum everyday ordinary mundane aspects of life and not feel bored or lonely. Shadow Chaser taught me that when I expand my vision and perceptions, I can go to many realms and be visited by many wondrous fascinating beings. Stargazing is no longer a time of sadness, longing, and yearning. Instead, it is a time of rejoicing and celebrating the light that animates and unites all life, matter, and creation.

CHAPTER TWELVE

SOUL-SHARING AND

COLLECTIVE SOUL-MERGING

A few weeks after the amazing experience with the shape-shifting shaman psychotherapist, I dreamed of a beautiful woman holding a red rose. When she stepped closer, I noticed that the heart was only an outline. There was no inside to it.

"What does this mean?" I asked the beautiful radiant lady who resembled an angel.

"Dear sweet soul," she gently said. "You are sad because your heart is more empty than full. Unfortunately, this applies to most people on your world. You will never be happy until you come into the fullness of your being. That can only happen when you open your heart and let love fill it. We shall be visiting soon outside of dream time. I have some things to teach you that I think can help you. Goodbye for now, and I look forward to spending time with you soon," she said and then disappeared.

I woke up smelling the scent of roses. The image of the heart was still in my mind. The lady had said that most people's hearts on this world were more empty than full. *Where was she from? Was she an angel or advanced being from another planet?*

I recalled her saying, "You will never be happy until you come into the fullness of your being. That can only happen when you open your heart and let love fill it." *How does love fill the heart?* I wondered. The lady's words had given me hope. She had said we would soon visit outside dream time. Perhaps I would receive answers then.

Shortly after the breakup with Mary, I had taken to spending more time alone at night because the night fascinates me. After being terribly frightened of the dark for many years as a child, now I derive much comfort and solace from the dark. I'd sometimes stay with my Mamaw and Papaw who owned over one hundred acres of land. Papaw was a hermit so he understood my need for nature and solitude. He used to say that having been raised in a household of ten with relatives close by, he vowed as a boy that he'd spend his later years with the trees, critters, and brooks as his neighbors. He often told me that solitude, fresh air, and exercise were good for body and soul. Papaw totally understood my predilection for the night time, and since there were no neighbors for quite a distance, I never feared being bothered.

The night is so much more exciting than the daytime to me. Sometimes I would lie out all night and stargaze until I fell asleep. When I returned to the house, Mamaw would chide me, but Papaw would wink at me. "The boy is a nature child," Papaw would say. "Leave him be."

When I was heartbroken over Mary, I took a few days off and visited my grandparents at the old home place. Papaw was up in years, but he still managed to cook and care for his entourage of dogs.

Mamaw would get mad and say, "You have to stop taking in those stupid stray dogs."

At one point, Papaw had fourteen dogs. After laughing about his dogs, (he was down to eight at that point) Papaw said, "Michael, make yourself at home. I know you will be roaming the fields."

After dinner I insisted on helping Mamaw with the dishes. "Michael, never mind the dishes, I'll tend to that," she said. "Just be sure to take a towel, a blanket, and some water if you are going to be camping outside beneath the trees stargazing."

"Sure. Mamaw, you know how I love to lie on the ground and stargaze. Sometimes I like to sit on the bench with the little stars that Papaw carved for me."

I got my things and gave Mamaw a kiss on the cheek. She straightened my collar. "Now you be sure and come back if it gets chilly."

"I will."

After walking about a mile, I arrived at my favorite spot. I took the brown beach towel from my backpack, spread it on the ground, and then lay down to stargaze.

Suddenly a strong feeling of melancholy descended upon me. It had happened before but never this intensely. It was as though I wanted to go to one of those stars. I stared at the stars near the Big Dipper for a long time. A sense of homesickness, which I could not explain, began to drain me of all the enthusiasm I had been feeling. Drowsiness overtook me.

As I lay there drifting off but not yet asleep, suddenly a bright light appeared a few feet away. I leaned back against the oak tree and adjusted my eyes, wondering where the light came from. It had disappeared but standing where I had seen the light was a very beautiful woman with a golden bright light encircling her. I noticed a cluster of what appeared to be diamond-shaped stars above her head. They seemed to be suspended in mid-air about an inch. Her long hair was radiant and golden and her skin fair. Her eyes were light pink, and she emitted the sweetest rose fragrance. She wore a loose flowing white robe with a golden sash tied around her waist.

Am I dreaming? I thought. If I can ask then I must not be, I concluded. I was too afraid to open my eyes. Part of me feared if I did, she might disappear. I closed them tighter and heard playful laughter. "Please, relax," the lady spoke softly. "Do not be so serious. You are not asleep and you are not dreaming."

I opened and closed my eyes several times. She was still there. I made a strong effort to relax, taking a few deep breaths. Soon the pitter-patter of my heart subsided, and my shaking hands were once again relaxed. I looked up at her. My eyes lit up in sudden joyous recognition.

"I know who you are. You are the beautiful lady who recently paid me a dream visit."

"Yes," she replied, smiling.

My heart raced with excitement. "Thank you so much for coming. I have missed you. Won't you please sit down?" I said, pointing to the bench. I hoped she did not hear the trembling in my voice. I was silently grateful that I had left the soft cushion on it and that it had not rained since the last time I was here.

"Thank you," she replied. It actually looked like she glided to the bench. "Won't you please come and sit next to me, Michael?"

I slowly made my way to the bench. I was so nervous and excited that I nearly fell off the bench. Her presence was so radiant and ethereal. She was so strikingly beautiful that I wondered if she came from the stars.

As though reading my mind, she smiled and pointed to the sky. "You are not dreaming, Michael, and the fact that you see the bright light around me is a very good sign."

I wanted to ask her how she knew that I noticed the light that encircled her but refrained, hesitant to say anything. "Who are you?" I managed to stammer, still astonished by her beauty and presence.

"My name is Rosara."

Being close to Rosara was like being in a rose garden. Her entire being emitted a rose fragrance.

"Do you always smell like this?" I wanted to ask but didn't dare. I soon learned that I couldn't keep any of my thoughts secret. She could read them all. I tried to pay special attention to what I was thinking.

She smiled. "Michael, my fragrance is so potent because we have a special link which I will tell you more about later."

"Oh, really?"

"Yes. My people don't always emit this fragrance," she added. "It is reserved for those with whom we plan to soul-share."

"It's nice," I managed to blurt out.

"It is quite nice," she replied softly, "especially during soul-sharing."

I was becoming very interesting in soul-sharing.

"Where are you from?" I asked, bursting with curiosity. The way she looked at me I could tell that she had read my thoughts again.

"I will tell you about soul-sharing and where I come from in a little while, but first things first. I have been observing you for a very long time. You have been struggling and feeling lonely for many years, and you do not feel that this earth is your home. Human love has disappointed you. This is because you seek a deeper more wholesome love."

She stepped closer and looked intently into my eyes. I thought I would faint, her presence was so intoxicating. "You seek soul-sharing, Michael. You seek soul-merging. You seek me. This is why you spend so much time alone in the woods and fields and stargaze.

"I am sorry for the dissolution of your relationship with your beloved and the emotional turmoil and hardship you have undergone. Even though it may not make sense to your conscious self, the pain you have been experiencing is actually pushing you to go deeper within. It is helping you to contact your soul who can help give you some needed answers and insights. You can also call upon angels because you are especially connected to the angelic realms. This should come as no surprise to you as you have had several visits. As a matter of fact, an angel inspired you to write the poem, "The Messenger of Love" just as she told you that you were ready to learn more about love."

"Most earth people know so little about true love and soul-sharing, let alone their own soul. I am here to teach you a few lessons. Michael, I have a secret to reveal to you. You and I have soul-shared from a world called Astellva which is very far away. Love on Astellva is so much more beautiful, intense, and fulfilling than human love. There really is no comparison. Your higher self and subconscious mind know about our connection, and they remember times we have soul-shared. This partially explains why there is emptiness in your soul and why you write so many profound and beautiful love poems.

Through your art you are capturing some of the beauty and essence of soul-sharing."

"Thank you, Rosara. I have been told that some of my poems have an *other-worldly* air and flavor."

"That is because so much of your essence is other-worldly, sweet poet. You will never completely feel at home on the earth. Nor do you need to. Now that I have made conscious contact with you, there will be many more wonderful life experiences for you to look forward to."

I wanted to ask Rosara to elucidate but refrained, assuming she would tell me when it was the right time.

Rosara looked up at the sky. "Michael, Astellva is very far away," she said softly. "It is out of reach of your scientific telescopes. We have the means to remain anonymous to any world we choose. Few on your world know anything about us. I come to you because we are soul-mates on some higher planes. I have been watching you for several years and monitoring your development."

"How do you do that?" I asked, puzzled.

"With a big computer that has a gigantic screen," she joked, laughing. "Seriously, I tune into your energy field. Just like you can see a light around me, likewise, a light emanates from you. Each person has a light which extends from his/her physical body. No two are the same. They are different colors depending on the thoughts and feelings the person projects. On my world we recognize people by this color. It is also what draws people together. Your light is almost the exact hue of gold as mine. On Astellva there are over a hundred variations of gold alone. It is the same with the other colors. We have many colors most of your people have never seen. Some of your artists and ultra-sensitive people are exceptions, and some have painted the soul light above the head, in what you call a halo."

"Like I said, your hue is identical to mine. We are soul-mates, beloved Michael. By attuning and utilizing my soul senses I can perceive people very far away. It is part of our training on Astellva. Anyone can do it. All it takes is for one to develop a sensitivity. Are you not wondering why I have come to you?"

"Yes," I replied, trying to absorb the experience without looking too shocked.

"I have come to you because you are ready to learn how to see with your soul vision. You already do to a degree. You have the sensitive temperament and disposition needed for such vision. Also, the increased frequency of your stargazing has shown me that you are ready to know and experience more. You spend a lot of time stargazing, and you have begun to feel an intense homesickness. This is a sign that your soul senses are awakening. I have come to awaken them even more. That is, if you wish for this experience," she said, tapping me gently on the forehead.

Her touch felt like a light current of electricity. It didn't hurt but rather sent pleasant tingles all through my body, and even my mind, if that is possible. When I looked at her soft, deep eyes, I felt that my soul was merging into her being—as strange as that might sound. Intrigued by the tingling sensations and a little scared, I quickly looked away.

"Michael, you are beginning to sense that who you think you are, is not really who you are, or at least completely," she continued. "Many on your world are beginning to realize that the earth is not the place of their origin. I am aware that you have felt since childhood that you are a stranger on the earth. In many ways you are. As you stargazed and dreamt, you began to wonder about other worlds. Do they truly exist? Where are they? How can you make contact with them? Along with your many questions, deep longings and yearnings for something you could not define as you star gazed began to stir. Is this not true?"

"Sort of," I replied, feeling embarrassed. It was not easy having a virtual stranger see into the very depths of my soul so I tried to remain evasive. "Well, sort of, I like I said. But I thought I was only imagining things when I looked at the stars. I think if you stare at anything long enough, you can put yourself in a reverie or trance, and your mind and eyes can start playing tricks on you."

Rosara smiled and touched my hand gently. "Tricks, you say, Michael. What an interesting word. The experience must have been pleasant because you keep coming back to this spot."

"Yes, I have been coming here ever since I was a boy. I love the night, the quiet, and the sounds of nature."

"I know. On Astellva night time is when we undergo soul expansion. You sense this unconsciously. I will show you how to project yourself up there sometime when you are ready. Let me assure you that the things you have sensed and seen were not dreams or the conjuring of your imagination. With your permission I am going to help you expand your soul in some of our future visits."

"Future visits," I murmured.

"Do you think I came all this way just to say hello and then goodbye?" she laughed. "Before I tell you about soul-sharing, let me tell you how we communicate on Astellva. We communicate by soft whispers, which most people on the earth never hear, and we also communicate through song. Many of your animals, especially porpoises and whales, can hear the sweet tones that we murmur and sing on our world, and they mimic some of them. It is natural that your whales love to sing. As you know, some people have a natural love for singing. You have always loved music, and you have a lovely singing voice, I might add."

"I am aware that you even pursued a singing career at one time. And why would you not? You will always be a singer. As a matter of fact, you will become so receptive to the stellar tone patterns and energies that you will actually hear the songs of the stars. You will come into contact with many beings who will teach you beautiful songs. I also know that you have written some beautiful songs. Let me just say that there is so much to come, as your earth saying goes."

"I admit that I love singing, and I do write songs."

"Singing is natural for you because in earlier times, many ages past, people on your world likewise communicated through song. Through telepathy we taught them many of our songs."

I wondered how old Rosara was. *She could be a million years old as far as I know. Perhaps her kind has achieved immortality.*

She paused. "No, I am not a million years old. Now back to what I was saying, "By 'we,' I mean my people. One rarely hears such beautiful songs anymore on your world. They contributed greatly to the serenity and tranquility prevalent in those times so long ago. A few poets, musicians, and other sensitive people sometimes hear our songs. Utilizing their highly developed pineal and pituitary glands and extraordinary soul senses, certain composers have transmitted some of our music to you. You often call such music *the music of the spheres.* In our training we learn to harness the power inherent in the pineal and pituitary glands. Now you know why you love music and are always humming and singing. You are recalling the music of your ancient ones. Your sensitivity lets you delve deeply into your mind where the ancestral memories are all recorded. You frequently make this contact unconsciously. You are not alone, Michael. This you need to know because you have struggled with loneliness most of your life."

I was so taken with and fascinated by Rosara that I was not even surprised that she knew my name.

"The wind carries memories of our ancient ways and magical times. When you are in nature, especially at night, some of these memories visit your conscious mind. The result is that you start humming or singing unusual or haunting songs unlike songs that are heard today on your world. I remember a song about the wind dance and the golden light beams you sang when you were six years old. You even wrote the words down, and your mother said they were lovely. You were tapping very deep ancestral memories."

"I do recall writing and singing such songs and poems. I came up with a lot of them. I even made up little dances."

"The contortions and movements of your body in those dances were not your everyday one-two-three steps. You were very supple. I will teach you some more dances if you would like."

"Some *more*? You mean *you* taught me those dances?"

"Let me just say that I mentally projected pictures in your mind of those dances. You translated them into moves. Would you not have had more fun with a partner than with the broomstick you sometimes danced with? Shall we dance?" Rosara said, standing up and twirling in semi-circles.

"Please, not now," I said, captivated by Rosara's presence. "I just want to listen to you talk. Otherwise, I think all of this excitement is going to be too much, and I might drop dead and wind up wherever dreamers go."

"Oh, yes, you are a dreamer, Michael, as am I. Long live the dreamers!" she said, sitting back down, this time closer to me.

We looked at each other in silence for several moments. My head was spinning, and my heart beating fast.

"Rosara, tell me about love on Astellva, please."

"Love," she sang in a sweet lyric soprano voice, looking at me so intently that I blushed. She held a high note for the longest time. *How could one do that in a solid breath?* I wondered. Her voice was lyrical, melodic, and divine all in one. There was a purity, sweetness, and vibrancy in it that was intoxicating. It made my mind soar, and my heart missed a few beats as well. It felt like my soul was exiting my body. I wanted to soar to the stars with Rosara and never come back.

She sang softer until the sound faded. Then she lovingly looked at me and resumed speaking.

"Love--that four letter word that brings some joy but far more heartbreak and sadness on your world—instead, it should bring joining and celebration. What can I tell you about love that you do not already know, at least deep in your soul?" she said, smiling, reaching for my hand. "Michael, you celebrate the joys of love quite often at night in your dreams," she whispered. "That is what brings you to this spot."

"Are you the one whom I dream about?"

"Tis I," she said, playfully. "Let me add—those experiences are much more than dreams. You would never come to these woods so late just to talk to trees and to dream when you can do that at home."

"I am not sure why I come here so much other than my love for the night and solitude."

"Now you know why. Let me get back to your questions about love. Something like marriage as understood by your people on earth cannot begin to compare to the bliss we enjoy and partake of on Astellva. True and complete soul-merging is virtually unheard of on the earth although most people long for it. To be able to soul-share and soul-merge with others you must first become acquainted and intimate with your own soul. Unfortunately, this understanding and lack of soul intimacy is lacking on your world. Your sacred institution of marriage is inadequate because people do not even know who *they* are, let alone who their beloved is. The concept of two souls joining is strong on your world, however, rarely realized. Magnify that joining that people feel with their beloveds with millions of souls, and you will have a glimpse of how much deeper your capacity to experience love truly is."

"This is amazing," I exclaimed, feeling much more relaxed in Rosara's presence. "No wonder I have no intention of marrying. How many couples remain happily married? The divorce rate is alarming. I don't know why people even bother to go through the marriage ceremony. It seems so pointless and useless."

"Sadly, that is very true. People on your world marry mostly for the wrong reasons: physical sexual chemistry, desire for companionship, material security, fear of growing old, of being alone, etc. It is called settling and ultimately does not satisfy the needs of the soul. Do not misunderstand me. Physical chemistry certainly has its place. It is exciting and attracts people to each other but without soul-sharing and soul-merging, the physical attraction sooner or later begins to wane. Then many people have affairs or move on to someone else."

"To give you an idea of soul-merging on Astellva, think about the feeling that you have when you take in a lovely breath of morning air and then sigh while thinking about your beloved. On Astellva we partake of a certain substance that is somewhat similar to air, except it is so much sweeter and more delicious than the oxygen people breathe on the earth. Two people who want to merge on Astellva (or share their merging more individually and intimately, as all are merged on Astellva), partake of the soul-sharing, soul-merging ritual in a lovely flower garden beneath a trellis entwined with garlands of beautiful roses. There are plants everywhere and a cool bubbly brook nearby."

"The forest creatures come to celebrate the union because they are also part of our family. Standing beside the couple is an elder woman with long white hair flowing down to her waist. She wears a pink robe with a red sash and tiara of blue diamonds on her head. Next to her is a long white-haired white bearded elder man with starry blue eyes. He wears a light blue and white robe with a golden sash. The elders will oversee the ceremony. The couple wear flowing translucent gowns which radiate hues of light greens, blues, pinks, and other pastel colors which your colors can only approximate in beauty and softness."

"The couple stands next to each other. They hold hands, close their eyes, and greet each other's soul in the silence. Then they open their eyes, and the elder woman and then the man kiss them on both cheeks. The woman takes out a phial of rose-scented oil from her robe and draws a heart upon the center of their brows. Then she steps aside, and the man gently touches the hearts of the couple with his left forefinger. This fills the couple with tingling sensations of love and bliss that saturate their entire bodies."

"The couple slowly breathes in the sweet substance that is so much more than air. What we breathe to sustain our physical bodies is not the same as what we breathe during soul-sharing. Through slow, sustained breathing while exuding and taking in love for the beloved, another set of lungs activates, receiving more and more of the sweet substance, which can be compared to breathing the scent of a freshly blossomed rose. This other set of lungs is only activated during the soul-sharing ceremony of joining. Energies are exchanged between the couple in ways you cannot imagine."

"There is intense passion, joy, and bliss that builds in electrifying excitement as the couple takes in the love and energy that millions of their soul family are sending them from their light bodies. Tingling pleasant sensations pour through their bodies as the higher centers become fully activated. It is an experience of complete bliss and ecstasy. The souls of the couple actually experience a total merging that is not possible on the earth."

"This is because at this time there is a lack of understanding of what love truly entails, and the heart and higher chakra energy centers are not opened sufficiently. Michael, one day you will experience soul-merging. Your heart and soul will know bliss that you have not known before. When the ceremony begins to wind down, the rose-like fragrance slowly begins to recede, then their other lungs slowly reactivate, and they take in oxygen once more."

"Please tell me more about this transfer of energy from the two sets of lungs."

"This transfer of energy from one set of lungs to another is accomplished by concentrating and the murmuring of tones. Through slowly breathing the fragrance, the higher energy chakras and centers are stimulated, and the couple begins reciting beautiful poetry which gently transforms into a lovely song. The tones from the song carry vibrational wave frequencies which enable their bodies to transfer the energy to their soul-sharing lungs. It is difficult to explain this ritual with words. One has to experience it to understand it."

"During soul-merging we are less corporeal. We are able to be in our light spirit body as well as our physical body simultaneously during soul-merging. The love and energy that we are given by the others from their light bodies helps us to sustain this less corporeal contact. This concept is not easy to convey, for it transcends human language."

"Please try. Rosara, this feels so familiar. I need to know more."

"I will try," she said, touching my hand gently, sending tingles from my head down to my toes. It was not a sexual sensation; it was better and more intense. It was a soulful sensation. That is the only way I know how to put it.

"Once the song is finished, the pure energy creates a gentle tingling swirl of energy that flows through our bodies. The human orgasm cannot compare to how intense and pleasurable it is, and it lasts far longer than an orgasm. You had a sensation of this when I touched your forehead earlier."

"Yes, it was very intense, and yes, I know it was not orgasmic; it was much more than that."

"Still, it was nothing compared to what awaits you when we soul-share and soul-merge after your training."

"I can hardly wait."

"Back to soul-sharing. The energy created is imbued with a pure rose fragrance. This experience is most pleasurable and even ecstatic. There is no comparison to it on your world. At some point the couple, the sweet fragrance, and their souls merge into oneness. Even so, they do not lose their sense of individuality. Soul-sharing enables the couple to lighten considerably although we are already much lighter than your people. If I were to make another comparison, let me say that a type of soul-sharing occurs on the earth when two soul-mates connect in mind and spirit and can feel intense energy stimulating their nerve and higher centers during close communion at the non-physical level. Everybody knows that he/she feels differently when he/she is in love. The senses are heightened. Everything looks more beautiful. Does this make sense?"

"I think so even if it's a lot to take in."

Rosara smiled and gently touched my hand, sending me reeling again. "Oh, this is nothing compared to what all there is to take in, but I understand the importance of taking this step by step. Michael, I am giving you a lot of information. You will have plenty of time to sort it out and assimilate it. In time you will come to understand and be able to fully experience soul-sharing and soul-merging. Do you remember the time when you dreamed about a man and woman standing with their heads tilted back as they were breathing softly as part of a ceremony?"

"Yes, I do. It was right here at this very spot. That dream was about three months ago. Was it really a dream, Rosara?"

"It was not just a dream although some dreams are more real than so-called reality. You were projecting part of your soul to Astellva just as I have projected part of my soul here today in the form of a woman standing beside you."

"And a very beautiful one, I might add," I said meekly. "If your form here contains only part of your soul, I cannot begin to fathom how else you could project aspects of your soul or in what form or forms. I don't think I'm ready to know more about that yet."

Rosara smiled and gently touched my hand. "All things in due time, Michael. Your curious mind serves you well. It will lead you to many more marvelous experiences. Let me say that I helped you to project part of your soul to Astellva. You did not know it consciously, so your subconscious symbolically translated the experience into a dream since it did not have access to your soul-knowing—something that will occur soon. You have been attending classes without knowing it for quite some time, and you have not skipped a single one," she said, inserting humor.

"That is nice to hear. Playing hooky was one of my favorite pasttimes in school. It got me into trouble several times."

"You only did that because you were bored. Your entire educational system is in need of radical transformation."

"Now back to love on Astellva. Sexual intercourse cannot begin to approximate the bliss and ecstasy that soul-sharing and soul-merging offers. On your world when two people love, they often close themselves off from others. They are in a type of self-created bubble which insulates and isolates them from others. On Astellva we never lose our soul connection to everyone else, even when we soul-share and soul-merge. We draw from the soul essence of everyone else who willingly and joyously gives us love and energy. The rose-like fragrance contains a bit of everyone else's soul essence, so soul-sharing is both a personal and a collective group experience.

"Separation and oneness exist simultaneously. On Astellva we draw on the collective energies to enhance the personal ones."

"Can I ask you one more thing, Rosara?"

"Of course, my beloved."

"Have I been imagining this, or is it true that every time you touched me, you exuded light and I could actually feel its warmth? There is a glow around you as well. Your presence and even the very words you speak seem to glow and exude a rose fragrance. I know this sounds pretty incredible, but I see a glow around the words as they come from your speech. I cannot properly articulate what I am trying to say because I don't think the words exist in English. Perhaps they do not exist in any language, except perhaps a star language, if that makes any sense. I cannot understand how words can take on a glow or emanate a rose fragrance."

Rosara took my hand in hers. The tingling warmth and glow was there again. "My beloved, there is much for you and your earth people to come to understand. Let me say that I am very pleased and impressed at how keen your soul-vision and senses are becoming. Most people would not have seen or detected my glow or the rose fragrance had I appeared to them. You truly are a star child and the star-love of my soul, Michael. My people will be very pleased to hear news of this visit with you."

"For now, let me say that my people's bodies is not as—how do I put it—dense as people's human bodies on the earth. We hold more light than earth people. This is why you feel such intense sensations when I touch you. We have ways of taking in light from our grand central sun that sustains the part of us that is a light body while inhabiting a physical body. Our soul contains a vaster portion of light than our physical body. When we communicate in any manner, light exudes from us and transfers to the person close to us. This is a type of soul-sharing that humans are not familiar with, except only to the extent that they long for a deeper understanding and expression of love."

"The fact that humans dream, yearn, hope, and seek out this greater love proves that it exists. The sad thing is that up to this point in human evolution, they have not yet experienced it to the degree that is not only possible, but it is the soul's destiny to experience and partake of this greater love. A call is being sent forth by many of you to your star family imploring them to teach and show you how to experience this all-encompassing greater love. You have called out to me in restless dreams many times, and this is why I have come to you. As some of your other-worldly teachers have and will be pointing out to you, dreams can serve as portals and gateways for other-worldly beings to come to your world and for you to go to theirs. You will learn more about this from some of your other visitors in the future."

"You mean I will be having other visits such as this one?"

"Well, no—no two beings or visits are ever alike. As you humans like to say, 'Variety is the spice of life.' You are going to have some astonishing mind-blowing visitors who are going to 'rock your world' as a friend of yours in the future is going to say. You will meet her when the time is right. You will love her very deeply because she is in your soul family. You two go *way back in time*, as the saying goes. You will actually be able to mentally communicate at times via a type of telepathy. You will engage in a type of soul-sharing such as you have only done with three others in this lifetime so far."

"I thought you said that humans don't know how to soul-share?"

"I did." Rosara bent close to my ear and whispered, "Beloved, Michael, you are much more than a human, as are those with whom you have and will soul-share. Actually, every human is divine, but most are unaware and oblivious as to who they really are. They will come around in time. As a matter of fact, you have quite a role to play in this long-needed and awaited awakening. This is part of your destiny and also part of the reason for my visit and for those future visits you will have from others."

"Wow is all I can say. I guess all my lonely years were not in vain if they will lead to such visits as this. I guess I *am* getting pretty good at calling out to angels and other-worldly beings in dreams."

"Yes, you are."

"The angel in my poem 'The Messenger of Love' said, 'I come to you because in dreams you asked for me.'"

"That is true. Now back to the rose fragrance you asked about. Part of my soul essence contains rose essence as well. It also contains part of the soul essence of all my beloved people. You are aware that you possess or inhabit many more bodies than the mere physical one. Your etheric body is capable of so much more than your physical body as your shamans and many indigenous healers know. They often refer to this other body as the 'double' or 'etheric double.' The etheric body is capable of extracting essence from the etheric body of plants or flowers and storing it. Since the rose is the most potent flower with its many healing properties, it is rose essence that my etheric body stores. Since the etheric body is intertwined and joined with the physical body, my people are able to transfer healing, loving energy to your etheric body in ways you are unaware."

"When I speak and communicate in whatever form I choose, in this instance, human words, part of my soul essence exudes this rose essence from my etheric or spirit body, permeating even the words I speak. Since my people constantly partake of soul-sharing and soul-merging, our energy or soul essence is never depleted. Just as some beings rejuvenate their energies with sunlight, we rejuvenate and replenish each other with our soul essence, which is, by the way, composed of light, as well as rose essence. I will tell you more about that another time. You have partaken of a type of soul-sharing with me today. Since I possess some of the soul essence of all my people, I have transferred some of it to you."

"I will teach you more about soul-sharing and soul-merging. You will one day share this knowledge with others in books that you will write. When people read the words, their heart chakra will pulsate in joyous recognition; as the truth of their being resonates deep within, love stirs and awakens their soul. Now that we have met on your world, I have imbued you with some of my soul essence and the essence of my people. You will be able to transfer that love and essence to your words onto the written page. Soul-sharing on my home world is much more intense and complex than what has taken place here with you today. Nonetheless, you should feel energized and rejuvenated for several days."

"Thank you, Rosara, for sharing this information with me. Your loving words ring true to the very core and depths of my heart and soul. I will never look at a rose the same way again, and I better understand why the rose is the most beloved flower on the earth."

Rosara smiled and gently touched my face. "Yes, Michael, the rose is the most beloved flower on the earth. People know somewhere in the depths of their soul the importance and the significance of roses. Your aromatherapy healers who use flowers and rose essences are aware of the healing qualities and properties of the rose and other flowers."

"You will come to know the fullness of love in this lifetime, my beloved Michael. When you come to my world, you shall bask in such rose essence and love from my people that you will never again feel alone. I eagerly await such spirit visits. You will experience far more than these words I have carefully chosen in my endeavor to convey to you the concepts of soul-sharing and soul-merging that all experience on Astellva."

"As limiting as the human language is, nonetheless, these words can serve to help activate many energies and open your heart chakra to take in more love. It can also help awaken soul memories. It can likewise do the same for those who read this story. These are my messages for now," Rosara said, moving closer to me, softly kissing my cheeks. "It is time for me to go. Think of me when you breathe in the lovely fragrance of a rose. Goodbye for now, my Beloved Michael."

Rosara rubbed my face gently and the tingling returned. It was even more intense and intoxicating than before. Then she stepped back, blew me a kiss, waved and disappeared.

A rose fragrance permeated the air around me. I sat stunned and bedazzled, tears falling down my cheeks for a solid hour before I could even get up to walk back to the house. I feared I might never be able to move. I was absolutely wonderstruck and speechless. The thought of trying to construct words and phrases seemed cumbersome as did the thought of moving my physical body to get back to the house. Papaw and Mamaw always get up before daybreak. If I were still gone, Mamaw would worry. Nothing seemed real or to have meaning after Rosara left. It was a major task to keep one foot in front of the other and to walk to the house. My physical body had never felt so dense and cumbersome. It was actually uncomfortable to be in this physical body.

Rosara had somehow put me more in touch with my essence and activated my soul, or my soul-body, if such a word can exist. I felt that my soul's essence was not matter or any kind of physical, tangible form. Perhaps, it was not even pure spirit. It was more. How I longed for more visits with Rosara. How I yearned to be able to consciously project part of my soul and spirit to Astellva so I could learn more about the soul-learning which would enable me to better experience and understand love, or dare I say *become* love? I knew that I would always think of Rosara every time I stargazed and when I wrote love poetry. I heard lines and verses forming in my mind and could not wait to write them down.

The front door was opened as usual when I got back to the house. I quietly walked upstairs to my room, still in a daze. I was glad the lights, all but a kerosene lamp on the dining room table, were out and that Mamaw and Papaw were still in bed. I looked at the grandfather clock which chimed. It was 4:00 a.m. I lay in bed until the sun rose, thinking about Rosara. How could I even talk to anyone again or deal with humans after such a fascinating encounter? How could I ever listen to all the noise around me or even think about turning on a television?

I never shared my secret spot with anyone, nor have I ever married. How could I love anyone else after meeting Rosara? I thought about her saying that she projected part of her soul into the form of the woman standing in front of me. I wondered what other glorious divine forms she was capable of taking on and when I would be able to consciously project part of my soul to Astellva. Rosara's words and my memories of that extraordinary visit give me much hope and strength to go on when ordinary mundane life weigh heavily upon me.

There were many more adventures. There is no time to tell them now. I will write them down some day. I met some of her friends and teachers. I made friends with many other-worldly beings. One thing is for certain. I no longer feel melancholy or homesick when I stargaze. The nights still fascinate me and in my solitude I derive much comfort and solace. I suppose I inherit that from my Papaw.

CHAPTER THIRTEEN

A VISIT WITH THE DREAM MAKERS

I often think about my poem "Individuality." Two lines stand out:

Maybe one day they will awaken to their own individuality,
Look in the mirror with pride and be glad at whom they see.

One day while looking in the mirror, I heard the question, "Just who is this 'self' that I am looking at?"

I recalled a verse from another of my poems which says, "I am a part of all that is; all that has been and all to be born."

This felt rather comforting as my spiritual and metaphysical beliefs support the idea that we are all part of each other; all life is interconnected and intertwined.

This theme is repeated continuously in many metaphysical books that I have read. I have concluded that since I am a part of all life, then all of life and creation must equally be a part of me. This realization led me to perceive everything as an extension of me rather than as being separate. I do not believe this means that our personal individuality dissolves into some collective all-encompassing bubble of oneness devoid of personal identity. On the contrary, I can perceive and feel my personality. I know that I have my own tastes, interests, abilities, skills, weaknesses, and other traits inherent to the human condition as does everyone else. In the early 1980's, I went through a period where I spent many hours in deep meditation. During this time, I began having some unusual visitors in dream time and outside dream time during the day and night. Sometimes dream time and awake time overlap. What especially interests me is that other-worldly visitors have interesting knowledge and teachings to impart. Their company reassures me that none of us is ever really alone. We can call out to these other-worldly beings for assistance and guidance. I now truly understand to the Biblical verse, "In my Father's house are many mansions." I have been blessed to meet some wonderful beings from some of these mansions of father mother beloved creator source. All can do the same if they do the inner work and preparation.

I frequently call out to these wonderful *other-worldly* teachers and friends and enjoy their company. I often do this unconsciously, and that is why I cannot predict when a visitor will show up. This reminds me how active the subconscious mind always is. The more contact we make with our subconscious, the less lonely we feel and the more we realize that we are connected to all that is. We are all part of the all-knowing that is available for everyone to access. We all have this ability. It is a gift bestowed unto us by our beloved creator source.

As time passed, other things began to happen, and my perceptions and outlook on life began to stretch and expand even more. Friendly other-worldly beings began appearing out of nowhere and often in the middle of the day. This happened one day when the spirit of an oak tree, Elora, paid me a visit. I had been having a bout of depression because no publishers were accepting the stories and novel I had submitted. I was beginning to think I would never break into the writing market and feeling tempted to give up on my writing dream altogether. Yet I also knew that when I didn't write, I was even more depressed. What to do? Well, every aspiring writer has no doubt dealt with similar feelings and circumstances. A couple of days later I was so depressed that I went to bed at 7:00 p.m.

I was staring blankly into space when I heard a voice say, "Don't be sad, Michael. I have come to cheer you. Maybe it will ease my own loneliness. I think we can help each other."

"Who are you?" I said, jumping out of bed. I put on my bathrobe and looked around, trying to figure out where the voice came from. "Who are you and what do you want?" There was no answer.

"Don't be sad, Michael," I heard again; the voice speaking so softly that I could barely make it out. It was definitely a female voice, and there was a gentle sweetness in her tone that made me smile. I wanted desperately to believe that she was real yet some part of me believed that it was my loneliness causing my imagination to work overtime.

Dancing shadows flickered through the window. *Another breezy night*, I thought, looking out at the full moon. *One of these nights that oak tree is going to extend one of her branches right into my room and shake my hand. Then what will I do? Visit the local mental ward and tell them that my loneliness is causing oak trees to talk with me. What makes me think the oak tree is female?*

The voice spoke again. "You refer to the oak tree as female because you prefer the company of females. I have been lonely ever since I died two years ago as you have been since your grandmother died."

"How do you know about my grandmother?" I blurted out.

"You tell me in dreams, silly boy. You tell me many things. Think a moment, Michael. You know that your dream recall is excellent. You recall me, don't you? I am Elora."

"Yes," I said, looking around my room. There was silence except for the sound of the wind and the oak tree's branches tapping against the window. "I do remember you. You are Elora, the spirit of the oak, or at least that is who you tell me you are."

"Yes, and I'm miserable. What I need is a miracle. I believe that we could both use one."

I didn't bother asking her to elaborate.

"Michael, do you believe in miracles?" Elora asked.

"To be honest, I don't know what I believe anymore."

"That could get you into trouble or into some exciting adventures."

"Before we think about going anywhere or doing anything, I've got to get something straight—are you saying that we are not dreaming now? How can this be?"

"Don't ask me. What do I know? I'm just a lonely spirit. Maybe it's because I'm a spirit now all of the time while you are a man in the daytime and a spirit at night when we visit in dreams."

"What does that mean? I'm getting more confused now. How can I be dreaming? I'm awake."

"The same way I can be awake when I dream in the daytime. I know I'm awake because the boredom and loneliness nearly drive me mad."

So do spirits recall their dreams better?" I stammered, searching for the right words.

"I don't know."

"How have we made this contact?"

"I don't know how we've made contact this way. It's not the usual order of things because you are not dreaming, and I have somehow made my way into your world."

"This is too much, Elora. This simply cannot be. It's one thing to think of you as a dream character. That I can accept but now you say you can be awake when you dream. Does this mean you are my dream? Or am I your dream? Or are we neither one's dreams? Heaven forbid we should be someone else's dreams? Do you think we are both losing our minds?"

"Questions, questions, Michael. You're worse than I am. I lost my mind a long time ago. We're really much better off without it. The mind only causes confusion if you ask me, but the heart is another matter. I never lost that, not even when I died. I wish I knew what I was searching for. The not knowing is even more depressing and sad. It's like being locked in a dark room."

"I know what you mean. My mind drives me half nuts trying to figure everything out."

"Now hold on for a moment, Michael."

I stood still, filled with nervous excitement and anticipation. Moments later there she was, standing right in front of me. I could hardly believe my eyes. Who or rather *what* was I looking at? I reached out to touch Elora's arm. She felt as solid as human flesh can feel. I noticed that she was very pretty, just like in the dreams. She had light blue eyes and strawberry blond hair that came to her shoulders. She was about four feet tall and had a nice figure. She wore a navy blue skirt, a pink blouse, and white stockings. There was a small silver chain around her neck with a star on it. I gasped.

"Elora, you are real! I'm not dreaming. Tell me, how did you get trapped in the oak tree and how did you get here?"

"I am not trapped. I always loved trees when I was human. When I drowned in the pond, my spirit came back to the tree it always loved, and since no one was occupying it, you could say that I was allowed to take residence there. Oh it's plenty big enough, and there is lots of room. I can shape-shift and be as tiny as I want to be. Spirits can think anything they want into existence. It's nice in there. One day when you are more adept at spirit travel, I'll show it to you. As for how I got here, I do not know."

"This is hard for me to take in. I mean it's one thing to read a fantasy story or watch a movie where anything is possible, but are you saying that you have stepped out of dream time and come to my world?"

"Michael, I really don't know what has happened to us. I sense it has something to do with perceptual shifting and spirit travel. Maybe the Dream Makers can help us. Therein lies our adventure. I think we are due some counsel. The Dream Makers live in a beautiful palace in Dream City a long way from here."

"Where is a long way from here, and how do we get there?"

"Dream City exists on another dimension on what you would call an alternate reality or parallel world. You get there by shifting your perceptions and vibration to a higher level.

One means to accomplish this is by speaking certain tones which my guide taught me. The sounds activate a portal. I have no spirit friends, and I live alone in the tree. I've always been afraid to go very far alone."

"I am your friend," I said softly. I don't care who you are or what you are. I like you."

"Thank you," Elora said shyly. "We need to be getting on our way. When I sound the tones and include our names, we will be there in no time."

My head was spinning. Everything looked hazy and dreamy. Elora gently touched my arms and gave me a lovely smile. I think she could read my mind.

"Michael, it is time for our spirit journey. Now lie down and close your eyes. You can trust me. I would never harm you, and I sense that we will learn a lot in Dream City."

I lay down and closed my eyes. A few minutes later there was a thud and then my spirit exited my body. Elora slowly began toning strange sounds I had never heard before. Then she spoke the following words:

We implore the Dream Makers, respectfully!
Dream Makers for all eternity.
Michael and Elora call out to you.
Please open your portal and bring us through.

There was a sudden gushing wind. Elora reached for my hand. Then it felt like we were spinning in the air. A few minutes later two tall white gates suddenly swung open before us. A beautiful woman with fiery red hair and star-like eyes welcomed us. She led us inside a magnificent palace.

"What has happened?" I asked. "Have we been bewitched?"

"Not at all," the lady replied, smiling. "Most people's soul vision is very dim. There is so much to see and experience. Everyone has this innate ability; it is a gift from our beloved Creator to us all. Few develop it, but more are beginning to do so. You are among these valiant, daring souls. You have the willingness and desire to see more of all that is and all that can be. This willingness and openness will help you to understand and get a glimpse of who you really are in your *fullness*. It will allow you to take in so much more of life than most people do. You are so much more than what you see when you look into a mirror," she said, looking at me. "Increasing your soul vision will open so many doors for you; it will also alleviate your loneliness. I am called Jelana. I am one of the Dream Makers. How can I be of service to you?"

"Due to my untimely death and Michael's loss of his grandmother, we have become quite confused," said Elora. "Our loneliness somehow brought us together. At first we only communicated at night in dreams. Something has changed. There is more taking place now. We are both wondering if we might be losing our minds."

"Elora came to me tonight, and I was not even asleep. Am I becoming a spirit? Is my spirit disentangling itself from my body?"

"Am I becoming more corporeal?" Elora asked the Dream Maker. "It's getting more difficult for me to appear and disappear at will. Lately it seems that I've become solid or semi-solid. I fear I will become human again even though I have no idea how that could happen unless I traded places with someone who wanted to check out. I have no desire to become a walk-in."

"I can understand why you feel that way," Jelana replied.

"I am content being a spirit in the oak tree. For the most part, humans do not appeal to me. Michael, of course, is an exception. Most people are mundane, selfish, materialistic, stupid egotists. How boring! I should not wish to go back and be among them. There has got to be more to life than amassing heaps of money, trying to impress others, and acquiring power."

Jelana looked at us both lovingly, her eyes full of concern and compassion. "On an optimistic note, more humans *are* tapping the resources within and discovering their own inner powers. Now how about you, young mortal, are you acquiring unusual powers?" she asked me.

"I never admitted it to myself, but I think that I am if that is what you call some of my experiences. I believe I actually disappeared from my room last week. I didn't tell anyone, not even Elora. It was a moment when the loneliness seemed unbearable. I remember thinking, *I want to go where my grandmother is.* I repeated this over and over.

The next thing I knew I was walking in a beautiful flower garden and saw her smelling roses. They were her favorite flowers. When I tried to speak to her, she placed a finger to her lips and motioned for me to remain silent. I said a few more words which I cannot recall and then returned to my room. I had the feeling that the talking brought me back. I was too frightened, and I talked because of fear and anxiety. Was that only a dream?"

"Only a dream," said Jelana softly. "Come with me. I want to show you something." She led us down several corridors. She began to sing softly:

Receive these Dreamers, O Dream Makers inside.
Help them see wonderful vistas far and wide.

We floated right through a door. We were greeted by a spirit encased in bright light. I saw many other spirits encased in different colors of light.

"There is so much light here, and it is so beautiful. Are we dead? Is this what the afterlife is like?" I asked.

"This is what life is like," said Jelana. "There is no before or after life. That is all a dream or illusion. Inside this chamber are the Dream Makers, including you. Look around awhile and enjoy yourselves," Jelana said then disappeared.

A spirit encased in blue light appeared and observed me from a side glance, concealing its face.

"I think you have a visitor, Michael," Elora said.

The spirit was still looking at me from the periphery. Elora reached for my hand.

"There is so much light and love here, Michael. Can't you feel the love?" she said, smiling, with a look of fascination and sheer delight on her face. "And the loneliness is gone. At least mine is. Wonderful things happen here. I could stay here forever."

"Yes, I feel the love. It is unlike anything I've ever experienced before, not even in dreams or astral travel."

The spirit moved closer to me and turned to face me.

"Mamaw," I whispered, "Can it really be you?"

"It is I, Michael," she said softly. She then hugged me tightly and spilled tears onto my face with her kisses. "I have waited for this day so long. I've been telling you in your dreams that I am still with you, but your doubting has blocked me."

"I remember some of those dreams, but I thought they were only dreams."

"They were. Everything here is only a dream, and everything out there as well."

"You mean like in the children's song "Row, row, row your boat gently down the stream. Merrily, merrily, merrily! Life is but a dream?" I asked.

Mamaw chuckled. "Yes, just like the song, Michael. There are often underlying truths in songs, stories, and myths for those who seek them out."

I scratched my head. "So everything is just a dream?"

She nodded. "You dream it all. We all do. There are so many kinds of dreams, and you are beginning to experience some of them. You have dreamed your loneliness, and Elora has dreamed hers. I dreamed my death, and you dreamed each other into your lives."

"In this place we learn that everyone is a dream maker. Most people have just forgotten it. Here we learn that we can dream anything into being. Dream makers can create any experience or form they want; however, do not misunderstand. This palace is not the only place where Dream Makers learn to remember who they are and how to manifest their hope and dreams. The true place of power is inside us."

"I remember how your eyes lit up so brightly when I would tell you that the secret dwelling place of happiness and magic is in the heart. You'd beg me to tell you some more stories, which I was always delighted to do. What I didn't realize is that even though I was dreaming them, they were not fantasy; they were real."

"So is this only a dream?"

"Yes, you could say it is a type of dream, but you are not sleeping, so it is not a sleeping dream, my dearest Michael. I suppose you could call it a type of spirit dream. There is so much about dreaming that people do not understand. It was a type of dream, or better put, an extension of consciousness that brought you to me in that rose garden last week. It is your loneliness that is leading you to discover the powers that you possess within yourself. It also brought you and Elora together. You need never feel lonely again, my dears. When you do, it is time to create and experience a different dream. Here we learn and teach people how to do that. We teach those outside this palace—at least those who are receptive to us. There is no need to feel sad or lonely."

"Dreams serve many different purposes. For example, they can serve as portals to many worlds and dimensions. They can be the means to bring you to me and to many people—and the means to bring us to you. With practice you learn that we don't need the dream portal to step into each other's world. We can shift our perceptions and extend our consciousness to go anywhere we want. You and your friend are becoming more proficient at it, and this explains some of what is happening to you. You are the daring mavericks and pioneers who are breaking the ground and will lead the way for many others."

"There will come a time in the future when all will easily access, maneuver, and extend their consciousness and awareness to be able to visit with anybody anywhere in the vast cosmos on all the planets, galaxies, other realms, and dimensions. Telephones and email will become extinct along with other gadgets people use to enable communication to take place. The cosmos will become your playground. Welcome your other-worldly friends, Michael. You have already met several, and there are more coming your way. There is plenty of room in God's worlds and vast kingdoms. 'In my Father's house are many mansions" is one of my favorite verses in the Bible, and I know how you love reading the Holy Bible, Michael."

"Life is going to be more interesting and fun from now on. You will be seeing a lot more of me and not just at night. Believe in magic and dreams, and remember that dreams don't just come true. They are already true. You can create anything if you believe strongly enough. Nowadays, I think people are calling it positive thinking and working with the universal law of attraction. It is all the same. Thoughts are things, and what you focus your intention on eventually comes true, depending upon how much energy and feeling you give it. Your loneliness and missing me have caused you to pour forth an enormous amount of intention and energy."

"Part of you believed and knew you could find me. That is what has allowed you to connect with Elora outside dream time and what has allowed you to come here. Believe in your dreams and dare to dream them, for they can and do come true. Never forget this, my dears. Well, that is my little positive thinking speech for today. It is time to leave now. Feel free to come back anytime."

My grandmother gave me a big hug and kiss and disappeared. Elora and I stood awestruck, holding hands.

"I always knew such to be true when I was human," Elora said. "I knew there was more to dreams and life. There is so much more knowledge available to seekers willing to access it," she said, pointing to her head. "I should have explored that more, but I did not. The few times that I commented on some experiences I had, people would tell me that such ideas were absurd and crazy, so I stopped talking. No wonder I was a miserable, unhappy human girl."

Jelana appeared in front of us. "Everyone creates their dreams," she said. "Many wish to see very little. They will pay us a visit here in Dream City when they are ready. I hope this has been a joyous experience for you. I will now escort you to the Chamber of Return."

"If it is okay, I'd like to use some spirit magic," said Elora.

"How wonderful," said Jelana gleefully. "So few learn this fast. All it takes is total belief and anything is possible."

We hugged Jelana and waved goodbye. Elora spoke some words and within moments we were back in my room. I looked at Elora and chuckled.

"That was some adventure, Michael. Are you still feeling lonely?"

"No, but I am a little tired. If it's okay with you, I will take a raincheck on a dream visit tonight."

"Michael, I think that henceforth I'll just show up in the daytime if you don't mind. We can reserve our night time dreams to visit with other friends who have yet to learn how to find each other in the daytime like we have."

"Sounds good to me. You know something—nobody would believe this story, Elora."

"They don't have to. Let it be our little secret. See you soon, my friend." She gave me a kiss then disappeared.

I kept this experience secret for a long time. The more I read and learned about parallel realms, worlds, and universes, the more my heart and guides began to tell me that those experiences were authentic and real. Via astral spirit travel and the extension and maneuvering of our consciousness, Elora and I visited a parallel world where we met the Dream Maker, Jelana, and visited my grand-mother.

I soon began recalling some of my other personal experiences, and this made me more eager to share them. I no longer fear these visits or feel like I am going crazy. I give gratitude to my guides and angels and inform them that I look forward to other adventures and friendly visitors. They never disappoint me.

CHAPTER FOURTEEN

SOUL-VISION AND CREATOR SOURCE

The Christmas season is especially magical for me and is my favorite holiday. I have always believed in magic but had learned to keep these ideas to myself. Certain holidays, especially Christmas, remind me of what I know deep in my heart—that magic and wonder exist all around us if we look for them. What a relief for me when the holidays arrive. During that time it is customary to be merry and cheerful. Then, I can hum, sing, and constantly smile without attracting undue attention. I can take in the magic and enjoy the twinkling glow in the eyes of others equally caught up in the spirit of the Christmas season.

The extraordinary Christmas of 1994 is one I shall never forget for as long as I live. I recall it as though it happened only yesterday. It would forever change the way I view the world and our place in it. I recall how one night about a week before Christmas I was feeling magic in the air. When I looked outside my window, big shimmering snowflakes were falling. Several melted on my nose and face, which made me snicker. My friend Pam was having a Christmas party at 8 p.m. That was a couple hours away, so I decided to go out and do a little shopping.

"What a beautiful night of lights and stars, and that *magical presence*," I cooed as I got into my car and headed to the store.

Maybe this evening it would identify itself and take some kind of form. Yes, tonight it would. I felt it more strongly than ever. The magical presence would appear. I knew something magnificent was about to happen without knowing how I knew—the same way I know many things I cannot explain. The crisp air and snow enhanced the feeling; it had something to do with the marvel soon to occur. I knew that as well without knowing how I knew. Then to confirm what I was feeling I got the tingles and chills that I usually get when something extraordinary is about to happen.

A little while later as I exited the dime store with a bag of Christmas goodies, I immediately noticed the big snowflakes falling from the sky. Several melted on my face and nose, making me snicker. I recalled times I had spent staring at snow-covered hills and tree branches. The white snow is so lovely and magical.

"What a beautiful night," I said as I walked to my car.

The snow continued falling as I drove to my friend Pam's house. I arrived at the party early, exchanged hugs with Pam, and then said that I wanted to take a stroll in the neighborhood before the other guests arrived.

"Enjoy your walk on this magical night and happy holidays to you, my friend," Pam said.

I could still see the twinkle in Pam's eyes as I began walking. I like that look and see it far too infrequently. *Why aren't people more childlike?* I thought. *Why does growing up have to be so serious? As for me, I'm never growing up.*

Soon I passed a neighbor's house where blinking colored lights immediately caught my eye. A large wreath with a bright red bow was attached on the outside door. Several bushes were lit up in reds, greens, blues, and yellows. The snow was falling at a steady pace. I looked upward, wondering how high the snow originated from. I stood in place with my eyes closed.

Where had childhood gone? I asked. Or had it? Maybe it is still as real as the beautiful falling snow. I know that my inner child still lives within me. At heart I am a big kid who believes in miracles and wonder. I know that magic is real.

It didn't take long for the brilliant scintillating lights to fill me with joy and wonder. I picked up my pace, wishing that I could cover the entire neighborhood. I wished I could transform into a giant. Then I could see even more lights. Or better still, grow wings and fly all over the place. I would like to circle the entire city, the state, even the entire nation. In my mind I could see lights everywhere. They seemed to twinkle and glow even brighter as though knowing that I wanted to see them. They were so colorful and radiant. I think they needed me to look at them and attempt to fathom their iridescent mysteries.

And not just one string of lights but *all* of them needed me to see them—from Cincinnati to Boston to Miami to Chicago to Los Angeles and further still to other countries. The fiery radiance of my own spirit wanted to merge with the lights.

"My goodness," I said aloud. "All of this pondering. My mind sure is busy tonight."

I sat under a street lamp and closed my eyes. I could still see the lights and with each passing moment they grew brighter in my mind. The colors magnified. I felt liquid pristine light pouring through me. The tingling increased until I burst into a smile and a hearty laugh.

Suddenly I jerked back, opened my eyes, and looked around, anxiety replacing the pleasurable sensations of magic and wonder. No one was there; yet I knew that I wasn't alone. I had felt this way many times before. My eyes did not see anyone. Doors were shut. People were snug inside their homes, cocooned for the night.

I looked about and lost myself once more in the lights. They took me outside myself.

"What secrets do the lights hold?" I remembered asking my mother once. "Every time I look at them—especially the bright colored ones—it's like I feel that if I look long enough, I'll come to some kind of knowing I don't possess now."

"Oh, you mean get illuminated or enlightened," she joked, explaining the new words to me. I recalled my second grade teacher telling me that if you stare at lights long enough, you will turn into a star.

"Really?" I had replied, believing her.

I got up and continued my stroll, mesmerized by the bright golden street light. I didn't want to be away too long. Pam would wonder if something had happened to me.

The snow began falling more heavily. More lights came into view. They made the falling snow look like sparkling diamonds gently dropping out of the sky, then glistening onto the white blanket below.

"Will I really turn into a star if I stare at the lights long enough?" I recalled asking my teacher so long ago. Long before I had met *sky people* and other-worldly beings, I knew even at the age of seven of my connection to light and the stars.

I became aware of how much I was enjoying my own company. Most people spend so little time alone. "How can we be with others, if we can't be with ourselves?" I often tell my friends.

My eyes darted back and forth from one house to the next, taking in each and every flickering light. I couldn't miss a single one. I found myself mentally counting the bulbs, distinguishing reds, greens, blues, yellows, and whites. I did this for several minutes. Counting and recounting to be sure. Not one light could be neglected. Each possessed its own beauty and magic.

A few minutes later I headed back. I was unable to keep from looking back every few seconds. Maybe I was supposed to look for all the people too busy to see them. I retraced my steps to view a couple of houses again which had extraordinary light displays, then advanced ahead.

Many years later, I realized why I am so fascinated by Christmas lights. My new visitor was to explain that to me in great detail on that magical, wintry, snowy evening in

December of 1994. One reason some of us are so drawn to bright, colorful lights is because they stir and awaken memories of lifetimes we have lived on starry realms. On some of those realms, entire cities are designed with magnificent light displays so bright and colorful that our colors cannot begin to imitate their luminescence and beauty. Viewing the lights activates subconscious memories which fill me with an inexplicable sense of joy, magic, and wonder. There is another reason why I was so drawn to bright lights, but I don't want to get ahead of myself. I'll let my visitor explain. Now back to that snowy December in 1994.

I stopped once more and gave the light displays a final gaze. My solar plexus actually tingled. I was thrilled to think how some families really get into the Christmas spirit and create lavish displays. I smiled as I wondered about the cost of their electric bill. Who cares when it gives them joy and pleasure to create their own version of the North Pole? I wonder what subconscious soul memories might be partly responsible for such extravagant displays and what starry realms those people may have lived upon. A car sped by, disturbing my musing. I waved at the lights and then began walking back.

When I approached Pam's house, several more cars were parked out front. In my mind, I saw an image of the big oak tree in her yard and felt drawn towards it. I slowly made my way out back, walking in the snow and humming "O Christmas tree." Moments later I greeted the oak tree. I threw my arms around it, recalling the How to Be an Artist poster which says to hug trees.

A tingle I had earlier felt returned, except it was more intense this time. It felt like something between a caress and a tickle. Lightheaded, I released my firm grip and slowly lowered myself until I was sitting under the colossal oak tree. Snowflakes melted on my face. I gazed upward. I sat still for a long time, lost in the beauty of the wintry snow and lovely night. Then suddenly the hair on my neck stood up as I sensed a presence such as I had when I sat under the street light. I put my hand over my mouth and gasped, slowly turning my head to the right. Standing a few inches away staring at me was a very odd looking man about two feet tall.

Black twinkling eyes stared at me. I had never seen such a sight before. Were my eyes playing tricks on me? My excitement mounted with each passing second. I placed my hands next to my side hoping the little man would not notice. Why do my hands have to tremble every time I get nervous and excited? I mustered the courage to look at the little man. He wore a rectangular brown hat. Thick black hair fell to his shoulders, and he wore a long black beard. He was of a stout build and wore green breeches, a red shirt, and black suspenders. He was certainly dressed for Christmas. I wondered if this was a coincidence, or was he aware of this holiday season?

I tried to greet him but could only voice a tiny screech. I knew something exciting was going to happen tonight, but I had never thought that I'd meet a genuine *whatever the little man was*. He smiled and stepped a little closer. I entertained the thought that perhaps I was dreaming or maybe I had died, and the man had come to escort my soul to the other world. He wiggled his hands and shook his head to the side.

"Ye no be dreaming and ye no be dead a'tall," he said, pointing a finger at me. "Ye ought no be afraid of me when ye been waiting all yer life to meet one of me kind."

How would you know that? I thought, looking at him intently. The little man winked at me and continued.

"The fact that ye be here tells me ye be a lover and friend of nature. I be a friend of the oak meself. As a matter of fact, this oak tree be me home and home to me friends and family as well."

"Be ye a snow faerie?" I asked with eyes big as saucers.

Whoa! I'm talking like he is! I thought.

"Be ye an ass," the man cried out, letting out a guffaw, moving closer and slapping me on the thigh. "I know ye be a dreamer and believer in the little folks. There be so few of ye mortals who believe in us. And fewer still who we take the time to make an appearance to. No offense to ye, of course." He tipped his hat and bowed. "No need to keep ye in mystery any longer. Me name be Nookles and I be a snow gnome."

"Nookles," I said softly. "I'm very pleased to meet you, Mr. Nookles."

"Ye no need be so formal. Makes me feel older than me eight hundred years I actually be." He moved closer. "Scoot yerself over a wee bit and make some room for me if ye no mind."

He took my hand and felt it. "Yer hand no feel like a mortal's. Much power be coursed in the lines of yer palms. Look here. This be yer lifeline. Ye got two of em, which is to say ye be living two lives, perhaps more, in one. I also see that ye be very in touch with the spirit realm. Ye see things and go places few ever go. And mind ye, yer experiences no all be on earth," he said, pointing to the sky. My mouth dropped and my eyes got as big as a saucer. *How could he know so much about me?*

As though reading my thoughts, he patted my hand and said, "Nookles know a lot of things and so do ye."

Then he stared into my eyes. "Ye no have the mortal stench that so disgusts me kind, and ye no feel human a'tall. As ye know the mind, body, and spirit all be intertwined. When thoughts and belief systems be self-centered this cloud up aura and create dense stench. As ye know, most human's nature be selfish; this be why we avoid most of them. But ye be very different, young mortal. Nookles be wondering if ye really be human?"

"Well, go ahead and touch me hand," I said, imitating his argot. "I be flesh, blood, muscles, and bone like all other humans."

"Nookles no need to touch ye. Yer flesh be so little of who ye be. It be yer soul that interests and appeals to me and that I can read, and yers be unlike any other humans Nookles ever encounter."

"Well, I am not surprised. Isn't everyone different?"

"Yes, to some extent, but ye be *very* different. Sure yer mother no be a faerie woman? In ages past under special circumstances, some faeries could love and mate with a mortal, giving the mortal special powers."

"Well, I don't believe that happened to me. My mother married my father when she was sixteen, and I was born four years later. She never mentioned any faerie man and besides I resemble my father."

"Well, ye still no feel mortal to me. Me great grandmother Elira, snow gnome prophetess, taught me to read hands, and I never be wrong. Me kind no like most mortals and we avoid most of them."

"Why did you come to me then?"

"Because Nookles can tell that ye be so much more than the average mortal on ye world."

"How do you know that?" I ventured to ask.

"I can feel yer presence and see yer soul-light and aura as ye humans call it. It be very bright, and I know that ye can see lot of things most people no see. Most humans exude a terrible stench that makes us half-sick. Since snow purifies, it be possible for we snow gnomes to make occasional appearance to those humans we deem worthy of contact, mind ye." Nookles nodded his head, folded his arms, then leaned and peered into my eyes.

I saw glittering stars then quickly looked away. Nookles flinched, a bit startled. "No be afraid. That just be me soul-light reflecting out of me eyes. Some fairies and other *little folks* can see the soul reflection through the eyes. Did ye notice any colors?"

"The white sparkle was beginning to shift. It scared me so I looked away."

"Michael, no be afraid to see with yer soul-vision. Ye already do and quite frequently. That be one reason why ye be so drawn to and fascinated by lights. Ye be stirring up yearnings of a time long ago when ye see much more on many faraway places than folks see here today," he said, pointing to the sky.

"The soul radiates outward from the eyes in diverse colors and in those far away times, even mortals could see it. So long ago it be. Even long before Nookles be here. Different people emanate different colors."

"In the olden times ye could lose yerself and merge with others, all from gazing into the eyes. T'was far more satisfying than, what do ye folks call it—lovemaking? Ye be wanting to dance with other spirits and letting yer soul-light flicker and swirl as ye merge one with each other. Indeed, 'tis one of the most pleasant sensations ye can imagine. It sort of be like bathing in a pool of rose-scented love. Do ye no feel some tingles and light headiness earlier when ye stare at the lights?"

I wondered how the snow gnome knew this about me. We were quiet a few minutes. I sensed that Nookles could read my mind just as Rosara could.

Awhile later I spoke softly. "Yes, I did feel light-headed and joyful and got tingles when I stared at the lights. It felt strange and yet not strange. I can't explain it."

"No need to. Words no can explain such marvels. Come with me. I want to show ye something."

Nookles jumped up off the ground. I was amazed at his quickness and agility. Could he really be eight-hundred years old? He led me a few feet down the hill to another oak tree. He cocked his ear and bent towards the tree. "Do the same. Be sure and touch the tree. Even better, lean yer full body against its trunk."

I did so and heard soft singing sounds, then whistles. Then whispers. Then laughter and humming and singing. The tunes were lovely and somehow felt familiar.

Close yer eyes, me friend, and let a snow gnome show ye some truly amazing marvels."

The moment I did so, I beheld twinkling star-like figures dancing and floating about. They were of diverse colors and hues I did not recognize. I also smelled the sweetest scent and took in several whiffs. Nookles and I remained glued to the spot several minutes. Then the voices began fading and the lights vanished. I wanted to stay there forever—to become a dancing spark of light and float about and smell the sweetness in the air. A few minutes later Nookles led me back to his tree. We were silent a long while. I wondered how much time had passed. I looked about. The snow had stopped. The sky had cleared and was filled with twinkling stars which flickered as though winking at me.

"Soul stars," Nookles whispered. "Certain faeries often dance on the stars and join them or *ensoul* with them. It makes them even brighter. Ye can tell which stars be ensouled by fairies by their brightness. It be blissful to behold such a marvel. Ye saw the fairies, didn't ye?"

"I think so, but it all seemed so unreal somehow, yet very real too."

"More real than not real, young mortal."

"Is that why people like to stargaze?"

"It be one reason. For a time they be filled with magic and wonder, something which mortals hunger for deep in their souls. Something they need. Something all life needs. The sense of wonder and magic be as much a part of yer nature as yer five senses. Mortals do themselves a grand disservice by denying something which can bring them glee and mirth. Sad it be indeed! Not know of any creatures that torture themselves more. Things they should disregard, they give undue attention to, and most tend to ignore magic and wonder. I no can figure people out. Can ye?"

"Magic and wonder!" I said, bright-eyed, looking upwards. "Can ye take me up there to the stars, Nookles? Can we see the soul stars and maybe even dance with a faerie? I'd give anything to do it just once."

"Once," huffed Nookles, pointing a finger at me and stomping about. "Ye still so much to learn. Magic be the norm for fairies, snow gnomes, and such folks. It be for mortals, too, if they be no be so rigid, stubborn, and ignorant. Life be simple and magical in olden times. People need to open their hearts and let their light shine," he said, gently tapping me on the chest. "When ye open yer heart and soul and align yer spirit and join with nature and all life, then all be possible. It be really quite simple. Magic and power be available every day. No limit to eternal supply. Never forget that, and ye be happy always."

We sat in the quiet for several minutes. Then Nookles looked at me. "What be on yer mind, Michael?"

"I just feel that I have come here for more than this. Please don't get me wrong. It's an honor to be here and to speak and listen to you. But something is missing. I feel it."

"So, ye do now, do ye? What do ye sense?"

"I sense there be more ye have to teach me."

Nookles rubbed his long beard as he looked at me intently for several moments. Then he spoke softly. "So ye be saying that ole Nookles, snow gnome, have more to teach ye. Perhaps he do," he said, snickering, then looking up at the sky once more. We were silent for several minutes then he picked up where he left off.

"Yes, indeed, life exist up there. Beloved Creator has many children, and all no live here or down in there," he said, pointing to the oak tree. Some be sky people."

"You know about *sky people*?" I said, filled with excitement.

"Nookles sure do as do some of yer Native American peoples. We snow gnomes love those people, for they be lovers of earth mother and respect her. We visit some of them quite frequently."

"It be a small world," I chuckled.

"Very small," he laughed, "but also very big."

"Speaking of sky people, you are not the first person, I mean, being, to tell me that my sky friends are not the creation of an overactive imagination."

"No a'tall. Ye no create any of them. What ye create be ability to make contact with them."

"So, how is it that I can make this contact so easily while so many others cannot?"

"Ye sure ask many questions," he said, laughing.

"That's true," I replied a little embarrassed. "My mother once said I practically came out of the womb talking and asking questions and have never since ceased to shut up."

"Nookles say curiosity no need kill cat, as mortals say."

"How do you know our sayings? To not like most earth people, you seem to know our language pretty well."

Nookles let out hearty laughter. "Guess ole Nookles do know human talk pretty good. Maybe ye ought to give Nookles silver or gold medal."

He winked at me. His eyes glowed like stars and radiated so much love.

I *have* felt that much love before. I thought of Mr. Divine in my book, *Morning Coffee with God*, who said I possess a deep capacity to love. I wanted to cry. To be blessed with this lovely snow, so many beautiful lights, and then to meet a snow gnome! What more could I want for Christmas? This I knew, would be my best Christmas ever. I also knew that my life would be transformed and my mind expanded after this visit. I knew it just as I knew that this meeting with the little snow gnome was not by chance. Nookles had things to teach me, and I knew that he was much more than he appeared to be.

Nookles tapped me on the knee. "Nookles seldom meet like-minded mortal whose thoughts soar like mighty eagle. Inquisitiveness be good quality—one that always serve ye well and create some fantastic adventures," he added, giving me another wink.

Then he scooted right next to me and gently tapped me on the head.

"Michael, I can know yer language because I can get in yer head, with yer permission, of course. Mind ye, all permission no always be given on a conscious level. Earlier as ye look at beautiful snow ye be sensing something special and unusual about to happen. Ye could feel it in yer gut, and ye got those tingles and chills too, did ye not?"

"That be very true."

"Well, it be Nookles who plant notion in yer mind and who suggest ye visit oak tree before ye return to friend's festivity."

"I see."

"Yes, ye see," he whispered. "That be big key. Ye see. The reason ye be able to make contact with beings like me and *sky people* be because of the marvelous soul-vision ye possess. Most mortals stumble about blindly, missing so many beautiful experiences because their soul-vision be shut down for most part. Too many computer games, television, and eating yer animal brothers and sisters numb ye and blind yer soul-vision."

"I've never felt that eating meat is the highest path. As a matter of fact, I've been vegetarian more than once, and I am headed back in that direction again. I watch no television."

"That because ye be bookworm," he teased.

"Yeah, I be bookworm as ye put it. As for computer games I never play them."

"Such mindless games, most, if no all, be designed to do in opponent. They be bad role models for children and teach them competition, war, violence and hate instead of cooperation, sharing and love which is what they should be teaching them."

"Don't get me going on that one. I was made fun of so much as a child because I never asked for toy guns or G. I. Joes for Christmas. I just wanted clothes, books, or a Casper the friendly ghost doll who talked."

"There be some nice spooks," Nookles chuckled. "I know ye seen some 'feny faces' and be seeing many more in future."

"Well, if you can get inside my head, I guess you can access my memories, can't you?"

"Some," he said, "no all and ye must never doubt the strength and power of yer soul-vision. Ye can go to so many places. Ye also be able to get inside other people's heads, and some can get in yers. I might add that ye do so quite frequently. This type of mind communication, or telepathy, soon to happen more for ye. It be no intrusion if ye ask permission, and ye do this often on a subconscious level."

"Well, that's good to know. Speaking of know, how is it that you know so much? I thought that gnomes were just simple guardians and caretakers of the earth."

"Be no deceived by appearances, Michael, or to quote mortal saying, "No judge book by cover." Some gnomes be simple and content to work with earth energies and purification. Others like Nookles like to take on more, shall we say. Just like people be different and at different stages in their souls' evolution and advancement, so be gnomes, faeries, sky people, and all beings. Variety be spice of life, as ye be known to say."

"That makes sense."

"We all be spirit sparks and children of Creator Source. That means we all be co-Creators. We can create and be anything we want."

"Wow," I exclaimed. "This be getting kind of deep, Nookles."

He snickered. "This be but tip of iceberg. To quote great earth teacher, Jesus, 'In me Father house be many mansions.'"

"That Bible verse seems to come up a lot. I've always been especially drawn to it."

"That be because no truer words ever be spoken before, and ye simply be visiting some of those mansions." He pointed at the oak tree. "Me humble abode in there be one of Creator's many mansions."

Then he shot his gaze upward and pointed at the sky. "Lovely morning star, Venus, be another of Creator's many mansions. Nookles know about yer deep love for and strong connection to Venus."

"Yes, I have a deep attraction to Venus."

"And why not? Ye live up there more than once and part of yer grand mighty soul be living there now."

"I've been told that I'm a multi-faceted soul. I can understand how part of me lives on Venus. That is probably why other parts of me misses Venus."

"Affirmative, but I say multi-faceted soul be too big word for Nookle's taste. Nookles say ye be big soul. Simple as that. As ye become more adept at soul travel, more parts of ye that be here can soar off and pay spirit visit to Venus, your beloved homeland, or at least one of them."

"I want to go there now."

"And leave yer new friend behind?" he chuckled.

"Come with me, Nookles. Show me how to get there. I bet you are an expert at soul travel."

"Nookles been on a few journeys, I have. Some been a bit bumpy, I might add. Ye got to know what ye be doing, or ye can sometimes encounter some souls whose intentions no be so benevolent, let me say."

"I'm sure. When you said you been on a few journeys I have, you remind me of Yoda, the Jedi Master Knight, in the Star Wars movies. He talks like that."

"Nookles see ye have much respect for Master Yoda. Much homage to great Master Yoda. Many grand powerful teachers like that one inhabit some of Creator's mansions. I might add that to be a master adept one no need be ten feet giant, or to quote one of yer sayings, 'Dynamite come in small packages.'"

"You can access my mind and memories?"

"Yes, it be easy to read yer mind and memories. Yer soul be very open and inviting to those it trusts."

"That is a very kind thing for you to say."

"It be true. Ye know that Nookles be friend not foe, and ye think that Nookles possess little bit of knowledge in head, so do ye?" he said, tapping himself on the top of the head. "Be ye sure about that? Nookles sometimes think his head be empty. What have ye to say about that, young mortal?"

"I say Nookles be trying to pull me leg," I said, laughing. "Ye no fool me. I know that Nookles be me friend and he know lots of things."

Nookles burst into hearty laughter and started pulling at my leg.

"To pull someone's leg is just a saying, Nookles. It means to kid, fool, trick, or as we sometimes say to 'bullshit.'"

"Nookles know what pull leg mean. He just want to make Michael laugh and no be so serious."

"Thank you. I appreciate that. I am too serious sometimes. Speaking of which, now to change the subject, will you please tell me more about our Creator. You said that we be spirit sparks and children of Creator. So who and what is Creator?"

Nookles looked at me for a long time then spoke. "Ye do be asking deep questions, Michael." Then he grinned and softly sang, "Ye be me sunshine, me only sunshine, ye make me happy when skies be gray."

"You are amazing. You even know our songs."

"Nookles no be amazing a'tall. I can know yer songs because Nookles can get in yer head as I said earlier. And yers be like open book to me. I can also get in some other mortals' heads as well to learn and store in me memory quite a few songs, words, phrases, and such. Eight hundred years give

Nookles bit of time to build up his vocabulary," he said, snickering. "This really no ought be big surprise for ye, Michael. Ye have big vocabulary yerself."

"I guess my mind does take in a lot."

"Ye no be seeing anything yet, as saying goes. Ye just be getting started. I see books ye be writing that ye no even yet begun. Ye going to write about some of Creator's mansions. Ye going to write about some past lives in Atlantis and how power be acquired, wielded, and later abused. Ye be going to expose some ancient sorcery that world be ready to know about."

"I was told once by a psychic that I was a minor player in the destruction of Atlantis. I've pretty much stayed away from books about Atlantis. Yet, I've always felt I had a karmic debt to go back in time to see and relive those experiences and then write about them. I'm not ready for that anytime soon."

"Ye be ready when time be right. Ye be going to write books about those times and yer memories of Atlantis. By the way, there be at least three of them and they be going to reveal much secret information, mysteries, and such. Nookles be yer first customer to purchase book when come out."

"I guess I got my work cut out for me, don't I?"

"Ye sure do."

We were quiet for a few moments. Then Nookles started singing, "Ye be me sunshine" again. I joined him. When he finished, he patted me on the knee and said, "So yer question be answered, be it not?"

"I think I know what you are implying and getting at."

"Nookles no get at or imply nothing. Nookles only state what be true. Creator Source be big golden central sun, and we children be little spirit sparks. Size of sparks and form depend on how much of light we take in from sun."

Then he moved his hands in a circular motion. "Ye, Michael, be taking in lots of Creator light so yer soul be growing and glowing until ye become like giant light bulb that can see and extend yer soul and soul-vision way up there, way down here, and in here," he said, touching his head and heart.

"In time ye can see and go any and everywhere, and ye no need car keys or space craft, let me remind ye," Nookles said, laughing. "In time ye be doing much more mind and soul travel. Or some people call it spirit journeys or astral projection. Funny how ye mortals have so many ways to say same things. Nookles find this amusing."

"Variety be the spice of life," I said, winking at him. "Wow, what you say sure is a lot to take in."

"I know. Ye assimilate it in time, Michael." He tapped my forehead. "When ye think about it, ye realize this concept no be really so strange to ye. Like day man put ye under and ye talk about when ye be a dancing flame and spirit spark long, long ago. Do ye no recall that day?"

"I do. I was hypnotized, or put under as you say, by a friend and I said some very far-out things. I even said that I had once been a reed swaying on the waters. I also said that I had been a cat and an old sage in a cave. That experience was very far-out."

Nookles snickered. "Far-out. Close by. It all be same. Time and space be but illusions created for convenience sake so mortals can experience more density and less light. The true essence of yer soul be light. Ye no just be light workers, to quote some new age people, ye be light, albeit it condensed light. Smoke that in yer pipe as ye papa used to say."

"Yeah, papa was a bit of a philosopher in his own way. He had a few sayings of his own, along with being a devil."

Nookles laughed. "Devil. What an interesting word. Devil. Evil. Lived if you spell devil backwards. Devil. Evil. Dead. Alive. All different shades and frequency patterns of light. Nothing more and nothing less. Yer papa's light no be like yer's or mine or Hitler's, but it no be extinguished. It be simply more dense and condensed. Hitler, too, have more opportunities to be enlightened, to take in more light as will all souls, including ye and me. Our soul-lights be very bright, but other souls and some *sky people*s' lights be brighter. Good news be there much more light available where our light come from—from Creator Source, big central sun. And so be cosmos world without end. Be delightful. Be full of light. Ye light up me life. Have ye got a light? Lighten up."

I laughed. "I've heard that before."

"I know," he said, giving me another wink. "When Jesus float away or ascend, as yer Bible put it, he simply drew in more light essence, or ye could say that he merged with his light body. He no be first to do this, and he no be last. As a matter of fact, ye be destined to merge with yer light body and higher self. Then ye no need look at glowing Christmas lights to be reminded of who ye truly be. For then ye become the light just as our Creator be pure radiant light. And please make sure and no fall in trap of thinking there be only one Creator or Source. Let it be said who be the Creator of the Creator? Where there be one, so there be many. There be many suns in many universes that provide light whence soul sparks and creation be given birth. One day light of yer higher self can be so bright, and ye, too, can become a creator god or goddess. Ye can give birth to yer own planets, people, and life forms. This time be many light years away when ye be far more advanced than ye be now. But remember that time be illusion, so what does it matter?"

"I don't understand. How could such a magnificent event happen?"

"Let Nookles try to explain. There be no limit to amount of light yer higher self can take in at mental, causal, and celestial levels. If ye be thinking these levels be most high that exist, I here to tell ye there be yet higher realms. Yer gods of all religions, Buddha and such evolved souls, dwell on celestial planes beyond mental and causal. Celestial planes be beyond comprehension of most people living on earth at this time. Beyond celestial planes, be cosmic planes. At these higher galactic universal cosmic planes, even more light be available. Souls here can choose to manifest and create or move on to higher levels where manifested creation ceases. From there be what ye call Nirvana and other higher states of consciousness beyond manifested creation."

"Whoa," I said, "this is over me head, Nookles. Ye be telling me that not only can we become a Creator and create our own planet, people, and life forms, but there be yet higher realms?"

"That be exactly what Nookles try to explain to ye. Ye folks say watch what ye ask for, for ye get it. I can read yer mind and see that ye wrote a poem once where ye want to see God's face and form. Nookles tell ye that such be possible, but there be higher realms should ye be daring, willing, and earn the right. Let us leave cosmic, non-manifested realms and Void alone for now and get back to talk about how ye and other souls have opportunity to become Creator gods."

"Okay. Thank you. I'll wait to try and ponder the void and the non-manifested realms of creation another time. My head be already spinning round and round from all that ye have so far told me."

"Can be fun to take a spin in car around block now and again," Nookles said, bursting into hilarious laughter. "Take a spin in car or play spin bottle for kisses." Then he quickly took on a serious look and continued speaking. "As Nookles say, there be no limit to amount of light yer higher self can take in at mental, causal, and celestial levels. At those levels of energy and consciousness, ye literally have capability to become a Creator god. Creation's ancient starry codes be implanted in yer DNA genetic codes. The potential power that can be wielded when ye light body be fully activated and fused with big central sun energy make atomic bombs look like fire crackers."

"It be possible to create enough energy to initiate yer own *big bang* creation blast. This knowledge be only available to advanced initiates worthy and spiritually evolved enough to receive keys to activate the codes which activate more cosmic divine light at those greater proportions. The higher beings and Lords of Karma no want repeats of destruction that took place on Atlantis, Maldek, and some other places. It be detrimental to soul evolution to create worlds and then to become power hungry, greedy and corrupt and then destroy them. Such wasted needless actions hinder and retard the soul's progress and creates karma that can take a long time to work off."

"I still don't see how one person could wield such power."

"One person, no. One completely Christed, actualized, enlightened, fully empowered divine soul, yes."

"Wow," I'm blown away. All this talk makes Superman and Spiderman look like a baby in a crib."

"I guess ye could say that. Needless to say, yer ultimate destiny be far greater than most ever perceive. The human part of ye could no take in nor sustain such light as yer actualized divine self can. This be why much of yer soul essence no dwell in yer human form. But yer higher self be a completely different story. It has access to unlimited amounts of light. To take in light from big central sun no drain or diminish Creator Source, at least for very long time. Think of yer computer when ye copy/paste a page or file to create new one. Ye no lose original. Ye simply create new one. Same be with drawing energy from Source. And yes, way down road suns eventually die, but from death always come new life as nature teaches us. No one or no thing ever really dies."

"All remaining essence goes back to grand cosmic recycle bin. Just as people be born, grow up, give birth to children, meet old age and die, so do suns and Creators. The purpose be to allow process to be natural one. When people interrupt and interfere with forces of nature, the sense of balance be disturbed and unnatural forces be set into motion. This leads to global chaos, violent unstable weather conditions, patterns, and destruction and finally to premature demise of world. This tarnishes soul and can set back human evolution tremendously as ye know from yer own cave man, dark ages, and medieval times."

"I am in awe of your words, Nookles. Nookles," I repeated. "What a strange name for one so wise."

"Nookles like things simple. Simplicity for simplicity sake be me motto."

"I understand. You don't need some special fancy name. I doubt that your ego ever works overtime. As a matter of fact, I doubt that you even possess an ego."

Nookles let out a hearty laugh. "Oh, please no put Nookles on pedestal. I most certainly possess ego. Just ask me lady or me kin. But Nookles learn long ago that secret be to tame ego. No one can be master until ego be completely tamed. Nookles have a ways to go as do Michael and most humans."

"Yes. I get chills when you said that one day my light could be bright enough that I could become a Creator Lord and create a planet, people, and life forms. I think of the verse in the Bible that says, "Abraham would be the father of many nations. And you are saying that I might be the father, or should I say mother, of all creations on some distant world in the faraway future?"

"Affirmative, and no only ye but many souls be given this grand and mighty opportunity. Such happen in past and such happen in future, for infinity be playground of all Creators and all creation."

"Wow. I need a drink. This sure gives added meaning to the line from the Christmas song "Mary did you know that your baby boy will be lord of all creation?"

"It surely do, and yer own Beloved Jesus say, "Ye can do even greater things than I?"

"You sure know how to quote the Bible, Nookles."

"No, ye do, Michael. "Ye have many Biblical verses memorized in that fine mind of yers since ye be lad. With yer soul permission, I simply be accessing some of yer stored information and memories by type of telepathic interaction. It be as simple as that. This goes on far more than most people realize. Ye becoming more aware of it. Part of purpose of this visit be to make ye even more aware of yer connection to all beings and life and infinite possibilities and different ways of communicating and connecting that exist. Ye no go crazy as ye sometimes fear. Ye becoming more enlightened as ye take in more light. Michael, ye be in process of becoming more of who ye truly be. And ye be going to spread yer light to many people."

I thought of the words to an old gospel song, *This little light of mine, I'm gonna let it shine.*

Nookles read my thoughts, and we sang it softly while holding hands. A few minutes later, he spoke. "No only can ye do greater things as Jesus say, but he also be going to do greater things than he so far ever done. The soul desires to move forward and become more perfected. Such be its nature. Evolution be its destiny."

"My little friend, this be a lot to take in. I thought Jesus was at the top of the mountain."

"He be pretty high, but he no be at top of the mountain as ye put it. Nookles know this be a lot for Michael to take in. Nookles also know that Michael be ready for information at this time, and in time ye be sharing it with others. That be why we meet on lovely, snowy, wintry evening. Ye going to integrate and assimilate information and pass it onto others who need be reminded of who they truly be and all the vast potential and infinite possibilities available to them. Ye have so much to accomplish, me friend. Now I need be on me way, but we meet again, Michael."

"Where?" I asked, looking despondent, not wanting to leave my new friend.

"Maybe up there on star or inside oak tree by spirit travel. And for starters, why don't ye leave yer lights up all year? Enjoy brilliant magical colors every day, no just a few. Why live in darkness when there be so much light?" He pointed at the stars, the tree, and his heart.

"I want to make you a gift, Nookles. You have brightened my night and life. What would bring you pleasure?"

"A bit of mistletoe about the tree if ye be so kind. We know about some of yer rituals, and we like some of them. Mistletoe bring romance in the air. Me lady like it." He moved closer to me and pointed to my ear. I bent down to listen.

Nookles whispered in my ear, "I have final important message for ye. I think we can help each other. There be some other mortals like yerself fascinated by lights. Some also spend hours stargazing and staring at bright lights, yearning, remembering, and piercing veil between our worlds. I can help ye help them along. Every time we help fellow souls to light, our own soul radiates more brightly. Now I must go back to me lady. She be wondering as to me whereabouts. Yer friends be wondering about yers as well."

"Oh my goodness. Pam is going to think something terrible has happened. It must be midnight or later. It feels like we've been talking for hours."

I looked at my watch. It was seven-thirty—only a half hour had transpired. "How can this be, Nookles. This is impossible."

Nookles grinned and winked at me. "Me friend, we step into what be known as *no-time*. It no be only faeries who can affect, bend, and step through time. Some snow gnomes such as meself be good at it as well. Time to go now. No be sad, me friend. We meet again sometime, Nookles promise ye. Maybe up there somewhere or down here somewhere as long as there be sufficient snow. I want ye to meet me friends and family sometime."

"I would very much like that," I said, wiping a tear away. Nookles stepped closer and threw his arms around me. I bent down and hugged him closely. "I do hope I see you again, my friend. Seems like so many come to teach me something, and then they leave and never return."

"Nookles no be like so many friends." He then bowed, tipped his hat, winked at me, and then vanished.

I stood by the tree several minutes, still mesmerized. The magic I had anticipated had come. Had my anticipating it caused it to manifest? I wondered. Did expecting and believing in magic make it come true? I wasn't sure. What I was sure of is how blown away I was. Nookles had taught me so much. It would take time to assimilate all that he said, and perhaps I would never understand it all. He said I was supposed to share the information. Do I dare? Who would believe me? I then realized that I don't need people to believe me. I knew what had happened, and I would never be the same. I couldn't wait to get home and write it all down.

I heard a gentle humming as I touched the tree and was tempted to stay outside, but I knew that Pam was expecting me, and she'd be delighted to hear about my new friend. I slowly made my way to the front door. Before I could open it, it opened before me.

Pam stood there smiling. "Oh, it's you, Michael. Welcome back. Did you have a nice walk?"

"Wonderful. Actually it was quite magical."

"Wonderful! Welcome back to my magical house. Your eyes are sparkling like the Christmas lights. You're just in time. The party is just beginning."

My thoughts were still on Nookles until a firm hand gripped me on the shoulders. "Great to see you, Michael," said my friend, Neil. "Happy holidays. Did you hang half a dozen strings of light this year? We all know you love lots of bright lights and how extravagant you are when it comes to holiday decorating."

"Happy Holidays to you, Neil. Yes, I have lots of bright lights strung all over the place. And guess what? The lights are not coming down this year. I have decided that every day is going to be Christmas at my place. This year and every year. I am going to create my own mini-version of the North Pole and add to it every year."

"Sure, sounds good to me. Can I get you some cider or eggnog?"

"After ye," I said. I tipped my hat and gave Neil a small bow.

CHAPTER FIFTEEN

MARVEL MANSION

AND THE CHAMBER OF BEAUTY

I think about Nookles often and am grateful for the things he taught. Thanks to him I now have a deeper understanding of my strong attraction to colorful lights and the stars. Some of the concepts he brought up I had already thought about while others were new to me, such as souls taking in enough of Creator's Source's light that they can become Lords of their own creation.

It seemed a lot to take in and was rather hard to swallow, as the saying goes. To be quite blunt, I was completely blown away for quite some time and had my doubts. But in time the concepts grew on me, and I began to accept them no matter how far-out or far-fetched they seemed. Now that I better understand why I love to stargaze and why I love bright colorful lights, I take in even more joy each time I behold all the lights in my mini-North Pole in my house.

As I look at each string of lights, I wonder where and what kinds of creator gods and goddesses will exist. What will their creations be? What color or colors will the people be? The houses and buildings? Temples? Animals? Flowers? Food? Clothing? You name it. Will they have shades and hues or different colors from the ones we have on Earth? How many souls will be drawn to these new worlds? And where will they come from? I am especially drawn to Venus, Arcturus, the Pleiades, Sirius, and Andromeda. If I advance and evolve to the point of becoming a *lord of creation*, will I be able to attract souls who have experienced lives in those places, or will I have to consult some karmic board or galactic overlords who are in charge of such matters?

There were so many questions I needed answers for. I had hoped for another visit with Nookles and called out to him often. He was either too busy, or it was not time for another visit because I did not feel his presence or receive any messages from him. I finally concluded that he was put on hold, so I asked my guides for a new visitor.

As though my call had gone out to the ethers, a few days later I had another encounter from an unusual and very interesting being. After doing some reading that evening, I had a glass of red wine and then decided to call it a night. I sat on my bed and leaned against the headboard. A few moments later I could feel my head becoming light-headed, which sometimes transpires when my guides adjust my energy before I receive a visitor. My heart began to pitter and pound as I became more excited. Who would visit me tonight? Rosara from Astellva? I had been thinking about her and missed her.

Suddenly in the midst of my musing, out of nowhere appeared a small man who said very clearly and succinctly, "Greetings to you, Michael, seeker on the path of spiritual knowledge. I am Mr. Toozles."

"Mr. Who?" I asked, snickering, thinking of the word *bamboozle*, which his name reminded me of.

"Mr. Toozles, if you please," the little man said, bowing to me.

The clock on my night table read 9:30 p.m. I looked at him again, and he was staring at me. I sensed that he was trying to decide whether to stay or not. I smiled at him, unsure what to say. I might feel uncomfortable breaking the ice communicating with my new friends, but this in no way implied I was not interested or fascinated by them.

I moved about and stepped towards the window. Snow was falling heavily.

"Isn't it beautiful?" I said. Then Mr. Toozles was not there. Where had he disappeared?

I looked at the trees outside my window a few more minutes and then sat back down. Moments later, he was back again—this time with the biggest grin on his face. That lightened me up to say the least.

Mr. Toozles was decked in a long blue robe with silver moons on it. Hanging from his neck was a thick silver chain with a big rose quartz heart. His long, snowy white hair and his thick beard reminded me of Merlin. His blue piercing eyes seemed to peer right into my soul. I kept looking at him, wondering where he was from and if his attire was the norm back home.

"Not exactly," he said, stepping a little closer to me. "I am not a magician or Merlin although I do possess certain powers." He bowed and then said, "I wore this attire especially for you, Michael."

"I suppose I should thank you for that. I do have this thing for Merlin."

"I know," he replied, winking at me.

"Thank you for returning. For a moment I feared you would not come back. Welcome back, sir."

"Why, thank you, good man," he replied congenially. "But you must decide whether you believe in me and whether you want me here or not. I am not in the mood to be zipping in and out of your world betwixt and between your doubts and uncertainty."

"I'm sorry. I didn't realize I was doubting that you are real. You'd think that by now I would know better."

"Yes, you should indeed know better. Doubt is for skeptics. You are no skeptic. You just pretend to be sometimes. It's your mind's way of feeling useful. Doubt does not serve you at all, Michael. It closes you up and blocks you from so many wonderful experiences. Although you think you have had some interesting experiences up to this point, there are so many more fascinating ones awaiting you in the future. We do not appear to most people because they tend to be skeptics or downright disbelievers. What would be the purpose? Doubting is for skeptical humans. You are so much more than a mere human. You are divine beings with unlimited powers and potential. How can you help to awaken others from their long slumbering if you allow doubts to creep into your mind—doubts that can confine and limit your experiences?"

"You are right. I never thought of it like that. I admit that my mind has been overworked as of late. It's rather exhausting to do so much thinking, analyzing, and trying to figure out everything. Please, don't go. I would like for you to stay," I said, smiling brightly. "Will you stay for a visit?"

"Gladly," Mr. Toozles said, plopping beside me on the bed. I had a spontaneous urge to put my arm around him. He was about the size of my teddy bear.

Well, if I'm dreaming, then it's a wonderful dream, I thought.

Mr. Toozles gave me a frown followed by a big twinkle in his eyes. "Watch your thoughts lest I disappear again. You are not dreaming any more than the rest of us. Life itself is a sort of dream, but this is a real one—or shall I say a *reality dream*," he snickered, tapping me on the knee. "In the absolute sense, this is not real. Neither you nor I are real, for on the absolute realms there is no individuality or separation. For our present purpose here, we are both real."

"That is kind of deep, but I think I sort of get your drift."

"Of course you do, Michael. You are a very deep person."

"Yeah, when I'm not depressed, and now that you are here it has lifted."

Mr. Toozles smiled and nodded.

Depression seemed a million miles away now. We were silent for several moments. Mr. Toozles looked around my room then he walked over to my poster of Charlie Brown on the wall and stared intently at it.

"I like that little boy," he said, still looking at it. "He's got soul in him, that one. He's very in touch with himself. A most sensitive character. Sadly misunderstood though. Don't ever think that his purpose is to be just a cartoon character. There are many people like Charlie Brown who have a lot of soul in them and feel misunderstood by others."

"Don't we all have soul in us?"

"Yes, but this Charlie Brown character has a lot. That is why you like him so much. Aren't you going to ask me where I come from?"

"I think I'll pass on that, sir. Actually, I don't care. It's just nice to have some company. I've been feeling rather lonely lately."

"Nice to join you as well, Michael," Mr. Toozles said. "I've been feeling kind of lonely myself. Nice to get away from all that back there." He pointed behind him.

I didn't dare ask him where back there was or what was there. I looked at him more closely. There was something unique about him. I couldn't pinpoint it, but I knew that this little man stood out from his own people—I assumed there were others where he came from. The twinkle in his eye was familiar. I had seen it before, but where? It made me relax.

He smiled at me. "Sometimes, we all need to step out of our personal traumas and dramas that life tosses our way, don't we? Tell me about how you've been feeling lately. I can tell you have been quite troubled. It never hurts to have someone lend a listening ear. It usually makes you feel better. Go ahead, Michael. I'm all ears."

I forced a smile. "Well, I guess you could say that I have been taking myself too seriously lately. I have been doing a lot of writing and making some creative breakthroughs. But then I also find myself having what I call one of my little existential crises where everything seems absurd and useless. I feel like there are so many people, characters, or sub-personalities inside of me. They are all so different. It can be difficult trying to deal with so many sides. This is a time when part of me craves for meaning and passion in life while another part says there is no meaning to life other than what we assign to it. I recently wrote two poems that talk about the passion I crave to express while another part of me could care less about passion or being filled with more life as my poems talk about. The past few days have been some of my bleaker days. I didn't really think I could get out of bed this morning when the phone rang at 7:30. After the woman apologized for dialing the wrong number, I crawled back in bed and slept another hour."

"When I awoke, I felt strangled by what I call the big black mire. It felt unbearable being in this mortal body. The feeling of being trapped has been with me a long time, but I can usually deal with it. Lately has been an exception. Sometimes, I fear that I'll be swallowed by this heavy, dense, choking physical existence."

"Yesterday I tossed and turned restlessly in bed, trying to entice myself to get up. What pleasure could I pursue today? I asked myself. I could pig out at McDonald's on greasy high fat hamburgers. Maybe see how much food I could put away without getting sick. Not in the mood for that today. I didn't feel like spending the money anyhow. I could write an erotic story or poem and send it to some religious magazines. Not in the mood to be shocking. Besides, I reminded myself, live and let live. There was a time when you were religious. It served a purpose as it's serving a purpose for some people now."

"Maybe I can pump iron for a couple hours, increase my weights today, and see how far I can take it without pulling a muscle. I lifted weights yesterday. I could do a Star Trek marathon and watch every movie and all of the TV episodes I have taped. That would keep me going for about a week nonstop. I thought of other things. Nothing appealed to me. What's left?"

"I couldn't dare commit suicide. I know how I feel about that. From what I've read and heard, it isn't safe to die that way. It would surely lead to nothing but more problems, so that ruled self-annihilation out, which I doubt can be done anyway."

"I lay immobile for a time longer. I felt so heavy. The bed seemed to weigh a ton. So did I. I couldn't take it much more. Something has to give, I recall telling myself. I can't go on like this. Life is not meant to bear down on us like this. There has to be more than this suffering. There must be more. I asked for a new visitor. Then you showed up. I am not even that surprised you are so small. I am just grateful for a star to brighten up my dim sky. When you're desperate and about to fade into darkness, any light is welcome. The twinkle in your eye somehow gives me hope. Still, I have to admit that my intellect cannot be satisfied without at least a minimal inquiry. I know you told me not to doubt, and I will do my best. But please help me. I need to ask if you are real, Mr. Toozles?"

The little man looked at me kindly with the patience one would extend to a child. "Of course I'm real, Michael. I'm here, and we are having an intelligent conversation. I know your name, don't I?" he said, grinning. "I know lots of things about you and your kind, by the way. Back to being real. Of course, I'm real although maybe not quite like you, and don't ask me to go into that. I'm not in the mood for long philosophical talks today. Save that for your books and academic friends. Just enjoy me while I am here."

"So I'm not just seeing things? Please don't fade or disappear," I added quickly, recalling his earlier comment. "I don't doubt you; I just need a little assurance. Am I seeing things?"

"Things, no. A little man, yes," he replied with that twinkle in his eye. "You see me because you have good eyes, real good eyes, I might add."

He was speaking in a softer tone, moving closer to me. It felt strange. "Can't you tell your mind to take a snooze?" he said, tapping my leg. "It'll drive you crazy. I'm here. What more proof do you need? Actually, we are not alone," he said, waving his hand in the air, "but you are not ready to see anyone else today—at least not here. But you *are* ready to see someone else somewhere far from here. Are you in the mood for an adventure?"

"I could definitely use an adventure," I blurted out. Mr. Toozles jumped up and down, exclaiming, "I was hoping you'd say that. Grab your coat. Get ready. We're going on one. All you have to do is trust me and hang onto me. Think of our contact as a portal to where we are going. No matter what you see, don't let go of me. If you do, you'll be in for trouble, and it won't be fun—I guarantee you."

"Okay, so when do we leave?"

"Now is as good a time as any. Lie down on your bed and with your permission I am going to awaken your spirit to take you on a spirit journey."

"Permission granted," I said, looking forward to another spirit journey. They are all so different, and I learn so much from them. Moments later I was standing next to Mr. Toozles, my body peacefully resting on the bed.

"Take hold of my hand, Michael." The next thing I knew we were walking down a long winding road. The sky hung overcast with dark clouds. Trees swayed fiercely. We were caught in some kind of gale.

"The least you could have done was put in a request for fair weather," I said, pulling my hood down over my head with one hand while holding his hand with the other. I didn't even bother asking how I'd gotten into these clothes when the last I knew I was wearing a t-shirt and shorts.

"You think mind power and magic can do everything," he asked, motioning for me to make a left turn.

"Mind power and magic," I repeated. "So this is a magical journey. Where's the flying carpet? It sure would beat walking."

"They're all in use," he teased, picking up his pace, which turned out to be rather fast for someone so little.

"I'm sorry, Mr. Toozles. Please humor me. I try to be funny when I don't understand something."

"I know. Just keep up with me. I am so eager to get to the Marvel Mansion."

"Marvel Mansion. Sounds like an amusement park."

"Amusement park. I like that word. Could be something like that."

He began walking faster. I had difficulty keeping up with this little man, which I found to be very funny. How did he move so quickly? I was about to ask when a screeching huge bird of a form I'd never seen before let out a squawk so loud I nearly fell down. I looked up and it appeared to be less than twenty feet above our heads.

"Wingle," Mr. Toozles said. "Ignore it. It can't hurt you unless you look at it eye to eye. Then it can kill you."

"This is not a good day for dying," I said, moving closer to him. I reached for his hand. The bird continued screeching and squawking and pursuing us. I gripped his hand a little tighter. I wasn't about to let go in spite of his assurance that the wingle, or whatever the thing was, could not hurt me as long as I did not look at it. Minutes later the creature flew away.

"You can let go of my hand now. We should be free of pursuit the rest of the way, but get yourself geared up. We're about to trek uphill for the final part of this journey to the Marvel Mansion."

He wasn't exaggerating. Before I knew what had happened, a huge tower appeared from behind a mass of clouds high in the sky. The road we had been traveling suddenly became vertical. It made the streets of San Francisco look like a Sunday walk in the park. I noticed that he slowed down. I was grateful for that. There was no way I could trek up that big hill at the pace we had been going, second wind or not. It must have taken two more hours before the Marvel Mansion was in view.

I was relieved when at last I did catch sight of it. This was a lot of walking even if I was in my spirit body. Mr. Toozles had seemed preoccupied and hadn't spoken for a long time. Surely there would be someone else to talk to or at least some interesting things to see. Hopefully, not any more of those strange-looking wingles. When we approached the colossal mansion, a huge door opened.

"You'll be okay on your own inside the mansion," he said, winking.

"On my own." I felt fear stir in my stomach. "You mean you've brought me here to abandon me?"

"All are on their own in the Marvel Mansion," he said, unaffected by my emotionally charged tone of voice. "You'll thank me later, I promise you." He stepped inside the door and instantly disappeared.

At least he said later, I thought, hesitant whether to go inside or not. *Just who did this little man think he was bringing me all the way to some strange place only to abandon me? He didn't even tell me what to expect, the reason for coming, or when and if I'd ever get back to earth.*

I looked about. This couldn't be my own planet. It looked like it, but the bird was too strange-looking, and if it was earth, why did I have to hang onto this man who pulled me into his world, or at least into *some* world?

"Existential crisis," I said looking about frantically. "Still bored, Michael?" I asked, stepping closer to the entrance.

Moments later the door opened, and a beautiful blond-haired lady dressed in a pink chiffon robe stood before me. She wore a diamond tiara and moonstone ear rings.

"Come in, Michael," she said softly. "I have been waiting for you."

"Well, I guess I either go inside or I don't," I said aloud.

The lady nodded and smiled.

"What the heck," I said, "life's been unbearably boring. What's the worst that could happen?"

I could die, a little voice inside my head said.

"That could be an adventure too," I told the voice then quickly stepped inside.

I looked about. The room was grand. There seemed to be no end to the walls or huge pillars extending upward. I strained my eyesight reaching higher and higher. There was no ceiling in this room. There was no sky either. I looked about. Glass walls sparkled like diamonds. The floor was made out of sparkling jewels. Iridescent colors were designed in various geometric patterns.

"Is this heaven?" I asked. "Maybe I have died after all." But there were no St. Peter or guardian angel or departed relatives to greet me.

The lady led me to a corner to what looked like an entrance to a smaller room. The room was lit up by a purplish glow. There was a fragrance in the air that I found extremely pleasant and a little intoxicating.

"Please enter," she said softly.

I looked at her again and was spellbound by her beauty. Even her silky hair radiated like sparkling jewels. And that star-like twinkle in her eyes reminded me of Rosara.

She approached me and gently taking my hand, she led me to yet another chamber, smaller still. I could barely fit in. I had to duck my head to enter this other chamber. A pure rose fragrance permeated it. The entire room was done in pink.

Pink veils with star and moon designs were hanging about. Bouquets of roses were everywhere.

"Where am I? I asked.

"You are in the Chamber of Beauty," she said, leading me to a plush pink reclining chair.

"Chamber of Beauty," I whispered, taking in all of it.

She nodded. Then she was silent. What was I supposed to do? I couldn't keep from looking at her. I leaned my head back against the comfortable headrest and closed my eyes. I must have fallen asleep because when I awoke a time later, I had a strong feeling that some time had lapsed.

The beautiful lady was sitting in the pink recliner, looking at me.

"How do you feel?" she asked gently.

"Like I died and went to heaven."

"Why die to go there, Michael, lover of beauty?"

This was too much. For some reason I was overcome with a desire to cry. I struggled but could not keep the tears away. She took a pink silk handkerchief and wiped away my tears. The touch of her hand sent me reeling. I didn't want this to end.

"You haven't even told me your name," I asked.

"Here we do not take names."

"Here," I said, hoping I could keep crying just to feel her touching me.

"The Marvel Mansion," she replied so softly I could barely hear her. "This is a place where we are reminded of who we really are. You are a lover of beauty and a poet at heart, Michael. I love your poems."

"You've read my poems?"

Her face glowed and her radiance brightened.

"I have not read them. You recite them to me in dream time and on spirit visits. They are lovely and some are quite profound and even exquisite. Through your command of words and rhyme, you portray beauty and love. You evoke many qualities and feelings that need to be awakened in people."

"You are very kind to say that. Sometimes I think that we poets, dreamers, and artists are a dying race."

"Not at all. On the contrary, you poets, dreamers, and artists are going to make a comeback. You are going to help the numbed masses come back to the realization of who they truly are—children of Creator Source whose essence is divine and whose destiny is to be magic makers and dreamers capable of manifesting their hopes and dreams. Your art will help stir the fires in their souls and awaken soul senses and sensitivities that have been numbed and dormant far too long. It is time for beauty and passion to be in the eyes of every beholder and for love to be awakened in her fullness. Then humanity shall create a paradise and golden age such as you have not known in ages upon ages."

"I have had such thoughts at times, but they don't last when I look around me and see all of the chaos, materialism, greed, violence, pain, and destruction in the world."

She reached for my hand.

"I know," she said softly. "The good news is that I am going to help you have more beautiful, loving, and peaceful thoughts and experiences. This will help to create the beautiful world you have envisioned. You spoke of this new world and new earth in a poem that the ascended beings gave you many years ago."

"Yes, it's called 'Hear What We Say' and is one of my favorites. I got chills when I wrote it, and I get chills even now recalling the words."

"It came from the realms of pure love and light, Michael, and more will be forth coming. More ascended angelic and highly evolved beings will be visiting you and others like you. They have many gifts for you and will help you make the transition to the higher energies of ascension."

"Thank you. Your words and amazing presence fill me with love and hope."

"Good. You need to be filled with love and hope. Everyone does."

"Hope," I said softly, recalling another poem I wrote called "Hope." The last verse said this:
Close your eyes and listen softly
to a voice that is always near.
The lady's name is Hope.
Let her wipe away your tears.

"That is one of the things that Hope does," she said then kissed my cheek. I thought I would die right then and there. It felt better than any human touch I had known before. If she would only do it again! And then she did so. She looked at me with unconditional love and kindness as she gently stroked my hair. I enjoyed her soft touch a few moments and then spoke.

"How is this a place to remind us who we really are?" I asked.

"Not how. It just is. It all began back in your room. You were feeling rather despondent. I'm sorry for that, Michael, I truly am. It hurts me to see you suffer when I know that you are so much more than your suffering. It is I who sent Mr. Toozles to you. He owes me a few favors from a time back. So he brought you here to make a payment on his little debt to me."

"Where is this? Is this really a place?

"Of course. It is one of the many mansions that your beloved teacher Jesus spoke about when he said, 'In my Father's house are many mansions.' And no, you cannot find the marvel mansion in the phone book or on the Internet, but that makes it no less real. Mr. Toozles, this mansion, and I exist on a parallel world that co-exists alongside your own. Your perceptual abilities have to be tremendously heightened and your soul senses developed before you can perceive this realm and come here. Your guides and some earth teachers have been adjusting your energies and strengthening your perceptual abilities so that you can make contact with other realms and realities."

"I could not send Mr. Toozles to you until your soul-vision had expanded to the point that you could see and perceive him. Many dimensions exist simultaneously alongside your own. Many different realities are interspersed at any given point in time. However, only those whose extrasensory soul senses or pineal and pituitary glands awaken from their dormant slumbers and become activated, can attain the heightened perceptions and soul-vision required for the other realms and realities to become apparent and visible."

"Your extrasensory soul senses have been somewhat activated most of your life. It was part of your soul contract you made before you were born that the veil between worlds would be thinner for you than it is for the average person. You also agreed to pierce the veil to the point that visiting and being visited by other-worldly beings would become as natural and common to you as getting in your car and driving to a friend's house. However, you did not contract to be able to completely pierce the veil between the worlds. Were such to be the case, then your extremely sensitive temperament would make you open to so many intense powerful energies that your neural circuitry would blow up and you would go insane."

"I've always had a fear of madness."

"Not to worry or fear. You have been there and done that, as the saying goes. This happened once in Atlantis, on another world, and a few other times. You do not need to repeat that experience. You have learned how to shut the door when too many energies start to bombard you."

"Yes, I am aware of that. I ground myself by engaging in activities, such as hiking, gardening, cooking, singing, talking to my plants, meditating, and listening to music in addition to writing poems, songs, and psychology and self-help articles."

"When things get too intense, just ground yourself and come back to terra firma for a time. Come with me," she said, reaching for my hand.

I was intoxicated in her presence. The next thing I knew we were back out front. The glass walls seemed to be staring at me. This time I felt more at ease. The Marvel Mansion seemed even more beautiful even though I had seen so little of it. She led me to another door. The new chamber was the brightest I had ever seen. There were heart designs imprinted on the walls, and pictures hanging on the walls of smiling faces full of passion and hunger for lovemaking. They looked alive. I cowered, fearing something would happen.

"Have no fear," my female companion said. "I am here. You are safe. These pictures cannot come to life unless you give them life."

"How would I do that?"

"You wouldn't. Let's leave it at that."

"Why are we in this room?" I asked.

"Magic," she whispered, "to remind you that you are a great magic maker. Everyone is but most have forgotten how. The secret of magic is that you make magic with your thoughts. You can think anything into existence if you think enough, focus your intention, give it enough energy, and follow the intuitive urges and promptings that your guides and subconscious give you. You will be returning with Mr. Toozles soon. We will meet up with him in a few minutes."

"But I cannot leave," I pleaded. "I've just arrived. There is so much to see and explore. I want to see the entire Marvel Mansion."

"Not possible. You can only see certain things here. It would be a violation to look in on someone else's creations."

"You mean all of that back there was my creation?"

"It certainly was. Everything you know and see is your own creation. Your existential crisis is nothing but a particular creation you have fabricated. You feel bored and lonely because you think that magic and wonder are dead. They aren't if you believe they are alive. It has been a day of wonder, hasn't it?"

"Yes, it has been, I admit. I'm not feeling depressed like I was."

"I'm glad. Think on me when you go back, and I'll be there with you in your little lonely room. You get sad because most of the people on your world have forgotten who they are. Your senses and perceptions are capable of seeing and perceiving so much more than you can begin to realize. You are beginning to stretch your perceptual muscles and your soul-vision. You easily pick up the feelings of those around you. When you see people chasing after ephemeral delights and physical pleasure as though that is all there is to life, you lose focus. You get scared. You think the physical life is all there is to your being. You are more than a physical being. You can know and love yourself as well as other people in ways people do not conceive or imagine."

"Someone else told me that not long ago."

"That does not surprise me as repetition seems to be necessary before humans grasp what we are endeavoring to teach and show you. I am sure you have heard this many times and will again. Michael, I am here to tell you that you can journey to countless worlds and dimensions and visit with your soul family. Some are human while others are non-human. Everyone is ensouled with the star spark of love and life that connects all life and creation. The powers of your mind and spirit are limitless. Opening the doors to other realms and worlds is the beginning of claiming your power. The maneuvering of your consciousness and perceptual alteration is one means to help bring that about. It comes very easily for you."

"When you vocally as well as telepathically put out the call for a new visitor, your plea and intense energy darted out like a bright light. It made its way to the Marvel Mansion. I read your aura and soulprint and knew that you were ready for a visit here. That is why Mr. Toozles came to you."

"In actuality, Mr. Toozles and I are not new visitors. We are members of your soul family as you are ours. We often meet in dream time and on spirit star journeys. Although your personal life is not very fulfilled or happy, you have advanced enough spiritually that you have earned the right to become consciously acquainted with some of your other-worldly soul family. This will help to ease your loneliness and remind you that you and everyone are so much more than your ego can know or perceive."

"Mr. Toozles, along with your other fascinating visitors, showed you that there is more than what you perceive with your five senses. He came to lead you to the portals where other worlds exist. He brought you to this mansion, but you had to find what you needed to see. You found me and I found you. You followed your intuition. You did not look into the eyes of the wingle. Many would have done so just because they were told not to. You will never go astray if you follow your intuition."

"What you say feels right," I said, gently squeezing her hand. The next thing I knew we were back at the door.

Mr. Toozles met us there. "Did you have a good time, Michael?" he asked, with that twinkle in his eyes and a smile on his face.

"I had a delightful time with this lovely lady," I exclaimed.

"Good," he said, tapping me on the arm. "It is time to return to your world and your room."

"Do I really have to go back?" I pleaded.

"Yes, indeed. You were one of the more adamant ones. Eons ago you chose to know physical density in its entirety so your wish was granted. Now you are bored with your mortal human limitations. The good news is that you are opening up and awakening your soul senses. You are going to learn that you can function as a divine being, an interstellar being, and a human being all at once, for you are truly all of these—a holy trinity, three separate facets of the same monad. There need be no conflict or contradiction. You can be a god and a man. And even more," he said, winking at me. "Ye can even one day become a lord of yer own creation as a friend of mine recently told ye."

I immediately picked up on the language shift and lit up like a light bulb. "Nookles told me that. Even though I've come to accept such a possibility and outlandish notion, it still fascinates and haunts me at times."

"Only to your human self are such concepts outlandish. Your higher self totally understands and accepts them. Your human self will come around in time."

"That makes sense. So you are friends with Nookles?"

"Much more. We are like star brothers. We constantly meet each other all over the place. In a certain sense, you could say that we have mastered time, space, and even form."

"I can see how you two can relate. You are getting real deep on me now just like Nookles did."

"This is just the tip of the iceberg," he said, grinning.

"How do you master time, space, and form, if I may ask?"

"There are many ways to do so but of utmost importance is the realization that time and space are illusions. Form is too. Once you completely realize this truth you are in a position to shift your perceptions and substitute one illusion for another. If you believe in anything strongly enough, there is nothing that you cannot create. Look at your own life. You have some experience with this.

You believed in angels as a youngster. You had two angelic visits within two years. You believed and knew you would go to college. It happened when all odds and outer circumstances seemed to dictate otherwise. You can even heal your body of disease. If your faith is strong enough, you can substitute the illusion of wellness for disease, and your very molecules and physical body will respond to your beliefs."

"I have heard this before."

"You are destined to become fully human, fully alive. When this happens, you will merge with your higher self and ascend. Then, as a god you can be, do, and create anything on a far grander scale than you can now. This is something you and all mortals have yet to learn. Today you have experienced more of yourself. Any time you feel overwhelmed by physical life, you can come here. Your lady awaits you. She preserves your chamber of beauty and constantly sends love and thinks of you because she is part of you. She is also one of your muses who inspires your poetry which, I might add, is very beautiful and soulful. You only get bored when you think that physical life is a trap. It is only if you accept it as that. Today should have proven that you can go to many places that your people claim do not exist. Yet, we know they do, and you now know also, do you not?"

"Yes," I said softly. "Life is only dense and restricted on the third dimension if I think so. Today I have basked in beauty and love that I dream and write poems about. I am now convinced of its validity."

"Yes, the things you write about are real and the love you long for is real. Just take a little break from your everyday life and call out to us. We will respond, won't we?" Mr. Toozles said.

His lady companion agreed. "It is time to go, Michael."

The beautiful lady hugged me tightly. Her fragrance made me giddy and my knees wobbly. "Beloved Michael, think of me and I am always nigh," she whispered. "Never doubt this."

Mr. Toozles reached for my hand. "We have quite a journey back. Remember not to let my hand go outside this mansion." I waved at the lady who blew me a kiss. Mr. Toozles led me out the front door. We journeyed back down the hill. When we reached the bottom, he said that his task was done. He had paid his debt. He could go back to his own world. I wondered how many worlds exist and how many intersect. Then I saw the image of a star-filled sky and knew that there are countless worlds out there.

Moments later, I was back in my room. The depression had lifted.

"Wow," I exclaimed, rubbing my forehead and having visions of a beautiful woman and a pink chamber. I took a can of pop from the fridge. I noticed three bags of Christmas decorations lying on the floor. I took a big swig of Pepsi and then began taking the decorations out.

"It's time to decorate this apartment. Add some color and magic around this place." I hung up some tinsel. The next day I bought a string of 150 lights, the new ones that blink in several different ways. Later that night I looked at the lights a long time. Nookles would be proud of me. The wonders of technology. I looked some more then went to bed.

Soon I saw an image of the lovely lady. "Hello," I whispered.

"Hello, sweet one. I told you that if you think of me, soon I am nigh. The magic is not gone. It took quite a lot of magic to come up with all those blinking lights all in one little contraption. You people really are amazing."

"So are you," I said, lovely lady with no name."

"On your world you can call me Belle Etoile," she said, then disappeared.

"Beautiful star," I said, smiling. "French is truly the language of love."

CHAPTER SIXTEEN

HEAD TALK AND SPIRIT JOURNEYS

I often lie in bed at night and ponder the mysteries of the universe. I wonder if I'll ever have answers to the myriad of questions I constantly formulate. Sometimes I think of Rosara's beautiful teachings and wonder if it really is possible to merge with every soul on the planet. Could one human being even begin to grasp or be able to handle an experience of such intensity and magnitude? Rosara had informed me about a universal group soul-merging that takes place when two people come together to unite in a soul-sharing ritual.

If that is not enough to keep my mind active as I lie restless in bed, I wonder if it is possible, and what it would be like to merge with every being and living life form—not only on the earth but on other planets, worlds, and even other star systems, galaxies, and universes? What would it be like to merge with Creator lords or ladies and then finally the beloved Creator Source—or Sources if there is more than one of them?

Another thought that occurs to me is that we are probably already merging with others on many planes and dimensions even though we are not consciously aware of this. Some of the metaphysical books I've read speak about the multi-faceted soul. Perhaps aspects of our multi-faceted soul are having such experiences. Mystics speak about experiencing a joining and merging with all that is and the ecstatic blissful state this puts them in. I have been told that I am a multi-faceted soul. We probably all are as we move closer to ascension, but some of us are becoming more consciously aware of it.

Nookles had told me that he preferred the word *big soul* to multi-faceted. He said that as a big soul, I am learning how to take in more light from Creator Source and the big central sun. This enables me to tune into dimensions and realms not perceived by the average person. I can shift my consciousness to deeper and higher levels of awareness beyond the ordinary—where most people's awareness is focused. I can take in more light and energy from the higher self or *great self.* This contact with my soul gives me access to its vast wells of information, secrets, and wisdom. As a vessel, receptacle, and conduit for the more inclusive, wise *greater knowing* or I Am self, I am able to tune in and shed insight upon any question or concern that people have. Thus has my spiritual work and service taken on a whole new dimension. I consider myself far more a soul-reader, guide, and healer than a psychic although I do psychic readings as well.

These skills and abilities do not make me unique or special. They are inherent in everyone although they lie dormant in most people. We are each destined to merge with our souls and higher selves to attain cosmic consciousness and access *collective unconsciousness*, a phrase coined by psychiatrist Carl Jung. Once we make contact with the collective unconscious mind that links all humanity, we have access to any and all knowledge. Telepathy, mind and spirit talk, and psychic clairvoyance then become commonplace along with many other forms of communicating. Many of the great metaphysical teachers tell us that these so-called occult esoteric abilities were highly developed in the mystery schools of Egypt, Atlantis, Lemuria, and other civilizations.

An extremely difficult abusive childhood with much soul and emotional wounding is what pushed open some of these doors, leading me to the vast domain of the inner self and the soul. Trauma or intense grieving have been known to open the door to the psychic realm for some people who, otherwise, have had no prior paranormal experiences. Some people are born attuned to the spirit and psychic realms. Others become interested at some point in their lives and explore the deeper metaphysical spiritual realities. At an early age I began tuning into other realms and receiving various visits from different guides and beings from many realms and worlds. After my psychic training was completed in 1985, I began to receive visits from ascended masters, angels, and benevolent ETs.

My energy shifts when I am about to channel angelic beings, such as the Blessed Mother Mary, Kuan Yin, Mary Magdalene, archangels, Nostradamus, Saint Francis, Helen Keller, Sun Bear, Mother Teresa, Vilura of Venus, ascended masters St. Germain and Hilarion, and others, all of whom I have publicly channeled. When in the presence of these ascended beings, I am filled with tranquility, gentleness, and a sense of love and peace. This loving, healing energy will remain with me several days after the channeling. My energy and perceptions equally shift, and I am filled with serenity, peace, and love when I encounter other-worldly beings, such as Rosara, Nookles, Mr. Toozles, Belle Etoile, Dresda, and others whose stories and teachings are found in this book.

When I am about to receive a visit from a *being*, it is like I am shot with a blast of cosmic fire, and my entire being seems to expand. It's like the eyes of an immortal cosmic being are looking through mine and its thoughts and ideas come to me. As my perceptions shift and heighten, I can feel my vision expanding. The words I speak are mine and yet not mine.

I used to spend hours pondering and speculating on the myriad beings whose voices fill pages and pages of my notebooks. I even asked a few for proof of who they were and where they came from. They said the encounters were proof enough and informed me that their teachings were what mattered most. Now I no longer question them. Instead, I offer humble gratitude when they show up. Their messages are uplifting, provocative, humorous, soul-stirring, and even poetic at times. As long as they keep coming to me, I will keep writing books. They have promised never to abandon me. This and their inspiring, hopeful messages often deeply move my soul to tears. To have so many wonderful other-worldly friends means a lot to my inner child who has not completely healed from the lonely foster home years from age thirteen to eighteen.

Since our muses, angelic guides, and other beings dwell in the *no-time*, they are not limited to time and space as we know it. Actually, we are not limited to time or space either, but most of us don't know or realize it. To illustrate my point, I will share a personal story. The other-worldly lady named Rosara (See chapter 12) came to me many years ago and taught me about soul-sharing and soul-merging as it is experienced on her far distant world, Astellva. Although I originally met Rosara many years ago, on the morning of October 29, 2010, she showed up at a little cottage I rented for my annual solitary retreat at Mammoth Cave, Kentucky. This was a time for solitude, prayer, meditation, reading, hiking, and writing for me. I do not take the cave tours, and there are fewer people during that time of year.

The previous night, I felt my old childhood abandonment issues coming up since I had not heard from my publisher for several months regarding the publishing of this book, *God's Many Mansions*, which had been accepted the previous April. My inner child ranted and raved, fretted, huffed and puffed, feeling hurt and angry. I was so upset that I went to bed in tears.

I woke up to the smell of roses in the air. A gentle calm washed over me. Then, in my mind I saw these lovely deep eyes looking at me with compassion, kindness, and love.

"Rosara," I whispered.

"It is I, dearest Michael," she said gently. "I have felt your sadness. I am here to assure you that your fear is invalid. Your editor has not abandoned you. She is extremely busy. You will hear from her, and she will publish your book as promised. I want you to spend your last day here at this lovely wooded park reading some of your stories from *God's Many Mansions*. You will be reminded of their depth and beauty and the many useful teachings contained therein."

"You will be inspired as you bask in the memories and teachings of the many wonderful and wise teachers and friends you have made who do not live on your world. As you bask in nature on this lovely cool autumn day, breathe in the fresh air, look at the beautiful, colorful falling leaves and trees. Revel in the serenity and solitude of nature and be at peace with yourself. I blow you a kiss as I take my leave. Goodbye for now, beloved Michael."

After Rosara's comforting visit and messages, I enjoyed my final stay at Mammoth Cave. The next night I took out *God's Many Mansions* and began reading the stories. I relived a beautiful experience and visit I had with a special kind of faerie many years ago. Enjoy this story and the teachings!

One morning shortly after getting up, I heard someone giggle. The prickling of the hair on my neck announced that I was not alone. I looked around. Nobody was in sight. I walked to the window and looked out at the moon. It was a beautiful, white full moon, and it seemed to be smiling upon me.

"I guess, I ask too many questions, don't I?" I said, half thinking the moon might hear me.

Then I heard laughter, but when I looked around, nobody was in sight. "This is not fair," I said. "You have to show yourself."

The laughter continued. It was very girlish and playful. "Why do you keep laughing?" I asked.

"For good reasons I will get into in a few moments," the voice said, "but first I laugh because you are so amusing. You 'crack me up,' to use one of your mortal expressions."

That comment led me to believe I was about to have another visit from a non-earthly being. It had been awhile, and I was always fascinated by who might show up and what I might learn. So, I just went along with it.

"So, I crack you up. Please tell me why that is?"

"Your problem—well, it's not really a problem; it's actually part of an adventure you are having—is that your mind is constantly going ninety miles an hour trying to figure out the workings of the universe. That is quite a bit for one mere mortal to take on, don't you think?"

"Who is there?"

My gaze slowly turned to my reading chair in the corner of the bedroom. Sitting there was a small lady who seemed to enjoy watching me. She stared at me with an intensity I was not familiar with but which I found exciting and most welcome. Are you real or am I dreaming?" I asked.

She grinned and said in a softly girlish tone, "What do you think?"

I touched my knees, my arms, hands, and my face. I felt solid and tangible. No, I was not sleeping or dreaming.

"I don't know," I replied just to see where she would take this.

She frowned as though expressing disappointment—then burst into laughter again. Then, just as suddenly as she started, she stopped and gave me a serious look.

"If it makes you feel any better, you are not dreaming, and you are not imagining me—but I think you already know this. At least you should since I am not your first friendly visitor from another realm. I would think that by now you would be used to these adventures and visitors who are coming to you from outside dream time."

"You don't need the dream portal anymore, Michael. You have raised your vibrational energy levels and shifted your perceptions enough that we are able to step through time, so to speak, and come to you directly. Does this not make sense?"

"It does, but how can one really ever get used to such experiences?" My face turned a shade red. "Don't get me wrong. I do believe that these experiences are real, but I have my doubts at times. It's not the average everyday person who gets visited by beings from other realms."

"That is because you are not average, and you should never want to be. The mundane and ordinary bore you."

"That is true."

"If you recall, in the past few years you have done a lot of work on the inner planes—developing and stretching your psychic abilities and muscles. You had some very long, intense meditations which allowed your guides to adjust your energies and raise them to higher levels so you can perceive other realities and beings that co-exist with you. You also did some intense, powerful energy work with a few special teachers whom your guides brought to you. These were very important teachers for you."

"Yes, they are all very gifted people whom I love dearly. I am very grateful for all they taught me."

"Yes, they all contributed to the expansion of your being. This expansion is what opens portals to other realms and allows you to step through. You have always been open to some extent. Many children are open. Other people have periodic psychic breakthroughs where portals to other dimensions open. On the higher planes their guides are orchestrating and overseeing the process."

"All have guides and spirit helpers assigned to them to assist in many different ways. You have advanced spirits who are skilled at restructuring your DNA levels. Your very genetic makeup can be altered so that you, in essence, become endowed with spiritual powers and skills that most people do not develop. You have always been hungry for deeper learning, knowing, and experience, and your spirit teachers have helped alter your makeup. It's as simple as that. You are becoming more of a light being, and this allows your spirit to venture out, so to speak, and draw all kinds of experiences and beings to you."

"I know you have heard this before, but repetition is a constructive teaching tool as you know from being a teacher yourself. You could say that you are in a more expanded state when we visit you, but this is not a dream state or an imaginary one. Your perceptual muscles are constantly being stretched. If you cannot perceive something, then it cannot become real to you. All matter begins first as thought and perception in the mind. You must become aware of something for it to become real."

"Your subconscious mind is so much more than a storehouse for memories, unconscious fears, and the like. It is a much larger part of your soul than the conscious mind. It is connected to the super conscious or all-knowing God mind.

The more you get in touch with it, the more paranormal, psychic, and cosmic experiences you can have. Just as there are many layers and levels of perception and thought, so are there many levels of reality. Is this to your understanding?"

"I think so. At least you did not tell me I am crazy and should be in a mental institution."

"Funny you should mention mental institution. We'll get to that, but first things first. I know you are wondering who I am and so forth."

"Yes, because as sure as the grass is green, you are not from here. That is obvious."

"That is obvious," she repeated and laughed again. For a moment I saw an image of me in a mental institution laughing hysterically and going on until the nurses finally drugged me to shut me up. I immediately pushed the thought aside and asked her why she laughed so much.

"I laugh because it is in my nature to laugh. But there is more. I am a *frample,* which is a type of faerie who heals through laughter. I hope my presence is not too shocking or upsetting to you," she said, softly.

Then with great agility she quickly jumped off the chair and was standing next to me as she touched me on the nose. That gave me a feeling of light shock which was not painful but on the contrary felt good. I was filled with chills and tingles as she softly rubbed my face. Then I became embarrassed and blushed, filled with fascination for this woman whose twinkling eyes told me there is a lot more to her than I could ever imagine.

I wondered what her name was, where she was from, and her reason for coming to me. "So, if you are a faerie, then why don't you have pointed ears?" I ventured to ask.

She laughed. "Pardon the pun, but what's the *point*, and who says that all faeries have pointed ears?"

"Good point."

"Good pun, Michael. "You are a *punny* man."

"I can be."

"That is a good thing. Humor is very healing."

We looked at each other a long time in the silence. I was filled with a strange desire to laugh but refrained. To burst out cackling would surely make me look like someone not playing with a full deck—a true mental case.

"You are definitely a mental case," she said, bursting into laughter, "as are most people on the earth. You think too much, and you laugh too little. When you do laugh, most of you fake it, resigning yourself to restrained snickers while you look around to see who might be watching you. Rare is the person who lets go and laughs from the gut. That kind of person is a delightful sight to behold. Such playful, uninhibited hearty laughter is the kind you hear constantly where I come from. It is the reason good health and magic abound as well. So many mortals won't even let their bodies respond to stimuli in ways that feel natural to it. Your body knows that I am a laughing faerie, and it wants to laugh with me and help awaken your power."

"So are you here to encourage me to laugh?" I asked.

"That's about the size of it," she said, nodding her head. "Just like the earth saying 'Laughter is the best medicine.' But it's so much more. We framples know that in laughter lies a key to awakening inner reserves of unlimited power and resources. And I don't mean the abracadabra magic in your faerie tales, although some advanced sorcerers and yogis can and do perform such feats, as Jesus and other masters do. It's more mind magic and head talk that my kind do and some humans do as well. Laughter helps move the energies. It can stimulate and activate the higher chakras and power centers. The best and most powerful laughter are those hearty outbursts where you laugh so hard you cry."

"Well, I'm known to let out hearty outbursts of laughter— that is, when I am not crying."

"Laughter is wonderful, but don't forget that tears also have their gifts."

"I agree. I think of those animated cartoon characters who laugh heartily before they perform magical feats. Witches are also known for their howling laughter. I think of the Wicked

Witch of the West in *The Wizard of Oz* howling in hysterical laughter before she takes off after confronting Dorothy over the ruby slippers. I think of lunatics in mental asylums bursting into hysterical laughter. I recall a lady in a bus station who was cackling so loudly that people were staring at her and giving her uncomfortable looks. It did not deter her in the least."

"You're wondering if I'm some crazy little person escaped from an asylum, aren't you?" she asked, trying to conceal a giggle. "Well I'm not, if that makes you feel better. And by the way, some people in asylums are not crazy."

"Want to learn about the healing power of laughter? Listen to children. They are full of laughter. Most adults lose their childlike spontaneous ability for unrestrained laughter. They are too busy trying to be grown-ups, and grown-ups are supposed to be serious, not child-like."

"Why do you think children laugh so freely and naturally? Because they believe in magic. Magic and laughter go together. Speaking of cartoons and faerie tales, there are elements of truth in faerie tales, myths and legends."

"I believe that, too. I always get dreamy when I hear the song "Somewhere over the Rainbow" from *The Wizard of Oz*. No matter how drugged out Judy Garland may have been on stage, the audience always begged her to sing that song."

"It's a lovely song full of truth. Over the rainbow is where the dreams that you dare to dream really do come true because in that place you go beyond reason, logic, categorizing, and labeling. You open yourself to synchronicity and magic which are available to everyone. Over the rainbow is also where star children live on other worlds. The sweet song touches and stirs a deep ancient archetypal chord in the soul of humanity."

"Yes, it does. You know something—my Aunt Mary Lou would love you. She has always been a hearty laugher. She used to tease me, saying I needed to come down from the clouds and laugh more. My friends used to say I was in the clouds half the time and way too serious. Surely, there's nothing wrong with dreaming."

"Not at all," she said, touching my arm.

I trembled from excitement. Her touch was electrifying. I wondered if she was aware of her effect on me. Every cell in my body seemed to vibrate. What had I gotten myself into? What had loneliness gotten me into? Maybe I should tell her to leave this very moment and forget the encounter. But a part of me said, *No way, foolish fellow. You've attracted a genuine faerie lady to you. Take it easy. See where things go. I guess I could do that*, I told this voice in my head. *What's there to lose and who knows maybe there's something to gain.*

I tried to gain my composure. I looked at the little woman who was staring at me and asked, "Why do you feel so familiar?"

She gently touched my face.

"Your voice sounds familiar, but I can't place it or you. Of course, I can't. You said you are not from this world."

"Nonetheless, I am familiar to you," she said softly. "Michael, we have a mutual friend whom I'll speak about soon."

"Thank you," I said, feeling more relaxed, not even surprised she knew my name.

"Where to begin?" she said, looking away into the distance. "Well, to begin—I am certainly not from this part of town, as you would put it." She tossed her long brown hair back with her other hand. "Actually, I come from a place that would be translated to something like 'The Wishful Valley' in your language. It is a parallel world on another dimension co-existing alongside your own. Because of your tremendous curiosity and insatiable hunger for new and unusual experiences, this has made it easier for some of us to make contact with you. Let me just say that your soul or 'deeper self' is very good at sending out calls. By the way, all of your 'feny faces' are not discarnate spirits, Michael."

I was surprised. "You know about my 'feny faces'? I have not thought of them in a long time."

"Not only do I know about them, I *am* one of them."

"This is amazing. I guess I was not born totally crazy. Not only was I seeing dead people when I was very young, I was also seeing other beings from all over the place."

She laughed. "That is true and, of course, you were not born crazy. You were just born more *opened up*, shall we say than many people."

"So, do I ever get to visit your world?"

"Yes. We will go there one day."

"I can hardly wait. The Wishful Valley doesn't sound like a place I am familiar with."

"Yes and no. It's a place that you have dreamed about. To get there from here in your non-dreaming spirit body takes special power," she whispered in my ear.

My mind was reeling now. *If she did not come to the earth often and yet we somehow knew each other, then where had we met before?*

She smiled at me. I knew she was reading my thoughts, but I said nothing. I didn't want an answer to my question.

I sat up and gave her a closer look. She was about three feet tall and wore a light blue silk blouse and a white mini-skirt. A mini-skirt of all things! I could not help but notice her nicely shaped legs in spite of how short she was. My heart fluttered every time I looked into her bright glowing eyes.

Then to confirm that she was reading my mind, she began shifting her body to various modeling poses. She was so cute. I fell in love with her smiles and laughter. Soon I was laughing. My inhibitions were completely gone. If this constituted losing my sanity and being a lunatic, I no longer cared. I was having a great time.

She seemed to like that a lot. Her face glowed like twinkling stars when she watched me laugh. It had been a long time since I had seen that kind of uninhibited warm smile. How I missed it. I had never let go like that before, and here I was doing so in front of a virtual stranger—and a faerie at that!

It was far past time for something like that in my life. I was tired of people being so serious, myself included. How I wanted to clown around and enjoy the light side of life! I continued my antics, adding dancing and jumping around. I was reminded of my first grade teacher who used to dance and jump around with us, telling us to pretend we were animals. She even gave us permission to be fairies, nymphs, and elves. I carried on until I was so exhausted that I fell on the floor and had to stop.

The faerie's face glowed like a star. She applauded loudly. "Didn't you feel the energy stirring, Michael? Wasn't it a wonderful feeling, a healing magical feeling?"

"Yes."

Next, she performed some kind of exotic dance for me. I was mesmerized watching her. I didn't know that the body could move with such graceful finesse. I wondered if everyone on her world could dance like that. Watching her dance was like seeing an exquisite statue come to life. She was absolutely captivating.

Her eyes had a mischievous twinkle in them. I was not even surprised that she looked so funny, at least according to human standards. Nothing surprised me these days. I had had such an overdose of what I call the 'monster mundane' that I welcomed anything out of the ordinary. Especially if it led to an adventure!

Then for the first time, I noticed that her eyes were violet. Why hadn't I noticed that before? I'd always noticed every minute detail when it came to eyes.

"What are you thinking?" she asked, smiling brightly.

"I am wondering why you look different."

"I look different because I am a laughing faerie. You'd look similar if you were faerie born. We laughing fairies are recognized by our violet eyes."

"You are very beautiful," I ventured to say, hoping not to be too bold. "Can you tell me your name? In this world people exchange names when they meet."

"I am called Frazura," she said so softly I could barely hear her.

"My name is Michael Dennis as if you didn't already know."

"Nice to meet you," she said, bowing in a curtsy. She looked awkward, making it appear as though it were the first time she had done so. Then she repeated herself several times as though trying to get the gesture down pat. I couldn't help but laugh.

She did a couple more and then said, "To make you laugh while trying to perform a graceful curtsy is a bit of a challenge."

"I wasn't laughing at you. It's just funny watching you do that when your modeling poses and dancing were so elegant."

"Thank you, Michael. Don't laugh *at* me. Laugh *with* me. Wonderful things happen to people who laugh a lot. And now are you up for a little adventure?"

"Absolutely," I replied excitedly.

"Let us be on our way. We are going on a spirit journey similar to what you call astral travel. I need you to lie on your bed and get comfortable. Take some deep breaths. You will feel dizzy and disoriented, but it will soon pass."

I did as she asked. A golden glow began to encase her. She stepped closer until she was directly in front of me. Warmth filled me as her glow encased me. Frazura reached for my hand which I nervously and eagerly extended to her. Then she uttered some strange words and waved her hands into the air.

Within moments we vanished into thin air. It felt like we were flying. It felt like we were Peter Pan and Wendy. I looked upward and clouds were racing overhead. *Yes, we had to be flying*, I thought. This was similar to some of my flying dreams. It was so thrilling that I never wanted it to end. I'd had a few astral travel experiences but never anything like this.

A time later, we began to descend. I recognized the area. We were arriving at the mental institution where my Aunt Mary Lou had been living for the past ten years.

What was this? I thought that we were going to The Wishful Valley.

Frazura only smiled as though we were completely on schedule and nothing was awry. As we gently landed, I was taken back to childhood visits to this place. Aunt Mary Lou was one of the few people who I felt understood me. I never understood it when my family referred to her as sick. She seemed fine to me. We'd play games when I visited her. She'd tell me stories and say that the institution was the best place for her since no one but her *other* friends understood her. She said that her spirit friends kept her company and that one day I'd meet some of them.

Moments later, we were inside and walking down a narrow hallway. Soon we were inside Aunt Mary Lou's room. There she sat, pretty as ever, staring into space, but the moment we entered she noticed us and started laughing. Frazura and Aunt Mary Lou fell into what I call a *laughing embrace;* then they held hands and looked deeply into each other's eyes. Aunt Mary Lou and Frazura seemed to be mind-communicating or head-talking as Frazura said when referring to telepathy. A few moments later they burst into laughter—this time for a long time. Then out of nowhere, faces appeared and the laughing increased.

Soon there was an entire chorus of laughing people in this room with us. An older woman kissed Aunt Mary Lou on the cheek and laughed with her. I knew that these were spirits. I wondered if they saw me. Then I started laughing. Every face turned towards me. There must have been over twenty of them. They floated over and looked at me. I kept laughing, and none of them attempted to speak to me. They began laughing once more, and this lasted for quite some time.

They smiled at me in unison and then disappeared. Aunt Mary Lou walked over to me and took hold of my hands. Then she spoke to me in my head. *Michael, boy, I told you that you'd meet some of my friends one day. Do you remember?*

I do remember, I thought. She nodded and continued mentally talking to me.

I'm also delighted that you can understand head-talk now, Michael. I tried it with you many times years ago, but you weren't ready for it then although I believe a few times you actually grasped my thoughts. This head-talk, as we call telepathy, takes some time getting used to. Now it's the way I prefer communicating. If you work at it, in time you can learn to do it without being in your spirit body. I know that you talk to spirits, and they talk to you in your head. There are also people who can do it—maybe not a lot—but there are some, and you will meet some of these people when the time is right.

The nurses and orderlies are always trying to get me to attend events and to socialize more. They say I spend too much time alone. If they only knew that I am not alone at all. But I don't say anything to them, and you must not either. Don't speak of this to anyone. To speak about it could cause you some problems. You'd be very misunderstood and could even wind up here. For now it's best to keep this a secret.

Frazura did not explain how Aunt Mary Lou could see me, but I felt it had something to do with me being in my spirit body. Maybe seeing me in my spirit or astral body is not much different than seeing spirits. I often see and feel the presence of spirits, and mediumship is part of my psychic work. She nodded as though she had read my thoughts. A chill came over me, and I concluded that she had.

Frazura stood next to Aunt Mary Lou who kneeled down on her knees. She and Frazura placed their hands upon each other's head. I knew they were communicating but not with the spoken word. *We are participating in head-talk*, I mentally heard. I watched them in silence. They embraced heartily and kissed each other on both cheeks then wiped tears from each other's face. The scene was very moving. Then Frazura blew Aunt Mary Lou a kiss.

Frazura looked at me and I heard the words, "Michael, take my arm." I did so, and within moments we were floating in the air. We looked at the dancing clouds in the sky and birds flying overhead.

Frazura looked at me and said, "Now it's time for our final adventure for today. We are going to The Wishful Valley to check up on your dreams and wishes. Are you ready?"

I nodded. Moments later we were standing in the greenest valley with the lushest foliage that I'd ever seen. Dappled sunlight danced through the trees. Roses and flowers of many colors scented the air. It was exhilarating. I was filled with the compulsion to laugh and did so. It felt more natural than talking. I ran about wildly, my senses heightened. I looked upward and was enchanted by the glistening reflection on the leaves of a tree as I hugged it. The leaves began falling, each one became something different. Many were books. I caught the title of one: *Soul Whispers of Love.*

I somehow knew that this was a book of love poems I would write. A leaf fell onto my hand. It turned into a book so translucent that I could scarcely make out that it was a book. It became more substantial and written in the most beautiful calligraphy was the title: *The Wishful Valley.*

I opened it randomly and read, "The secret of creating anything you want is belief. All can manifest their hopes and dreams and learn how to engage in head-talk. Those outside The Wishful Valley will learn this great truth in time."

I was filled with exhilaration, and I wondered if Ant Mary Lou had visited The Wishful Valley and read the book. I started running in the glade and soon came upon a bubbling brook. Children appeared everywhere and hugged me. Then, one by one they began laughing. They held hands and a small boy reached for mine. We walked and skipped and laughed for what seemed hours. We played games. A time later they took leave, each waving and laughing as they strolled away until they disappeared into thin air. I closed my eyes and called Frazura's name. She instantly appeared.

"Weren't the children adorable?"

"Yes. I felt like Peter Pan in Never Never Land."

"More like forever land," she said, manifesting something delicious to eat. She winked at me. Michael, you can learn how to manifest anything you want while in your spirit body. You simply think, focus, visualize it strongly, and it appears out of nowhere. Physical manifestations, miracles, and magic usually take longer. Haven't you noticed that the things you concentrate and focus on have a way of making their way into your life?"

"Yes, we call it being in the flow with the Universal Law of Attraction. I have many wonderful books on the subject. I teach the Universal Law of Attraction and constantly apply the techniques in my own life."

"I like the phrase, 'the Universal Law of Attraction.' It's catchy and according to this law of attraction, your dreams and hopes come true. They can come from anyone, any place, or any circumstance. And yes, some people even win the lottery," she said, grinning. "That is a magic all of its own."

"My brother-in-law is constantly winning money playing scratch off. He believes and expects to win. I, on the other hand, never gamble. I don't believe it's wrong; I just am not drawn to it. Maybe I robbed a bank in another life and do not subconsciously feel that I am entitled to have money manifest via a scratch off card or playing dice, cards, or slot machines."

"Money most likely will never manifest for you in that manner. As you know, belief is the key to manifesting as you've heard many times and constantly teach others."

"Well, I could have some fun manifesting all types of goodies in my spirit body. Maybe you can teach me how sometime."

"I'll consider it," she replied, grinning. "Michael, remember that everyone can learn to maneuver in their spirit bodies and not just at night time during dream excursions. Spirit journeys can be taken at any time as this proves. I came to your room in the morning, and you were not sleeping. Spirit travel is wonderful. You will become more adept at it, and you might even teach this to some people one day. Those children and the spirits who visit your aunt are in their spirit bodies. Some live here, some halfway across your country and in other countries, and even on other worlds you do not know about. Some are what you call departed or discarnates."

"This is all so amazing."

"Life is about to become more amazing for you, Michael. Now it's time to get back. I can teach you how to come here anytime that you wish. In time I can show you how to bring others here when they are ready."

We held hands, laughed, and moments later I was back in my room. I looked about. Clouds had gathered overhead. It looked like it would rain any moment. I thought about the visit as I looked at the clouds and sighed in wonder. I had had a genuine encounter with a faerie. I would never be the same again!

CHAPTER SEVENTEEN

PERSONAL EXPERIENCES WITH TELEPATHY

I thought a lot about Frazura after our wonderful adventure. I kept thinking about the spirits in the institution. I thought of The Wishful Valley. I knew that I would never quite think the same way about mental institutions. I also thought a lot about head-talk, which was a central theme in my spirit journey with the faerie Frazura and had come up in other visits as well.

Since I was a young child, I have been able to sometimes sense things that people are thinking. Sometimes I hear actual words. However, I was too shy to ever mention anything or really try to develop it. To be honest, it kind of scared me, and I did not think my parents, my pastor, or the people at church would welcome such talk from a child who was trying to be a good Christian boy. So I kept quiet. Due to later experiences, I have come to the conclusion that telepathy is very real, and many of the metaphysical books I have read state that in ancient civilizations, such as Atlantis and Lemuria, telepathy was a commonly utilized form of communication.

I was able to validate that belief when I began my psychic development back in the mid-eighties. I had been training for about three years and was still not able to do full readings. I would pick up impressions, images, and bits of information, but I wanted to be able to do an entire psychic reading. So I named my intention and put it out to the universe. A week later the least likely person would become my teacher.

My own beloved friend and partner, Mary, had had some powerful psychic awakenings with a spiritual teacher at a weekend conference she attended. The man told her that she had been a high Initiate priestess in Ancient Egypt, and he had been her teacher. He said it would not take long to activate her higher chakras, energy centers, and her memories. After a few visits with the man, Mary's *third eye* was completely opened up. She became highly clairvoyant nearly overnight. She could also interpret complex, intricate dreams, and to my delightful surprise and pleasure, she was able to teach and train me.

We spent several hours a day for six weeks working intensely. We covered symbology, past lives, clairvoyance, mediumship, and other topics. After about a month Mary said, "Michael, we are going to work with telepathy. We did this in ancient Atlantis and Lemuria, and we still have that skill."

"Okay, I am game."

One day we meditated, and Mary told me to concentrate on an animal. "See only that animal in your mind, Michael. Feel its texture and see its color. Look into its eyes. Let no other thoughts or images enter your mind. You can do this. Concentrate."

I took a few deep breaths and tried to calm my mind. Then I conjured the image of a white Persian cat and tried to only see that image while utilizing my other senses to keep into focus the image that I had created of the cat.

Mary said, "I see white fur and am sensing a cat. Is this what you are concentrating on?"

"Yes," I said full of exuberance.

"Now I want you to concentrate on some person that you admire. See his/her features. What he/she is wearing. What he/she looks like and where he/she might be."

I concentrated on Mahatma Gandhi whom I admire.

A few moments later Mary said, "I am seeing a holy man. Is this who you concentrated upon?"

"Yes, I was thinking about Mahatma Gandhi."

"We need to relax a few moments," Mary said. "This takes a lot of energy, but as with everything else, it gets easier with practice."

A few minutes later she let out a small cry and a gasp. "What have you done to me, Michael? You have zapped me. There is a red flare in your aura. You are angry at someone."

I blushed and realized my thoughts had wandered. I was feeling hurt and anger towards a friend who recently stood me up, and he had blown me off when I confronted him. Mary said it was the anger that created a electrical type of current that zapped her.

"It felt like an electrical shock. You can't let your thoughts wander," she chided me. "This is very fragile and delicate work. Your concentration must not waver; it has to be impeccable."

I felt bad and was so frightened by the experience that I ended our telepathy work. I never forgot the experience and what potential it revealed, as well as how careful we must be when participating in telepathy exercises.

Many years later I have come to believe that many of us often engage in telepathy with various people even though we may be totally unconscious of it. We all know about some of these experiences. For example, we find ourselves thinking about a friend, and the phone rings or we receive a letter, card, email, text message, or a spontaneous visit from them. Or we call someone, and he/she says, "I was just thinking about you." I think that to some extent we are engaging in telepathy when we are working with the universal law of attraction.

When I want more psychic readings and parties, I put out my intention and constantly repeat, affirm, think about, and visualize it. Just the other day I said very clearly and concisely, "Spirit, please bring me a party for July."

A few minutes later the phone rang, and a lady booked a party. I think she may have subconsciously picked up on my request, and we tuned into each other's energy and connected on a deeper level. It is also possible that she had been thinking about having a party because she told me that she had. But it could have been my thoughts that she subconsciously picked up on that prodded her to make the phone call and book the party.

I smile when I recall the time I was going through the yellow pages while saying, "I need a new radio show." When I came to the Mix 94 radio ad, I felt something urge me to call them. The lady laughed after hearing that I was a psychic and responded that they had just said, "We need to get a psychic on our show." Perhaps, I was picking up on their thoughts.

I recall my mother telling me many years ago about the time that she wanted to take her mother to dinner at this new restaurant. My grandmother cordially thanked Mom and said, "I cannot go, because Billy is going to call tonight."

Sure enough that night Billy called Mamaw from Germany where he was stationed in the army. Was Mamaw receiving a psychic impression or premonition? Could Billy have unconsciously and telepathically told Mamaw that he was going to call her, and did she unconsciously pick up on his thoughts? I am not sure that we can ever totally know what all is going on when we have such experiences. I still find them fascinating all the same.

I think about the times when I am doing psychic readings, and I receive names of people, places, and relevant information that mean something to the client. I often hear names or initials and give messages about such people. Recently at a conference where I did a spirit guide channeling, I was talking to a lady in the audience. In my mind I heard the song "Bali Hai" from the musical *South Pacific*.

"How interesting," she said, "I just played that song on the piano yesterday."

"It is a very enchanting and spiritual, I might add, song which I happen to know so I sang it." Did some spirit guide (mine or hers) plant the thought of "Bali Hai" in my mind, or were the client and I engaging in some form of telepathy? Could such experiences be a combination of psychic occurrences? I think that is possible as I don't believe that psychic phenomena can be categorized so simply. Such unusual experiences continually convince me of the vast potential inherent in human beings.

I believe that the powers of the mind and psyche know no limits for the brave mavericks who dare to go where many dare not venture. Long live the mavericks and pioneers! May they constantly reach out to bolder frontiers and bring back knowledge and wisdom that improves and enriches the human condition and experience. I make a toast to them, one and all!

CHAPTER EIGHTEEN

THE SISTERS OF THE POINTED FLAME

My first contact with the Sisters of the Pointed Flame was at my friend Elaine's home some years ago. While giving me a tour of her house on the way to the basement, a voice in my head very distinctly said, "These women know very little about real power and true witchcraft."

I mentally asked the voice, *Who are you?*

I heard these words in response, "We are the Sisters of the Pointed Flame, and we have some important information to relay to the women who attend your friend's events. We also have some adventures for you and some things to teach you as well."

I told my friend Elaine what I had heard, and she giggled in glee and excitement. "Let's set up a channeling of the Sisters of the Pointed Flame. The basement will be the perfect place as I have my candles, crystals, oils, totems, and power objects there."

The channeling took place in Elaine's home at 7:30 p.m. on a Friday evening almost a month later. I sat in a blue cushioned straight back chair in the middle of the carpeted basement room. Some twenty eager exuberant women sat spread about on the floor on pillows, sofas, and love seats. Elaine lit white candles and incense. She saged, and there was drumming and chanting. She offered a prayer, and then she invoked the spirits of the four directions. She then invited the Sisters of the Pointed Flame to come through.

I closed my eyes (all my channelings are done with my eyes closed), took a few deep breaths and then burst into a strong accented voice. A spirit who called herself Fiorella spoke first. She said that we had had many lifetimes together and this is why our connection is so strong. In one past life we were sisters and white witches in Italy where we honored both God and Goddess—the masculine and the feminine aspects of divinity. We practiced sacred magical crafts and earth-based rituals. We also worked with healing, herbs, astrology, moon and sex magic, and divination.

Fiorella pointed out that the knowledge and secrets of magic, healing, power, and divination dwell in the soul. "You have to invoke and make contact with your soul, otherwise known as your higher power, higher self, or inner deeper self. People can serve as guides and mentors, but they are only authentic if they teach and help you to discover that all that you seek is inside you waiting to come forth. The answers to your questions reside within the sanctuary of your own soul."

"When you have connected with and touched your soul, then you are on your way to wholeness and enlightenment. Until that happens, you are constantly besieged by sadness, loneliness, and alienation. Emptiness tears at your heart. You can only know and experience completion when you merge with your own soul. To touch your soul, you must merge with the essence of the Great Mother Goddess through her moon deities."

After Fiorella gave her blessing and took departure, two more sisters, Pathena and Geliana spoke about making and evolving the magic and personal empowerment. They offered several techniques to enhance spiritual, psychic and intuitive awakening and then responded to questions. I came out of the trance to the sounds of the women who were amazed at what had occurred. As I was leaving, I looked up at the moon and felt a shiver run down my spine. The next day I listened to the tape of the channeling and wondered what it all meant.

I found myself constantly thinking about the Sisters of the Pointed Flame. I often felt their presence when I took walks, enjoying the autumn breeze and the gift of the beautiful, colorful leaf-changing display that the trees provided. I love the autumn season, and soon my second favorite holiday, Halloween, would be upon us.

I kept thinking about what Fiorella had said, "People can guide you and be your mentors, but they are only authentic if they teach and help you to discover that all that you seek is waiting inside you to come forth. The answers to your questions reside within the sanctuary of your own soul. When you have connected with and touched your own soul, then you are on your way to wholeness and enlightenment. Until that happens, you are constantly besieged by loneliness, sadness, and alienation. Emptiness tears at your heart. To touch your soul, you must merge with the essence of the Great Mother Goddess through her moon deities."

I was very drawn to and fascinated by the part about merging with the essence of the Great Mother Goddess through her moon deities. What did that exactly mean, and what all did it entail? I wondered. I certainly knew about sadness, loneliness, and feeling dead and empty inside.

A few days later I had a dream where I was sitting in the woods, looking at the full moon. It was so radiant and seemed to smile down upon me. Soon the image of Fiorella appeared. Then Pathena's. Then Geliana's.

"It is time for you to come to us outside dream time," they said in unison and then disappeared. I woke up with tears dripping down my face.

"I cannot bear the loneliness of being separated from my soul," I muttered, wiping away tears. "Great Mother, I invoke you. Please help me merge with my soul. I beg you." I recalled the dream near verbatim and took notes.

"It is time for you to come to us outside of dream time," they had said.

I was determined to contact the Sisters of the Pointed Flame. I would do whatever it took. My shaman psychotherapist, Elizabeth, often told me that sometimes you have to take risks even if everyone else advises you against it and it goes against your reasoning mind. If your heart and intuition guide you, then you are obliged to follow it, no matter how much you question or how scared you might be. I knew that my heart was guiding me to contact the Sisters, and the dream confirmed it.

A few nights later there was a beautiful, radiant full moon just like in my dream. I felt an urge to drive to a little wooded area behind a friend's house a few miles away where I often go to meditate and to get away from people. I arrived at 11:00 p.m. and walked to my usual spot beneath an oak tree. No one was there.

I greeted the trees and then stared at the moon. Minutes passed. An hour. Two hours. Although the crisp, autumn wind chilled my skin, I would not leave. The Sisters had said I was to come to them outside dream time. Well, I certainly was not dreaming. The chill on my skin, giving me quite a sting and bite, was as real and tangible as the oak tree I was leaning against. If I was to come to them outside dream time, then surely they would show me how. I would wait all night if I had to.

A few more minutes passed. I took in a few deep breaths, taking air in on the counts of seven, holding my breath for seven seconds, and then exhaling on the count of seven. I did this for a total of seven times. I was drawn to look at the moon. I began shifting my energy and perceptions and entered a deeper, more expanded frame of awareness. I felt light-headed, and my solar plexus began to tingle. I leaned back against the tree and took a few deep breaths. As strange as it sounds, I saw images of the Sisters of the Pointed Flame in the moon.

"She comes closer," they whispered. "Luminara, the moon deity, comes closer."

Sure enough, the moon somehow began drawing closer to me. It moved very slowly until it was right above the top tree branch.

Without knowing what words came out, I said "Thank you, Luminara," and whispered my gratitude several times, not taking my eyes away. I sensed that part of me could lose myself in its roundness. The moon descended more, and I could feel its powerful tug and pull at me.

It will soon be time to merge with the moon deity, that is, if you pass a very important test, a soft voice spoke in my mind.

The thought exhilarated me, for I had been waiting so long to find the seat of my soul, my passion. Warm swirls of energy moved through me, and my grip on this reality began to more feel more tenuous.

"It will soon be time to merge with the moon deity," I heard again. "Pass your test, and you will then be able to merge with the Great Mother moon via one of her deities. If that happens, you will experience ecstasy, enlightenment, and wholeness as you have never known before—at least in this lifetime. Your powers will be greatly magnified, and you will be in a position to become a mighty healer and guide to many people. If you succeed in your initiations, you will be able to come into the fullness of your power and have the opportunity to fulfill your destiny."

"I am scared," I said, feeling resistant. "I do not know what this entails and if I will survive."

"Of course, you will survive—even if you fail the test, Michael," Luminara said.

"What test?" I wanted to ask, but I sensed that now was not the time so I remained silent.

"Let me tell you something, child," Luminara continued. "You are very much a child of the mother moon. You have several primary astrological placements in the sun sign of Cancer which is ruled by the moon."

"I know. My sun, moon, and Venus placements are all in the sign of Cancer. That makes me an emotional basket case," I added, trying to insert some humor.

"I suppose you have been known to be a basket case a few times, as you put it, but, Michael, you possess many of the gifts the moon deities offer. Your lunar placements give you many of the feminine qualities of the goddess. You are extremely sensitive and intuitive to the point of being telepathic at times. You draw upon the lunar energies and power of the moon far more than you realize, as well as the energy and power of the sun to bring and keep you in lunar and solar balance."

"That makes sense to me. Not only do I have a lot of lunar placements in my astrology chart, I also have a lot of Leo placements, and Leo is ruled by the sun. My natal Mars, Uranus, Pluto, and Ascendant sign are all located in the fiery sign of Leo. All that fire gives me boundless energy, ambition, enthusiasm, stamina, and the ability to act upon caution or impulse depending upon the need or situation. If I don't walk or jog and do my daily exercises, I get all bent out of shape so to speak. I can really get fired up at times and have to control it. If not, I can become too intense to the point of being overbearing. This was often the case in my younger years. I've mellowed out quite a bit over the years, but I can still get very intense and fired up. I guess all of this fire has its place."

"Yes, as everything does. Without that masculine fiery energy, you would not accomplish and give material manifestation to your dreams and spiritual and artistic pursuits. The key is to walk the path of balance, and you must never again try to repress or shut down your feelings. They have a life of their own and are there for a reason. Your feelings have much to teach you, even the so-called negative or bad ones. It is totally unnatural for one of your emotional caliber to shut down their feelings. It does a lot of damage to the heart and emotional body and can account for a lot of the rage and pain you have carried with you for a long time. I know that you have tried to shut down emotionally on many occasions in the past when you have been hurt. To deny your passionate feelings is to deny your very nature. Your highly developed emotional body allows you to feel more deeply than most people."

"You are capable of experiencing depth and intimacy with people in intense and powerful ways, such as occurred in ancient Lemuria, Atlantis, Egypt, Peru, and other times in your history. You have very strong muse energy in your soul essence. This enables you to translate the emotions of the goddess into beautiful songs, poems, and stories that deeply move people and arouse and awaken their ancient soul knowing and greater nature."

"Your empathic nature allows you to go right to the heart of the soul past ego so that you can help others get more in contact with their inner selves and souls. You help awaken the power, love, and energy of the divine feminine, the goddess that is so much needed at this time. Michael, before you were born, you agreed to carry strong feminine goddess energy and essence into your soul for this particular incarnation. You have far more than the average person—male or female."

"You would never know that by looking at me."

"Things are seldom as they appear, and neither are people. Michael, the goddess feminine essence and energy radiate from your eyes."

"That is interesting. Women often tell me I have beautiful eyes, and they even comment on my long eye lashes. So are the eyes the window to the soul?"

"A window—let me say that there are many others. As I said, you came back in this lifetime to experience and express more of the totality of the goddess's love and energy. You have the ability to tap endless fountains and wells of creativity, passion, and nurturing. You will find that doing so will open your heart chakra in ways you never thought or believed possible. The more the heart chakra/energy love center is opened, the more love you will feel for yourself and others. You will experience a greater need to share with others the great outpouring of love that the Great Mother has to offer you."

"In a sense, your destiny is to become a type of universal mother to humanity. Your words, poems, and books will help heal sad and broken hearts and radiate light to dissipate the darkness that so enshrouds and imprisons the souls of so many people. Why do you think you can read people so easily? Women. Men. You are even able to pick up on the soul imprint and lessons needed for unborn children still in the womb. As a partial incarnation and expression of the Great Mother, you know on a soul level that everybody is your child, and you deeply love everyone as a mother unconditionally loves her child."

"This is why you did not choose to take a wife and have children in this lifetime. You agreed to become a type of universal mother to all humanity. This is why there are no strangers to you and why people are drawn to and find you. They send out the prayerful plea for help, and you receive their calls and telepathically reply and invite and welcome them. Thus does your phone constantly ring, and you are busy tending to the Great Mother's children."

"I feel speechless. I've been called lots of things but never a universal mother although I know about my maternal nurturing side. It *is* very strong even though I fight it at times. I find your comments very interesting and relevant. When I was a teacher, I used to frequently call the students, 'mes enfants,' my children, even the junior high, high school, and college students for I have taught all grades from kindergarten to college levels. To me they felt like my children. When they would impress me on an exam or win one of the French or Spanish games we'd play, I'd think or even say to myself I'm so proud of my child."

When I am in front of adult groups preparing to do a public class or channeling, I will say, "Come closer, my children. Gather closer. There is plenty of room and chairs up front. Nobody need sit in the back. I want you close to me."

Luminara chuckled. "Yes, you can be quite the mother hen, wanting the children nearby, to quote one of your earth sayings. Now you know why."

"So please tell me, is it possible for me to be a mother hen and a moon child? Even though I've always possessed a strong maternal nurturing tendency, I've also always attracted women who mother me."

"Of course, you can be a mother hen and a moon child. Mothers need to be mothered, too, and in your case I see that you have had several strong mother figures in your life."

"Yes, and they all kind of adopted me. Usually, I called them mom and that seemed to make them feel good. They were all very strong, successful, independent, and resourceful. They helped me learn to believe in myself and to find my own way."

"As any good mother does."

"Well, I guess I know why I never believed in the phrase, "The man in the moon."

Luminara laughed. "Nor is the moon made of green cheese."

"Yeah, I have no idea where that idea came from."

"You cannot eat the moon for nutrition like you can cheese, but you can absorb lunar energy to feed your soul. You have been doing it for many years. Many others do it as well, not consciously aware of what they are doing. Haven't you been filled with inspiration and bursts of creative energy after some of your moon gazing times?"

"Now that you mention it, yes, I have."

"The moon's love and passion have literally saturated your heart and soul many times, resulting in huge, powerful creative breakthroughs which led to some powerful soul-stirring writings, poems, and stories filled with emotion, depth, and passion."

"Wow."

"More to come as the saying goes. And no, you will not go crazy or wind up in a mental institution, Michael."

"Well, that's good to know."

"On a lighter note, my friend Leiah calls me mother Michael. She says that if it moves, I mother it, and if it doesn't move, then I worry about it. Maybe this can relate to a prophecy given to me in college when I was having a very hard time."

"One day at a spiritual meeting this young woman, Mona Madison, who had long black hair and very dark piercing eyes came up to me and said, 'Michael, you shall survive the dark times ahead. Your destiny is to become a minister of deliverance.' Chills went through me, and I never forgot her prophecy."

"What do you think? Can a person be a minister of deliverance? I'd never want to get the 'big head' or anything like that. Sometimes having substantial power can cause one to give into temptation, and it can lead to abuse and misuse of power."

"I say that you will not become a minister of deliverance but rather a *way-shower/shower of the way* to help lead people to their own paths of deliverance and liberation. In other words, you will help them discover their soul treasures and teach them that all that they seek is within. As a beloved master said, "The kingdom of God lies within.""

"I like how you put it. Mona's words didn't make sense in a way because I was so lost and imprisoned in my own darkness at that time of my life. And yet in a way her words did make sense somehow, and they gave me comfort. I have always felt I had an important mission in this life to help others."

"You do, and the darkness has been one of your best, albeit, most difficult teachers. You have befriended your darkness that, in turn, has helped you transmute much of your suffering to joy. Your darkness has led you to my light—the lunar light, which is as powerful as the solar light in its own unique ways. The moon deities honor all that you and other sensitive people have gone through. You have a special place in their heart, and they have a soft spot for all of you. It can be very challenging and difficult living on the earth with so much dissonance and density prevalent and rampant. It is a constant challenge not to allow the dissonant negative energies to bombard you, deplete you, and keep you depressed and pessimistic. The moon deities lovingly extend their light to you as the darkness does."

"This is one reason you come to this spot so often when the moon is full. You seek the power, energy, and solace that the moon offers you although you might not express it in these words. You have not consciously known that the moon has been regenerating you, but you know it subconsciously. This knowing is what brings you back here. You have always been a moongazer, as well as stargazer. You are always deeply affected by the energy and power of the full moon and during other cycles of the moon as well. You know that I am speaking the truth. On a soul level, you know about your affinity to the moon, and you ache to take in more of her powerful loving essence and energy."

"Just as the sun is a living vital entity and energy source of its own, so is the moon. Her consciousness is far more advanced than most humans can begin to fathom. Her depth, understanding, and power propel her to express and experience her essence in her lunar children. No, she is not alive or aware in the sense that people are. The truth is that she is more alive. She is also aware of her connection to the souls that embody more of her essence."

"All have both lunar and solar essence, or they could not live in a dualistic world of polarity where sun rules by day, and the moon rules by night, as the saying goes. You, Michael, happen to possess more lunar essence than the average person. This means that you are a deeply spiritual person capable of feeling and experiencing the hurts, pains, joys, and successes of everyone because in that sense you are a cosmic lunar being connected to everyone just as a mother has a strong connection to her children. To hurt a child is to hurt a mother because the child has been borne of her and is part of her. To hurt a mother is also to hurt her children because they are part of each other."

"That is very interesting. I recall a psychic telling me many years ago that when my father abused and hurt my mother, he also battered and abused me. She said that was how connected and close to my mother that I was/am. That always haunted me, and in my soul I knew it somehow made sense. I used to cry, and it felt like my heart was breaking when my father would hurt her. I so much wanted to heal her. I even aspired to become a psychiatrist because I thought that would give me the ability to save my mother. I later learned that we can't save or heal anyone, except ourselves. Still I was obsessed with my mother, and I was extremely sensitive to her energy and vulnerable to her feelings and moods. What you are saying makes a lot of sense."

"Michael, you have come to know so much. You have come to feel so much. Yes, you have tried to shut down and block your deep feelings because they can be so intense to the point of frightening or overwhelming you. But you have always known that you can't really erase or efface them. They are a part of you. You have made a lot of progress in your search and your growth, Michael. You have had many unique experiences that have stretched your spiritual muscles to the limits, let me say. You have been taking in the moon's energy and power all of your life because your soul vibration is very lunar due to your sun, moon, and Venus astrological placements all being placed in the sign of Cancer. The moon or lunar placement is very important in determining the emotional and feeling nature."

"Your moon placement in its natural sign of Cancer makes you much more sensitive and receptive to lunar energies, feelings, and moods than the average person. It gives you special and powerful abilities to connect with people on many different levels. Not only have you been able to attract powerful, resourceful, and loving women to nurture and help you, you have also been able to step through the corridors of time and space to make contact with other members of your soul family on other worlds and dimensions."

"Your own beloved spirit muse, Dresda, is a powerful moon goddess who befriended you many years ago. She watches over you and walks with you on many pathways on many planes and dimensions. She takes you to places deep in your soul. She teaches you the laws of the universe that most mortals do not comprehend. She helps you to make magic and create what you need on the third dimensional mundane level while you pursue your writing, spiritual and healing goals, and dreams. She shows and teaches you that anything is possible. How many times has your telephone rung with clients booking appointments when you talked to her or after you had spent hours working on your poetry, books, stories, and other writings? She always rewards you for putting in the sacred time and labor."

"As an adept magic maker and telepath, Dresda helps drum up business for you from people who need your services and are drawn to what you have to offer. It is not by chance that your phone is constantly ringing. Dresda is the best agent you could ever have. She constantly promotes you and your psychic and spiritual work. Is this to your understanding?"

"Oh yes. Dresda constantly promises me that as long as I continually write and remain faithful to my writing dream, my telephone will ring and I'll have what I need on a daily basis.

She has not let me down a single time. Of course, I do my part to market and promote myself. With the help of Dresda, my website, phone listing, advertising, and word of mouth, I am busy but not to the point that I cannot write and promote my books. If I had a regular full-time job, there is no way I could accomplish my goals. I feel very blessed, but I also feel that I have earned the title of entrepreneur. I do put in the time, as the saying goes."

"Yes, you do and your beloved Dresda is always there for you. She is a moon goddess, a sister of my own heart and soul. I bow to her and salute her light, which is very bright, and her eternal love and devotion to you. She inspires your writing. With a moon goddess as your muse and inspiration, your internal creative life is always rich, fertile, and very active. With Dresda so much a part of your life, how can you not embody the lunar goddess energy of the moon?"

"I am aware that your heart has been deeply wounded in many life times. Your struggles are part of your learning and evolving—you have chosen this. In actuality, all of this pain has served to open your soul and heart to take in even more love and passion. This heightened sensitivity that you possess, along with a tremendous receptivity to lunar energy, has helped to open your heart to the point that it is now time for you to know and experience much more of the moon's power and energy in ways you never imagined or believed possible."

"However, I must tell you that this assimilation must take place in phases after a series of tests. The Mother Moon goddess wishes that you dance and merge with the moon deities. As a matter of fact, you shall soon have the opportunity to do that with a very powerful moon deity named Lunara; however, first, you must pass a test with the Sisters of the Pointed Flame, a test that I am not at liberty to share with you. I will say that if you listen to your heart instead of your mind and do not hold back, you shall pass all your tests".

"Should you pass your test with Lunara, then your soul-light will brighten immensely, and your spiritual, psychic, and healing powers will be incredibly enhanced. You will be able to awaken in many women and men the eternal, feminine goddess energy that can bring polarity balance and healing to humanity and help lead you to your long-awaited ascension. It is time for the rift between the masculine and feminine to heal. Men and women are gods and goddesses in the making. It is the core of who they truly are beyond ego entrapments and appearances. The gods and goddesses need to acknowledge and celebrate each other's magic and power. The time is approaching for them to unite. It is time for separation to cease and oneness to guide and rule. It is time for paradise to be restored upon the earth once more. You and others have a role in creating this golden age."

"But you shall only be worthy and in a position to fulfill your destiny if you pass your tests. The first test is to successfully merge with the Sisters of the Pointed Flame. Then you will be able to take in enough power and energy to be able to attempt to merge with Lunara. I know this is a lot to absorb and may sound strange, but I also know that part of you knows I am speaking the truth. This is because you have had many lifetimes as a female where you honored, served, preserved, and taught the ways of the goddess and the moon mother."

"You have also been up here with me and other moon deities, and part of your soul visits us in dream time and on spirit journeys. As you know from your studies, the entire soul never incarnates into a physical human form. To bring in the entire soul energy and essence would create too much light. The body could not absorb it, and it would destroy your human form. Does this make sense?"

"Yes, as far out as it seems, what you are saying feels right."

"Yes, it *feels* right. That is a key word as feelings are so much a part of who you are. You always feel truth when it resonates to your soul. Always trust your feelings and intuition, Michael, and you will never go astray. I have spoken enough for now," Luminara said. Then her image faded.

For several minutes I was left alone with the sounds of the crickets and other night critters and creatures. What was I to do now? Was I supposed to go home and write down this experience? Something told me I was not done here tonight, so I just closed my eyes and thought about some of the things Luminara, the moon deity, had said.

A short time later I opened my eyes, and a golden light emanated from the moon. It was so bright it almost hurt my eyes. Nonetheless something compelled me to keep looking at this beautiful full moon. Then the strangest thing happened. The moon actually descended more, and its pull became stronger and more enticing.

"Hear the sweet moon song, and let it lure your spirit into her loving maternal embrace," a voice sang softly. Then a haunting melody was sung in a high soprano voice. The song gave me chills and brought tears to my eyes.

"I am afraid," I said, still resisting, having no idea of what this *merging* entailed.

I closed my eyes and looked away. I felt that if I stared at the moon much longer I would disappear. But I could not keep my eyes away from the moon for long. Finally, something snapped inside me, melting the resistance, and I surrendered.

"Okay, encircle, enfold me, and do whatever you need to do," I said in resignation. I also intuitively sensed that the moon deity and the Sisters of the Pointed Flame meant me no harm. They had reason for my being here. It involved my connection with the power of the moon, I reminded myself. I stared at the beautiful moon a few more minutes, intense energy passing from me to the moon and back into me. Moments later, the moon descended until it was directly in front of me. It encircled me three times and then assumed the most beautiful radiant silver light I had ever seen. I was bedazzled, having never beheld so much bright light before. I wondered what Abraham felt when he beheld the burning light, and Yahweh told him not to look directly for such radiance could indeed blind him. It seemed that the light should blind me, but it did not. It was not even hot or warm."

I continued to stare. I seemed to be in some kind of trance. I didn't want this moment to end. Then the glow dimmed, and a beautiful woman's face looked at me from the moon. She had tiny stars in her eyes. I gasped, feeling awe and wonder. Then she spoke.

"I am one of the moon deities who has overseen your growth and development in this lifetime. As Luminara pointed out, my name is Lunara, or at least that is one of the names that I go by when I am on the moon. Little brother, you have much power inside you waiting to come to the light of day to heal and serve humanity and the goddess," Lunara said, looking me deeply in the eyes. "Many people fear the power of the eternal feminine. Many men are threatened by women who are empowered by their lunar feminine essence, which gives them much magic and power."

"Many fear being consumed or absorbed and this accounts for so many witch hunts, burnings, and the patriarchal attempts to control and subdue women—especially the powerful ones. Although much progress has been made, there is still a long way to go. You have no reason to fear or to worry. I have no desire to absorb your spirit. Few have the strength or courage to resist my pull. Please tell me how may I serve you?"

"Luminara told me that I would have the opportunity to merge with you, but first I have to merge with the Sisters of the Pointed Flame. The Sisters told me said I can never be whole until I touch my soul and to touch my soul I had to merge with the essence of the Great Mother Moon Goddess via the moon deities. I believe you can help me."

"Anyone who has had the honor of associating with that sisterhood is never truly satisfied in the world of form. The sisters are part of my soul family, as well as yours. You have known them in many past lives. They are only part mortal—just as you are only part mortal. To look into their eyes is like beholding the light in the center of a flame. The spark of light in the center of the flame is the light that does not burn but rather illuminates the soul, allowing one to see everything as it truly is. If you pass your test with them, it is they who will help you merge with me. If you merge with them, they can bring you to me. To take in my essence and light without preparation and intermediaries would be very dangerous."

"I seek the power and the light of the flame and to merge with you into wholeness. I will gladly merge with them as well to gain enough strength and power so that I may attempt to merge with you. I will do this, for I seek complete emotional expression, liberation, and wholeness more than anything."

"Michael, little moon child, you speak with much conviction and determination. Yet, I must remind you that you have no idea of the powerful tugs the moon can have over you. Few can withstand her more powerful intense tugs, and I assure you that your test with the Sisters of the Pointed Flame will not be an easy one. Failure is more likely than success. Nonetheless, it is possible for your wish to be granted."

"Listen carefully to me and be sure to do the following things: On the night of the next full moon, light a white candle and let it burn for twelve hours. Then light another one the next day for twelve more hours. Do so until you have burned twelve candles for twelve days. On the thirteenth day at precisely fifteen minutes before midnight, place all the candles in a crystal circle with a pentagram in the center and your special crystal wand next to it. Then light all of the candles. Move your eyes from one candle to the next in a clockwise manner. Then close your eyes and speak the words:

'Far beyond this world where power transcends names,
I invoke the Sisters of the Pointed Flame.'"

"Chant the words until you build a momentum so strong
that the words merge into one tone. Chant the sacred words
until the clock strikes twelve and then open your eyes. What
you will see and what happens next will depend upon the will
of the Sisters."

"They can manifest in their fiery ethereal flame essence,
take on other forms, or just mentally communicate with you. It
depends upon their will and the manner in which they wish to
merge with you."

"Hopefully, they will consider me worthy of merging."

"You are worthy. I can assure you of that. The test will be
whether you can take in all the energy they have to give you.
Let me rephrase this. It is not a matter of can you take in their
energy, but the question is *will you*? That will determine the
next step on your journey."

"I wish I could consult with an oracle. If I knew the
outcome, that might make the test less difficult. Are you an
oracle, Lunara?"

"Yes, I am, but there are certain things that even the oracles
are not allowed to reveal. Besides, there is always the element
of free will constantly in motion. The future is never totally set
in stone no matter how many prophets, seers, or oracles insist
otherwise."

"That makes sense, Lunara. Thank you very much," I said,
waving as the moon began moving away.

Quickly, I jerked.

"Was I out there?" I asked, pointing at the full moon.

I felt light-headed and strange. Suddenly the thought
occurred to me to write down the instructions. I took pen and
paper out of my backpack, turned on my flashlight, and wrote
down what the moon deity had told me. I made my way back
to my car, drove home, then undressed, and crawled into bed.

The next few days I did as Lunara instructed. Finally the long awaited thirteenth day arrived. I listened to my return of the goddess songs. Finally the time passed, and it was time for the ritual. I placed the candles in the crystal circle with a pentagram in the center and my crystal wand next to it. Then I lit the candles. I moved my eyes from one candle to the next in a clockwise manner and then as instructed, I closed them and spoke the words:

"Far beyond this world where power transcends names,

I invoke the Sisters of the Pointed Flame."

There was utter dead silence. The breeze had died. Still there was a chill in the air as I continued to speak the words. I spoke with as much conviction as I could. If the Sisters were able to be reached, I would reach them. I continued speaking the words.

Moments later the huge grandfather clock chimed. It was the midnight hour. I slowly opened my eyes. All was pitch black. The candles had gone out. I looked out the window and saw a faint glow outside. Had some enchantment come upon me?

"What is your will, Sisters of the Pointed Flame?" I asked, softly.

The image of a flame appeared in front of my face. The heat drew closer and closer. Sweat droplets formed and trickled from my face onto my neck. I did not move a finger. The image of a woman appeared in the flame. Her eyes burned through my entire being, awakening the kundalini fire within. I felt like I was melting. Still, I would not move. The heat grew more intense. I felt that my soul and every cell in my body was afire. The most amazing thing was that I felt no pain. Trembling with delight, I let out a cry. The glow did not diminish.

Suddenly, I was drawn to the window, and the brightest light I had ever seen began to shine. I heard a faint whisper telling me to go to the window. The moon was the brightest I had ever seen—a full moon. How could this be when the last full moon was a mere thirteen days ago? As my curiosity mounted, swirling sparks of red flame darted from the moon, encircling it—then disappearing inside it.

I experienced warmth in my solar plexus which created a tingling sensation in my stomach. It was like the flames were playing with my energy. I wanted to dance. I began moving and swaying my arms in swirling motions. Several flames danced in front of me—then encircled me. They did not burn me even though they touched me in many areas. I danced with the flames for a long time. Then suddenly the bright glow began dissipating. Within moments the brightness had vanished.

I felt a loneliness I had never experienced before. It was a deep yearning for something beyond my comprehension. I actually longed to become a flame and dance around the moon with the Sisters. In that instant, I somehow knew that the moon was a true living entity, full of power, and there are entities living there. Not only did I believe what the moon deities said, but my heart and soul told me this was true.

Then quicker than thought, my spirit left my body, and I was flying and spinning around the moon. My mind and thoughts were intact. I was overwhelmed with awe and wonder. Never in my wildest dreams had I imagined that I could encircle the moon, not even in my astral spirit body. Spinning faster and faster, the moon sent waves of ecstasy all through me.

How can this be? I thought. *How can I feel when I don't even have a body now?*

Then I heard the following words in my mind, *You are in the heart of the flame of your soul. Let your thoughts pass so your spirit can join with us. This is the first joining that must take place before you complete the merging and wholeness and take in power from our great moon mother. Before this can happen, you must become the flame of your true light essence. This can only occur when you release your thoughts and attachments to your individual self. You must completely surrender and fully take in our essence. You must temporarily lose yourself, and let the moon's lunar intensity engulf you. You must temporarily allow us to absorb you.*

So much energy poured into me that I felt like I could absorb or swallow the very moon itself if I wanted to. The flame of my soul spark soared faster and faster. It first made its way to Fiorella whose form had transformed into the brightest, most scintillating flame I had ever seen. At lightning speed we crashed into each other. Then our soul flame seemed to shatter into a million pieces. The soul pieces took a life of their own and sought out each other, dancing and merging into oneness. Although they were separate pieces, they were also parts of us. Each set of sparks darted off and flew around the moon. The sheer force of their dynamic movement felt like some kind of seismic or volcanic explosion. Waves and surges of pleasant sensations I had never felt before flooded my entire being, filling me with so much pleasure and ecstasy that I thought my very heart was going to burst.

Then the flames suddenly disappeared and all became darkness.

"No," I cried out. "It is the light I seek, not the darkness."

"The darkness is but the other face of the moon," a soft voice said, and then the images of Pathena and Geliana appeared superimposed on two different halves of the moon. They were encased in a radiant golden glow.

"Come drink of our sweet essence," Pathena said. "Be submerged in our love and take in our light. Come to us and rest upon the daughters of the Great Mother moon's bosom. You are in your spirit light body, Michael. Will yourself, and you will instantly be here. Come to us, moon child, and take in our love!"

The next thing I knew I was standing in front of them. Their glow was so bright that I had to look away. "You must lose yourself in our radiance," Pathena said softly. "Surrender and fully let go!"

They reached out and took me by the hands. Energy poured through my entire being, saturating me with jolting currents of what felt like liquid electricity and light. It was not painful. On the contrary, the sensations were exhilarating. My spirit body jerked and the more of their light I took in, the more pleasure poured through me. It was not a sexual sensation; it was like my entire being was plugged into an electrical outlet with Pathena and Geliana as the generators of these intense electrifying currents of ecstasy. It was like every cell, molecule, and atom in my spirit body were copulating in a sea of cosmic bliss. I managed to look at my arms and hands, and they glowed so brightly that I had to look away. It was difficult to behold so much light.

"Release your thoughts and come closer," Geliana said. "Become the flame of your true light essence and merge with us. Come closer and embrace us," she whispered, slowly moving her hand up my left arm. Pathena did the same thing with my right one. The tingling, tickling sensation increased. Their gentle touch sent surges of more pleasurable currents that filled my entire being. My kundalini fires seemed to be completely activated and ignited. My soul was ablaze. My brain seemed to be on fire, and what surprised me was that the heat did not burn me. I felt like a 1000 watt light bulb or a giant generator. It was like I had enough power pouring through me to light up an entire planet.

Then suddenly they both withdrew their hands and stepped back. "It is time to fully surrender and let go, Michael. Completely release your ego and humanity and merge into your divinity. Step fully into the light!"

At that moment, their luminosity brightened even more, if such is possible, and their image shifted until they had transformed into a golden ball of light. I jerked and stepped back, astonished at what was happening. Then something even stranger happened. My image radiated from the ball of light and looked out at me.

"It is time to join," a voice said that sounded exactly like my voice. "It is time to join your higher self. We are one! Step inside the heart of the ball of light and become one with yourself. Become one with everyone. Become one with God. Transcend your ego. Dissolve the wave of your lesser being, and become the ocean of your Greater Being. Michael, dare to become All That Is!"

"This is too much," I cried out, gasping. I cannot lose myself in myself. I can't be absorbed by my own self. It is too frightening and makes no sense to me."

My image in the moon faded and disappeared, and then the images of Pathena and Geliana returned.

"This was not supposed to make sense," Pathena said. "The truth is that you possess no *self*. In reality you, me, your higher self, the moon deities, the moon mother, and all life are one. We are myriad expressions of Creator Source who wishes to know itself fully and intimately through countless expressions. Here the ego is temporarily tossed aside to allow joining with the greater self—that which is joined to all life and whose essence is Light."

"You are right," I said, desperately. "For a moment I guess I forgot that."

"You were not supposed to nor did you have to forget the truth of who you really are," Geliana added. "Your fear and your ego have once again kept you from experiencing your true and complete self. They have kept you from the light which absorbs all ignorance and individuality and all sense of separation. They have stolen your bliss. You have failed your test, Michael."

There was a loud swish and suddenly I was back in my body in my room.

"No!" I cried out. "Take me back! I have to go back. I must merge with the Sisters of the Pointed Flame. Please take me back."

I was filled with immense sadness and despair. I had come so close to becoming one with the Sisters. I knew they sent me back because I had not completely released my thoughts and attachment to my ego and mortal human self. I had allowed fear to prevent me from becoming the flame of my light essence. Although I had no idea how to do that, I instinctively knew that my inner self knew exactly what it was doing, and my ego and fear had blocked it.

"To come so close—then to look away," I chided myself.

"I'm sorry," I said, softly, looking at the moon. "It was too beautiful, too wonderful. I've never before experienced anything so marvelous. Please give me another chance. I will get beyond my thoughts and release them all. I will become the flame. I will surrender my individuality to experience my greater being and yours. I want to merge with you, my sisters, with all of you and the moon deities and the great moon mother and all of life."

Nothing transpired. I knew they were gone and might never come back. I felt like part of me was gone, like my soul was gone. I knew I would never be able to look at a flame again without yearning for the sisters and the merging of our soul-light flame.

"That will be the price for holding back," I said aloud. I slowly undressed then crawled into bed.

When I woke up at noon the next day, I was still disoriented and felt a touch of vertigo when I tried to get up. My solar plexus was still warm. I slowly got out of bed and looked at the window.

"Was it real?" I asked, lost in the dazzling glow of the full moon.

It was very real, a voice in my head said. *The Sisters of the Pointed Flame did come to you last night. They took you on a spirit journey with them to the moon, and it was a bright full moon even though the last full moon was but thirteen days ago. You must recall that the Sisters are master adepts. They can slow down or speed up time. Michael, you almost merged with them but not completely. It was so exhilarating, and you have never known such euphoric rapture.*

"Yes, but I blocked it. I know I could have experienced even more rapture and wholeness."

That is true. There are no words to explain what it was like. You may have the opportunity to complete your merging another time, Michael. Until that time you will have your memories. We helped you touch your soul, even if only for a few moments. It only takes one such moment to give you the strength to get through any trial and tribulation and to deal with the limitations and restrictions that are a part of being human. Your destiny has changed. You will come into the fullness of many of your powers. Until then we take our leave and give you our love and blessings.

There was a shift in my energy, and I knew that the Sisters had taken their leave. I also knew that I would spend a lot of time thinking about, reliving, and trying to figure out what had happened that day in the woods and back in my apartment whenever I looked out at the full moon. I smiled and reminded myself that things are not as they appear. There is no way that the mortal mind can comprehend or know all of the secrets of the universe and the soul. Mystery and awe are a part of life, and if we had everything figured out, there would be no adventures. And I *live* for adventures!

I was fascinated by this experience and ached to have more understanding. Luminara had told me that I would become a type of universal mother for humanity. That would be no easy task to say the least. I think of beautiful souls like Mother Teresa and wonder from what internal spiritual fountains she derived her strength, hope, and faith *when the going got tough*, as the saying goes. She was probably such an advanced soul that she was never bound by human attachments or desires, but surely there were moments when she doubted, when her spirit was weary, and when she questioned her destiny.

What tests and inner conflicts, struggles and dark nights do such holy souls have to endure to be worthy to do the work they wish to do? I had two important tests. I did not get to take the second one because I failed the first. The first had been to merge with the Sisters of the Pointed Flame. I had allowed fear and ego attachment to end that powerful exchange of energy with my higher self and whatever else was going on that I might never be able to fully comprehend or figure out.

My soul gave me a gentle recognition that I had failed similar tests before. I recall a couple of times when my kundalini energy began to surge and pour through my chakras. It felt like liquid fire was going through me, baptizing, cleansing, and stimulating every cell, atom, and molecule of my being. It was like I was merging in a sea of bliss with all that is, with the creative forces of the universe, and with the souls of every human being and every other life form as well. The pleasure and energy moved through me with such a rampage and force that I allowed fear to interfere, and I blocked the energy. I let my fear block the energy from making its way to my crown chakra so I could meld into cosmic union and bliss.

Now that I had failed to complete my merging with the Sisters of the Pointed Flame, I had set my soul evolution back. *How* far I did not care to ponder or even attempt to ask or dare think about.

Yet, a little voice in my soul said, *Be not distressed. There is always another turn. Another try. Another attempt to get it right. To breathe in and become pure love and bliss. To merge with all life.*

I tried to make sense of the words. My babbling mind did not make much sense of it. I tried to envision a world of peace, harmony, and happiness—a world where men and women unite, embrace, empower each other, celebrate life, and remember part of the I Am divine presence—a world where magic, awe, and wonder delight the soul every day.

In the upcoming days, I reread the copious notes I took of my experience with the Sisters of the Pointed Flame and the two moon deities. My heart sank as I was forced to see that I had once more blocked the higher energies of ecstasy and bliss when they wanted nothing more than to purge me of my mortal dross and to envelop me in the loving embrace of the infinite Great Cosmic Mother's love and energy. I read two paragraphs over and over so many times that I had them memorized, for they both haunted me and ignited a small spark of hope that I would be given another chance to redeem myself.

Paragraph one:

Should you pass your test with Lunara, then your soul-light will brighten immensely, and your spiritual, psychic, and healing powers will be incredibly enhanced. You will be able to awaken in many women and men the eternal, feminine goddess energy that can bring polarity balance and healing to humanity and help lead you to your long-awaited ascension.

Paragraph two:

But you shall only be worthy and in a position to fulfill your grand destiny if you pass your tests. The first test is to successfully merge with the Sisters of the Pointed Flame. Then you will be able to take in enough power and energy to be able to attempt to merge with Lunara. I know this is a lot to absorb at once and may sound very strange, but I also know that part of you knows I am speaking the truth. This is because you have had many lifetimes as a female where you honored, served, preserved, and taught the ways of the goddess and the moon mother. You have also been up here with me, Luminara, and other moon deities, and part of your soul visits us in dream time and on spirit journeys.

I know that I shall recall and try to figure out that experience with the Sisters of the Pointed Flame and the moon deities. Hopefully, one day I shall be given a second chance at passing the tests that I failed for there is a part of me that has a tendency to shut down when I fail a major test. I sometimes allow my ego to fall into fear mode. I close the door, so to speak, such as I closed the door to further experiments with telepathy for a long time after a bad experience with my teacher Mary.

I sense that the moon deities and the goddess herself have need of me, and I believe that the door to the divine feminine will open to me again. If much of my soul essence is of the divine feminine as was pointed out to me, how can I ever be happy or satisfied until I allow myself to express and fully be who I truly am? How can anyone be happy or satisfied until doing likewise?

In the meantime I try to keep my sense of humor. I think and hear the words and tune of that famous song "Fly Me to the Moon" sung and recorded by such celebrities as Frank Sinatra, Nat King Cole, Tony Bennett, Johnny Mathis, Andy Williams, and others.

Fly me to the moon.

Let me play among those stars.

Let me see what spring is like on Jupiter or Mars.

I read that John Glenn (who landed on the moon in that historic 1969 world history-making moment) and Neil Armstrong were fond of that song as well, and I could see why. Quincy Jones presented platinum copies of "Fly Me to the Moon" to John Glenn and Neil Armstrong. Sinatra's version of the song was a hit and was played by the astronauts of Apollo 10 on their lunar orbital mission. I read that it was also played on the moon itself by the Apollo 11 astronaut, Buzz Aldrin. Astronauts Aldrin and Neil Armstrong were the first humans to land on the moon. Sinatra performed the song in the 1969 TV show "Sinatra" and dedicated it to the Apollo astronauts who made the impossible possible.

It occurred to me that perhaps the composer of this beloved song was a very evolved soul, albeit it perhaps unconsciously, and was offering a beautiful gift via this song that is sung and loved by so many people to the point that is has become a classic.

It makes me think of other songs where the moon is mentioned in songs, such as "Moon River" and "Shine on Harvest Moon." In the old Lynn Anderson song "I Never Promised You a Rose Garden," she says in one line "I could sing you a tune or promise you the moon." It's as though a chord in the human soul and psyche is touched when the moon is mentioned and the beauty and power of this loving entity somehow makes its way and moves through us all and reminds us all of the need for passionate feelings, emotions, and love.

I think of Shirley MaClaine's book, *Out on a Limb*, where she supposedly engages in astral travel and soars to the moon. I don't know if she claims to have seen or met any moon beings or entities. I don't think she talks about that in her book. But who knows—maybe she did. And isn't it interesting that in the metaphysical circles we say that it is the silver cord that connects the soul to the body. The silver cord stretches and can extend itself to long distances when we astral travel. If it can take someone to the moon without its breaking, I guess it is pretty resilient and long, I might add. They say that when the cord severs, we then die. I find the words *silver cord* interesting because silver is a *feminine* energy and vibration *connecting* us to the Great Mother and her fertility and creativity that brings life into the world.

I am convinced that the moon deities can fly me to the moon if I pass the tests again.

As I was typing this story, I paused to take a lunch break. I removed the big jar of white pike fish from the fridge and was immediately drawn to the product name label. It was titled "Mother."

"Of all the days for me to eat white pike fish and notice that label!" I said aloud. I smiled and thought of the moon deities as I enjoyed my lunch.

CHAPTER NINETEEN

A MAGICAL KALI PENDANT AND A

SHAMANIC HEALING

This shamanic healing experience took place several years ago. It began with my acquisition of a Kali pendant in a local Cincinnati, Ohio, New Age store where I worked part time. The moment I saw the pendant of Kali, the Hindu goddess of death and rebirth, creativity and destruction, I was instantly taken with the pendant. It seemed to be calling out to me. Several people picked up the pendant and looked at it, but nobody bought it. I now know that I was meant to have it. I kept thinking of the goddess Kali and the pendant.

Kali's archetypal symbolism has universal implications, and I can personally relate to this goddess of destruction and radical transformation. Kali is said to be beyond names. She cuts through *maya* (illusion) or false consciousness and ignorance that enslave people. I had read that Kali can help rid us of unhealthy attachments. I had also read that we must be careful what we request from her because powerful, no-nonsense Kali is known to rip attachments from us. She can help bring death to the illusory self-centered attachments of ego.

I could not get Kali out of my mind. I am convinced that things happen for reasons. There were some lessons that my soul and guides were endeavoring to impart to me, and I had the feeling that this Kali pendant had something to do with them. To ease my mind, a few days later I went to the store on my day off and told the owner, Terry, about the pendant and how drawn to it I was.

"Well, Michael dear, you should have it by all means," she said in her sweet charming voice. She took the pendant out of the glass case and gently hung it over my neck. "And you don't owe me anything. It's a little gift for all the help you have given me in the store."

As I wore my Kali pendant the next few days, I kept repeating the words *death*, *rebirth*, and *transformation* over and over. It was like a chant in my mind that would not stop. I began to have strong feelings that it was again time for me to undergo a symbolic death or deaths to *rip* some unhealthy attachments from my life. Rip is a strong term—one that I associate with Kali. I have heard that we create our own reality by our thoughts and actions. Perhaps my dwelling on thoughts of a partial death of my ego as a path toward spiritual transformation is what attracted the following experiences to me.

The first big *rip* came when my sweetheart dumped me. Needless to say, I was very upset as no doubt all lovers are when such a bomb has been hurled upon them. I cried and grieved for a few weeks. Then the pain dissipated to the point that I could move on, despite the emptiness and loneliness I still felt.

"This was your doing, Kali," I said, holding the pendant tightly. "You knew this relationship wasn't good for me, so you just ripped it out of my life." Looking back, I see that the death of the relationship was a necessary step in my growth. It had been slowly deTerryorating for several months while I was trying to convince myself that things were not so bad. The more I thought about it, the more I realized that I had settled for much less than I truly desired in a relationship. I also realized that I had begun to resent the way I was being treated. In retrospect, we often realize that the ending of a relationship turns out to be positive—something that we needed.

Life was less chaotic with few emotional upheavals for awhile as I was still recuperating from the breakup. About three weeks later, I began touching the pendant again and calling out Kali's name.

I felt like Aladdin rubbing the lamp as I repeated the words, "Death, rebirth, transformation."

This continued for a few days.

"Are you sure you want to go through another death so soon?" Terry said when I told her what was going on.

"When it rains, it pours," I replied. "Bring it on. I might as well get these symbolic deaths over with."

The next day I received a letter from the public school system, regarding my position as a substitute teacher. In the letter the principal of one of the high schools said that I had allowed several students to run around in the hallway and did not maintain classroom control. At the bottom was his request that I not be assigned to his school anymore.

My first reaction was one of anger and hurt. "You jerk!" I yelled as though he were there. "What do you know about my teaching abilities? I have one bad day, and you toss me. How about all the things I did for your students? I helped them write their English papers, tutored them in French and Spanish, encouraged them to go to college, and listened to their problems."

After getting my anger out, I took a few deep breaths and saw the image of Kali in my mind.

"This was *your* doing, wasn't it?" I yelled, banging my fist in the air.

After all my energy was spent on that rampage, I felt the urge to meditate. Alone in the quiet, I began to think about that school. Working with inner city kids was draining and difficult for my sensitive temperament. I came home exhausted every time I worked at that school.

"So you've ripped another unhealthy attachment out of my life, Kali. Gee thanks." I said with a little resentfulness but then with gladness. "You'd think I'd had enough of that school when I taught there full-time four years ago. It was time to move on. Kali took away my attachment to that school. She helped create the circumstances to allow what needed to happen.

Again, I realized that something that I initially resented turned out to be a needed experience for me. Sure, it's natural to feel loss when things like this happen; however, like the unhappy relationship, here was another situation where something I was hanging onto turned out to be something I needed to let go of. With a little help from Kali, I was removed from that school.

I threw the principal's letter in the trash and said, "There are lots of better schools than his." Another loss. Another death.

I could feel myself becoming lighter. "I wonder what my next death will be?" I asked as I went to bed that night.

The following week passed without any losses. I was glad. I didn't want any more for while. The next week I found myself holding the Kali pendant again and chanting those words, "Death, rebirth, transformation."

"Something is up," I told Terry at the crystal shop the next day. "I can feel it in the air."

"Something is definitely up with me," she replied, looking pale and distressed. "I am a mess, Michael. I promised myself that next week I would give up my twenty year cigarette habit. I'm going to be a royal witch, replace the 'w' with a 'b' and you have it. If I will ever find out who my friends are, it will be during this time. I become a monster when I don't smoke."

I felt sympathy for Terry. I had been through similar experiences, struggling with over-eating and other issues.

That evening I called Terry, "How you holding up?"

"I'm smoking like a chimney like this is the last day of my life. As a matter of fact, it feels like it is. I'm a raging monster. I guess you could say that my inner child is furious because I am making her give up the cigs."

I tried to be there for Terry. On her second day of not smoking, she asked me to run the store while she stayed at home and had a little breakdown. I worked at the shop then called her after closing.

"How are you holding up, Terry?"

"Not very well. As a matter of fact, I can barely hold myself up. I can't hold onto anything. My head hurts. My hands are sweating, and I think I'm going insane."

I offered what consolation and encouragement I could and tried to assure her that this would pass—this was part of the detoxification that her body was going through.

I concluded saying, "Terry, I'm praying and thinking of you. I'm here for you. I know you will get through this."

Then in my mind I saw the image of a big feather fanning the air around Terry. Somehow I felt that if she fanned the air around her with a big feather, this would somehow dissipate the negative chaotic energy which surrounded her.

"Now, how do I know this?" I asked myself. "Where in the world did that idea come from?" I concluded I had been reading too much Carlos Castenada lately. Yet the image of the feather persisted, and I had a strong feeling that Terry would benefit by carrying out a feather ritual.

"I'm going bonkers," I said as I dialed her number. "The little men in white coats may as well come after me and take me to the nuthouse," I said. Then I told Terry what I had been instructed to do.

"I trust you, Michael. I know that spirit works with you, and who is to say that unorthodox practices don't have their place and can't be useful? I'm desperate. I'll do whatever you say. I'll be over in about a half hour.

I looked at my bedroom wall where I had three large red feathers hanging beside a dream catcher and other Native American paraphernalia. The sociologist and anthropologist in me likes to have things around to remind me of the cultures that fascinate me. Can they be of benefit in shamanistic rituals? I think so and try to keep an open mind as I am deeply interested in shamanism. Every time I read Joseph Campbell, Carlos Castenada, and other books on shamanism, something rings true in my soul, activating some deep innate knowing within me.

With that in mind, I carried out the feather ritual. I smudged the room with sage and sweetgrass. I lit three green candles because green is a healing color. I called upon the healing spirit helpers and guides and gave a prayer of gratitude. I did some shamanistic breathing on Terry and touched some various points on her head and forehead. She said my hands became very hot, and she could feel energy being passed. When we were done, she said the headache was not entirely gone, but it was much better. I gave her one of the red feathers and told her to do some deep breathing when she felt the pain return and to fan the air around her with the feather. She thanked me and kissed me on the cheek.

I also gave her a piece of tree bark I had acquired from a big sycamore tree. When I had hugged the tree, the small piece of bark literally fell into my hands. My friend Elizabeth said it was a gift from the tree. I told Terry to hold the bark against her solar plexus and call upon her healing spirits to circulate the energy and to help ease her pain. She could also light sage and give herself some smoke baths to help clear negative energy. Terry called three days later and said the headaches were completely gone, and she was doing much better with her battle against cigarette smoking.

"I'm no longer a bit_ _h. I'm even nice to be around."

"I'm proud of you," I said, giving Terry a hug.

I thought a lot about goddesses and gods after those experiences. I read one of my favorite psychology books, *Goddesses in Every Woman,* by Jungian Psychotherapist, Jean Shinoda Bolen M.D. She says there are goddesses in every woman, and the more complex a woman is, the more goddesses are active within her. Since I believe we experience lifetimes as male and female, it would seem to me that there is no reason there cannot be goddesses active in men, as well as gods active in women. I know that Dr. Bolen is speaking in metaphorical terminology when discussing and exploring these archetypal mythological beings. She calls these powerful influential forces within "inner patterns." She introduces those patterns in the guise of archetypal goddesses or personality types. Reading her books, *Goddesses in Every Woman* and *Gods in Every Man,* helped me understand many of the psychological and archetypal forces and energies active in the psyche and personality.

For example, I strongly relate to Aphrodite, the goddess of love, beauty, and sensuality. I also strongly identify and relate to Hermes or Mercury, messenger of the gods and god of speech. Hermes personifies quickness of movement, agility with words, and easy flowing communication. I especially relate to Dionysus, god of wine and ecstasy, mystic, lover, and wanderer. Dionysus was close to nature and women; the mystical and feminine domain is very familiar to him. When I need help in any area of my life, I often invoke these beings and have discovered that help appears. By acknowledging the qualities, strengths, and power of these gods and goddesses, archetypal beings, or inner patterns, I am able to understand myself better and make more progress on my soul journey back home to Creator Source.

I no longer need a Kali pendant, Venus love oil, tree bark, feathers, gemstones, crystals, or other objects to stir and activate the energies representative of the particular gods, goddesses, and archetypes. I respect and honor those people who are drawn to amulets, talismans, and other powerful or healing objects. If these items awaken and stir the creative healing fires within an individual, then they serve their purpose. For that reason alone, they are beneficial and have their place.

CHAPTER TWENTY

A SORCERESS REPAYS AN OLD DEBT

I visited Terry a few days later. I told her that I felt I could now directly connect with the spirit and energy of Kali when I needed help in uprooting and ridding myself of any unhealthy attachments. We visited awhile until some customers came in. Then I went to the back room and read my book *The Teachings of Don Juan-A Yaqui Way of Knowledge* by Carlos Castenada.

After finishing the chapter, I laid the book on the table and closed my eyes. I drifted off into some kind of reverie and soon beheld the image of a tall, muscular, bronze Indian. Although he was older, his face showed few wrinkles. I was immediately drawn to the gray feather in his long, thick black hair, silver star earrings, beaded red cotton shirt, and the beautiful heart-shaped jade necklace on a thick silver chain that rested over his heart chakra. He wore blue jeans and a black leather belt with a turquoise-embedded silver buckle. Tall brown suede leather laced moccasins completed his look. He exuded strength, power, and wisdom as his dark piercing eyes studied me. I gasped in surprise.

The shock brought me back to ordinary awareness, but his image remained in my mind as though he was standing physically next to me. The next thing I knew, he *was* standing in front of me. For some reason I felt no fear.

"Who are you?" I asked him.

"I am called Chief Arrow Heart, a spirit shaman who comes from spirit dreamlands where we sometimes meet. If you think about it, you will recall that many of your visitors come to you in dreams, reveries, or meditations. When you wake up, some of them are still there. This is because you are a dreamwalker. You walk in dream and spirit time and meet with friends from many planes of existence. Then you invite them to come to your day world out there," he said, pointing a few feet away. "Because you are an adept dreamwalker, dreams serve as a portal for beings from many realms and dimensions to come to you. Is this to your understanding?"

"I think so, and I have heard this before. Thank you for coming. May I ask why you are here outside dreamtime?"

"All life is played and lived in dreamtime, young spiritual warrior. Just like your childhood nursery rhyme says, 'Row, row, row boat gently down stream. Merrily. Life is but a dream.' It just appears that life on the third dimensional earth plane is more real than dreams. Such is not true at all, but then such is true. Because you live on a dualistic world, there is a place for paradox where things that seem to contradict each other can actually complement each other and exist side by side. Let me just say that Chief Arrow heart has stepped from one dream into another. It is easy for him to do so and for you as well since you are becoming more of your *big self,* as I like to refer to the total and complete person."

"I like to think so. One thing for certain is that my mind and perceptions have stretched and expanded, and I've had some very interesting *other-worldly* visitors."

Arrow heart let out a hearty laugh. "More on the way, as saying goes. Let's get on with why I am here today in this spiritual place where energy is powerful and good. This is a good healing place for you, and you also earn a few dollars to help pay bills," he snickered. "I am here to share a very powerful vision."

"Michael, you are coming closer to the time when you carry out your big mission to earth family near and far. You are a very old soul and wounded healer who has been through a lot. Your darkness and despair have led you to your powerful inner world and soul. Your calling, mission, and primary purpose in this lifetime is to be a servant of Great Spirit and humanity. You will attain and then help others to attain spiritual awakening and personal liberation. You will teach other people how to heal their hearts after you heal your own."

"Before you are ready to begin your humanitarian mission, your heart must be fully opened. There is a big blockage in here," he said, gently tapping my heart.

"Yes, I've heard that my heart chakra has some blockages. This is not new information."

"New information is that your heart not only has blockages, but it is not all there."

Needless to say, I was rather stunned and startled by such a remark.

"I'm not sure what you mean. How can the heart not all be there?"

"I am not referring to your physical heart but rather your etheric one. You know that you possess an etheric and spirit body, as well as a physical one. There is the spirit counterpart of the physical body in which there is as much, if not more, activity occurring. Adept sorcerers and sorceresses can damage the soul and spirit body, which in turn can harm the physical body and lead to illness or in extreme cases, death. This is a well-known occurrence in certain voodoo practices

"I think that makes sense."

"Of course it does. Have you not had this big emptiness inside you all of your life?"

"Yes. For a long time I've had the feeling that some woman I had loved with all of my heart betrayed me in a past life. I have always felt that is partly why I have never been able to completely trust women."

"That is true, but there is more than one woman who hurt you and caused big heartaches and blockages."

"I'm not surprised," I said, feeling sadness wash over me. "I've had some heartaches in this lifetime, as well—recently too, so I am not surprised that you would show up at this time. I know that I am not completely over the breakup with my lover. I have been reliving many of our good times in my mind. I am experiencing a terrible time missing my lover. I find myself wanting to make a phone call although my mind tells me that such is futile because the relationship is over."

Chief Arrow Heart gave me a look of compassion and kindness that showed he understood my sadness. We were quiet a few moments. Then he spoke again. "Michael, I want you to get an arrowhead and place it on your heart. I can use this object to render you some healing." Then, as though sensing something, Terry came back and greeted me.

"Hey, Terry, have you got an arrowhead?"

"Why?"

"This spirit shaman who calls himself Chief Arrow Heart just told me to get one. He said he wants to help heal my broken heart."

We walked to the front of the store. Terri opened a drawer and took out a brown arrowhead about three inches long.

"I've had this for a long time, Michael. Now I know why. It's for you," she said, giving it to me. I'm going to lock up the store for fifteen minutes. I am feeling the urge to smudge you."

Terry locked the door, and we went to the back room. I lay down on the massage table and placed the arrow head on my heart. Terry lit the sage and made swirling motions all around me. I teased her saying "I wonder what kind of shaman you were in a past life."

"I don't know, and I don't care, Michael. If this ritual helps, then I'm all for it. Doctors don't have all the answers, and neither do the clergy or the psychologists. Why can't the shamans and healers have some answers, too?"

I felt heat coming from my hands. The arrowhead grew very warm. My head tingled and my heart fluttered, but neither was painful or uncomfortable. A few minutes later we ended the ritual.

"Michael, someone was here. I felt a presence. I think your spirit shaman was working on you, too."

"I think so, too, Terry, and I felt him as well. Well, to be honest, I could actually see him, but I didn't want you to think I was crazy."

Terry laughed and kissed me on the cheek. "Of course you are crazy, Michael. That is why I love you so much. Hey, do you think my third-eye is opening up more? I could actually see a shadowy image of the Indian with a gray feather in his hair."

"Good job, yes, Chief Arrow heart was wearing a gray feather in his long thick black hair."

"Well, there is hope for me yet. I guess I had better return to the storefront."

I felt the urge to lie back on the massage table. Once again I placed the arrowhead on my heart. I took a few deep breaths and thanked Chief Arrow Heart for whatever healing he had given me.

Then I whispered, "What's wrong with my heart? How can anyone really break our heart?" I saw the image of three women with long dark hair and very piercing eyes. Chills went through me. The women stared at me, which made my spine shiver.

"Who are you?" I asked.

I saw Chief Arrow Heart's image. Then he spoke in my mind. *"Those women are the three powerful sorceresses who bewitched you long ago. They stole part of your heart. You were a big-mouthed, daring young blacksmith in a past life who walked where angels feared to tread, as the saying goes. Everyone knew to avoid those witches. They were known to lure men and use black magic to capture their hearts. You were cocky and confident they could not harm you. So away you trudged like an idiot until you met up with them. They did you in, and your heart has partly been broken ever since. You will not be fully healed until you get the rest of your heart pieces back."*

"How do I do that, Chief Arrow Heart?"

"A few years from now, you will meet a very unusual woman. She will come to you first as a student. For a time, you will be her teacher and mentor. In time, you will become close confidantes. She will slowly begin to come into her power, and in time she will become your equal. You are

309

destined to do much healing work together. She will know this from the beginning, but it will take awhile before you completely believe it and are willing to work with her. This woman will tell you the story of what happened in the past life with the three sorceresses. I have given you some healing and protection, but your healing will not be complete until you meet this shaman healer and get the missing pieces of your heart back."

I wanted to ask Chief Arrow Heart when I would meet this woman, but I did not. I intuitively sensed that I would meet her when I was supposed to. I looked up, and he was gone.

"Whoa," I said, as I opened my eyes and slowly stood up. "You'd think I smoked some pretty strong stuff to have a vision like that!"

The Native Americans believe that our guides and Great Spirit can give us powerful visions if we are receptive, respectful, and ready. Even though my heart believed in the authenticity of the experience, my questioning mind would, as usual, have to put in its two cents worth.

Over the next few days, I found myself in an intellectual quandary, trying to figure out the Indian's mysTerryous messages. Part of me thought the vision was nothing more than my imagination working overtime; however, a deeper part of me felt that there was more going on. A few days later at the store I went to the back room and meditated awhile when it was rather obvious that the rain was keeping people away.

I lit some incense and fanned smoke in my direction, making little smoke designs. Staring at the smoke and the designs made me lightheaded and dreamy. I wasn't asleep, and I wasn't awake. I was in one of those in-between waking states. I saw the image of three hearts dancing before my eyes.

"What does this mean?" I asked aloud. Then Chief Arrow Heart's image appeared. His captivating, intense eyes held a childlike twinkle in them which made them glow.

He nodded and then spoke. "Let me tell you about the hearts you saw in your vision. They are the stolen three pieces of your heart taken with black magic by three sorceresses. I told you about them in our last visit."

"Where are the heart pieces now?" I asked, feeling apprehensive and dreading to hear what he might say.

Chief Arrow Heart pointed his long finger in the distance. "They are inside the sorceresses—somewhere in their souls, you could say. But there is more. The good news for you is that these three sorceresses are all in your soul family. They are not totally evil, and each in her own way loved you very much and still does."

"In here," I whispered. "You mean to imply that each of them has a part of my heart in her soul. This sounds totally crazy."

"Do not be so quick to dismiss that which is not yet obvious or apparent. Nothing is impossible, Michael. Things are seldom as they appear. When you learn who these women are, you will understand much more than I can tell you now. I just wanted to give you a partial understanding. When you meet them, you will feel a powerful connection because you are all in the same soul family. Some people think that just because someone is in our soul family, such relationships are all *hunky dory* and *sugar and spice*, as the sayings go. This is not true. Soul-mate connections can be some of the most challenging of all relationships. These three sorceresses all have many gifts for you, and you have gifts for them as well. Michael, it is time for me to go. Goodbye for now."

"Goodbye, Chief Arrow Heart. Thanks for everything."

He gave me a nod and a little bow and disappeared.

My heart was racing, and my mind was reeling. How can such a notion exist? This all sounds crazy in spite of what Chief Arrow Heart said. How can one person carry part of someone's heart (albeit a spirit counterpart) inside him/her, let alone three? This was almost too much to even attempt to fathom. I poured myself a glass of water and guzzled it down. I slowly began to come back to normal awareness. I tried to sort out what he had said, and the implications seemed more than my rational mind could absorb.

Chief Arrow Heart noted that this experience was some kind of vision—and a powerful one at that. I have to admit that it did touch something deep in my soul. I tried to tell myself that he had been speaking in a metaphorical sense. It's often said that when you love someone, he/she is in your heart and a part of you, but he didn't say that I loved them. If anything, it would seem that I would dislike them if they performed black magic, invaded my being, and stole part of my heart. And yet there was probably more going on. According to him, I was very connected to these three women/sorceresses. Hmmm, and why was his name Chief Arrow Heart? I had also forgotten to ask him about his name.

The more I thought about it, the more I realized I have always had a profound capacity to love. I used to even say that I had enough love inside me that could suffice for several people, and I have always felt there are many different people, or sub-personalities inside all of us. Perhaps I was closer to the truth than I realized. Perhaps what Chief Arrow Heart said explained more of this mystery and helped some things to make sense that I had been trying to figure out for years.

I kept trying to forget the incident. No matter how hard I tried, it simply did not work.

"Is this your idea of another symbolic death?" I said to Kali. I wondered if someone, through sorcery, could invade a soul and steal part of its heart.

Then I wondered, *Just what is the soul? Can we really ever know? Can we catch glimpses of our soul, receive hints of its essence, and/or even make contact with it?* The questions continued to formulate in my mind. Six o'clock arrived. I closed up the store and turned out the lights.

"What a day this has been," I said, as I headed to my car.

It would be some fourteen years before I received the answers to my questions regarding the three sorceresses that Chief Arrow Heart said had stolen parts of my heart. It occurred on September 1, 2009, when my friend, Arielle, from Indianapolis came for a visit. As a shaman, intuitive, sound healer, and channel, she was also developing her writing skills. She had been doing some healing work on me for a few months. It was always a joy to see her because being the *good and faithful* shaman that she was, she always brought her tools, candles, crystals, sage, gemstones, wand, singing bowl, and drum.

She had quite a collection of beautiful crystals and gemstones of many different colors. She did her layouts on various energy centers and areas of the body where her guides advised. In the few healings she had done for me, she had gone into trance and channeled for me. A couple of days before her scheduled arrival time, I had found my original 1995 story of Chief Arrow Heart in a pile of papers.

I was drawn to read it, and a little voice had said, "This story belongs in *God's Many Mansions* as well.

Arielle arrived perky and cheerful as usual. I helped her bring her *shaman goodies* (as I called them) up the narrow staircase. We visited and then went to the Golden Corral restaurant for lunch. When we came back to my apartment, I felt the urge to read her the story I had written based on what Chief Arrow Heart told me. Arielle listened raptly, and I noticed that she was staring intently at me, hardly blinking. I felt a little anxious as I sensed that this story was affecting her. When I finished reading, she smiled and softly said, "This story is not done."

"More writing," I replied, "I never get off the hook."

"You know you love to write, Michael. You live for it almost as much as you live for my wonderful company. Now to speak on a serious note." Arielle moved closer to me. She reached for my hand and softly said, "I was one of the sorceresses."

"Oh Jesus, Mary, and Joseph," I exclaimed, astonished. "Please tell me you didn't just say what I thought you did."

Arielle stood frozen, still. Her eyes had a faraway look. We looked at each other a few moments, and then I sat back in my recliner and covered my eyes with a towel. I had promised to do a channeling for Arielle. Merlin is one of the guides she works with, so he was the one that came through for her. He gave her some advice and encouraged her to continue her healing spiritual path. He told her that Victoria, who had been a close friend and teacher to me, was the second sorceress. Arielle said that my muse/spirit guide, Dresda, was the third one. Merlin added that Arielle would tell the story of what happened so long ago with the three sorceresses.

After the channeling was done, I gathered my pillows and lay on the floor. Arielle lit a white candle, did a gemstone crystal layout on me, and played some tones on the bowl. She called in the guides, did some soft chanting, and then some energy work on me. She turned on the tape recording device, placed her hands against my temple and began speaking softly.

"We are walking up the crystal stairway; it's a spiral stairway that leads to the Magdalena and Sananda. We are standing before them, and we kneel. They give us a blessing for our willingness to move forward at these times to integrate and assimilate the energies that are coming in from other dimensions and worlds. Sananda kisses my forehead, and then he kisses your forehead. He puts his hand on each of our foreheads and chants something I don't understand; it is a very powerful frequency and vibration. Words do not matter. He says we have done well. We shall continue walking and moving forward on our journey. We are just beginning to see a glimpse of the light that lies on the other side. For this we should rejoice and be glad. We are assimilating energies from many planets and solar systems. They are moving into terra's atmosphere and realigning humanity's DNA structure with intense energies."

"My 9/9/09 (September 9, 2009) trip to Arkansas shall be an awakening to a new frequency vibration and a new energy. When I come back, I shall align you with the same energies, for you are the same vibration and frequency as I am. Sananda tells us to go forth on our journey with grace, ease, and gratitude."

"The Magdalena gives us a kiss on our forehead as well and says, "My lovely children, you are my lineage as you know. Yes, Arielle, the book is coming forth sooner than you can imagine for your powers and gifts are growing by leaps and bounds."

"Michael is moving more into the proficient writer that he has always been. The words shall flow from the paper with such ease that he will not remember typing them, and he will have to go back and see what he has said. He will be in bliss and joy during these times of writing. You two shall write together. You shall get back in alignment on the path of the writer when things slow down some in the next few months. You will get back to your *Memories from Atlantis* trilogy. These stories need to be told as you have agreed and promised to tell them before you even took your first breath."

"As the Magdalene speaks these words to us, we turn to walk away and move forward until we are in the *no-time*. We are in the blue crystal castle once again. One thinks it, and one is there. The crystal castle holds many secrets. There are many trappings and new doors that have not been opened. We are walking, and all at once you go another way. I look but I do not see you. You have gone somewhere else. I see a door that is somehow calling to me to open it and enter. As I open the door, I transfer to a different time and realm. In actuality, there is no time or space. As I pass through the door, I am transformed into an aspect of my higher self known as Arianna Isabella."

"I quickly cover myself with a cloak of illusion as I step into the lifetime of the three sorceresses. I have come to rectify that which was wronged—rather, one aspect of that which was wronged. The part of me that holds part of your heart is another aspect of my soul known as Erionda. This is a moment that we all have longed and waited for—the chance for redemption at last."

"As I adjust to my surroundings, I can see a table set in the middle of an airy and open room. There are three sorceresses standing around the table, chanting aloud something that I can't understand. I recognize all three of them: myself as Erionda, Victoria who was Tiranne, and Dresda who was Kirrione. All three sorceresses have flowing long dark hair and are wearing beautiful gowns. I have sparkling violet eyes. Kirrione has dark emerald green eyes, and Tiranne has piercing azure blue eyes. All are very rapturous and beautiful. They are not aware of my presence, but they seem to be looking around as if they know something is amiss."

"As I watch, I am remembering just how it all transpired so very long ago. It is being played out again as if watching a play in a dream. As the story is told, Erionda loved you very deeply, Michael. She conspired to make you hers. To mate with you, merge with you, and to shatter the darkness of her heart with your purity. She was a masterful sorceress. She was at a level of mastery far superior to the others. She could time-travel, so she was aware of many lifetimes of love that you two had shared. You had loved her many times before in many places. It was this love that she needed in order to bring herself back to the light to merge once more into the wholeness of her being. She did not know that the other two sisters had a different plan. Erionda did not understand that the other two sisters were also aspects of the same soul and were also connected to you, for they had loved you as well."

"Erionda thought she would lure you in with a spell to make you hers. In your innocence and in her greed and lust to entrap you, more damage was done than she ever could have imagined. Since Erionda had been given the gift of time-travel, only she knew of the many lifetimes of love that you two had shared. The other two knew nothing of this, for they could not time-travel as she could. All had been given special gifts unique to each of them. As each was given her gifts, the other two used theirs for illusion as a way to trick Erionda. So the spell was cast. The two sisters tricked Erionda into luring you there through a song. They called to you upon the winds with a song. You heard the song in your head. You heard it on the winds calling out to you, whispering to you of a love that would never die, never end."

"It was calling you, calling you, luring you in, and whispering to you of this great love that you had known in other lifetimes but could not quite remember where or when. It was only Erionda's song that you could hear. Softly, gently calling out your name on the wind. Once you arrived, they all set out to prepare a spell for what Erionda thought would be her wedding day. For once mating with you and aligning the energies, she thought it would align her soul with yours and bring her back to the light. But before she could finish her spell on you, Kirrione reached into your spirit body and took out your heart."

"As Kirrione laughed at her own trickery, she thought, *Now at last he is mine!*"

"Let it be known that Tirianne was the go-between for the other two sisters. She was meek and the mildest of the three and the one with the most light. She also loved you but did not know why. She tried to stop the taking of your heart but was not powerful enough to stop Kirrionne. She crystallized your heart into a beautiful rainbow heart. Then she placed a less potent crystal inside your etheric form so you would still live. Tirianne quickly sealed up what she could for you to save you, but you would walk with the emotional entrapping of hurt and heartbreak in many lives. This was just one aspect of your hurt and heartbreak. You have had many lives of sorrow and heartbreak."

"As Erionda stood in shock, the tears fell. As she tried to reach for the rainbow heart, it fell to the floor and shattered into pieces. With the crystal on the floor she could do nothing to save you, and she knew that her soul would not be released in that lifetime. She vowed to give your heart back to you in another lifetime as she sought her redemption. Suddenly each one picked up the shattered pieces of your etheric heart and hid them in their hearts, where they could not be easily accessed. None of them wanted to share your essence with the others. What none realized was that in the taking of your heart pieces, they each gave you a piece of theirs as well."

"As I (as my higher self Arianna Isabella) focus my attention back on the sorceresses, I realize that as I was remembering the story, tears were flowing softly down my cheeks."

"I see you lying on a table in a somnolent stupor. You appear to have no comprehension of anything occurring around you. The three sorceresses are still chanting something as they are standing around you. I keep myself cloaked. It keeps them from seeing or feeling my essence. As I ready myself for what is about to happen, once again I ask for this to be the moment of my soul's redemption at last. I have waited so long to see this day come to fruition. As I watch in horror, I see it all unfold just as it has so many times before. As the sorceresses turn to me, one has a crystalline heart. Pure pristine blue. Pink. Violet. Rainbow colors all emanating scintillating radiance. Green. Yellow. Orange. Red. Colors that we do not know the names for on the earth realm."

"It is sparkling and glitTerryng. It is like a delicious essence to them. There is more than just the crystal heart. It is some of the heart essence they have trapped. Instinctively, I pull my cloak of illusion closer to me so as not to be seen or felt. As Kirionne holds up the heart, I seize the opportunity and swiftly run past her as I grab the heart from her hands. They cannot see me, so they are not certain what has just taken place."

"I flee with the heart as I hear them shouting at each other, 'Where did it go? Where did it go?'"

"I have waited many millenniums for this moment. Many lifetimes for resolution. I step back through the door into the crystal castle and into Arielle's consciousness, where I will help her to put the heart back into your etheric body to fulfill a grand promise. The filaments go through the electromagnetic system of rainbow colors. I hear the thump thump of the rainbow heart beating. This one portion of the heart is not all there is. You will have other portions of your heart given back to you as you journey forward and follow your soul's destiny."

At that point, Arielle took a small phial of scented oil from her medicine bag and with her left forefinger she drew a heart on my chest. She began chanting softly, and for several moments, her fingers traced the heart. Her fingers were very warm. I could feel her flowing energy. There was a slight pulse which felt like a mild shock of electricity. My chest was tingling, and my head felt lighter than a feather. It felt like I was not even in my body although I knew that I was.

A few moments later she said, "Now I put the crystal heart piece back, and I seal it with the shaman's breath."

She blew several long breaths on my heart area and then bent over and kissed my forehead.

Arielle began to speak softly to me. "The filaments go through the electromagnetic system of rainbow colors. The strands of anguish, sorrow, and hurt shall meld into the rainbow heart and be transformed into strands of love. They align and integrate with the strands that you carry now. The frequency and vibration of your heart coming back to you will heal a part of your emotional body, and you shall know love again with the depth and passion as you did in lives past."

Next, Arielle began to speak the prophecy to change my destiny. "You are not done, beloved of power. The power that you pull back in will more than make up for that which was stolen from you. In the plane not of the light, you shall align with the aspect of your spirit, that which was broken. And it shall be as if it had never occurred at all. The spirit that is you shall be aligned with your heart's desire."

"The heart pieces brought back to you will allow you to integrate the strands that align you with the star brothers and sisters. This corrects that which was wronged in that lifetime. You will align with the heart essence that was bestowed upon you to connect to the star people of Andromeda. For you it is Andromedan, for that alliance and alignment on many levels will serve many souls in the days to come. The stories you will write, every wrong that you right, brings you back into your alignment with the star people. It is a very strong connection. It is more a recognized frequency than an integration. You may align with the star brothers and sisters at any moment for yourself and others. As you do this, your power will magnify and you will be blessed with many gifts. You are to be a beacon of light that shines for humanity."

"As Arianna Isabella spoke these words, she began to cry and wiped away the tears from her cheeks. She knew that she had succeeded in achieving redemption. She withdrew her energy from Arielle."

As Arielle became more conscious of her surroundings she said, "My hands are absolutely numb, and I am crying. What is this all about?"

I was very moved at how emotional Arielle became while telling the story. It sent chills through me as its truth resonated deep within my soul. I have met the three sorceresses in this lifetime.

This story validates why I have a strong psychic and telepathic connection to these women, who can get into my head so easily. Even though Victoria died in October of 2005 and Dresda is not in human form at this time, I often feel their loving presence and inspiration. Dresda, my spirit muse, often gives me guidance. Sometimes she awakens me in the wee hours of the morn with insights that lead me to do automatic writing that can go on for pages. Likewise, Victoria and Arielle support me with my writing.

I feel that Victoria and Dresda have more than repaid that old debt while Arielle has taught me about human love and helped me to heal. She has returned pieces of my heart, and my life is much more complete and happy because of it. Nothing is ever as it appears. Arielle has informed me that I still hold a portion of each of their hearts, which must be returned to them. That story is yet to be told. The score is settled for now.

CHAPTER TWENTY-ONE

ROTAH, THE MIGHTY WHALE

(A Parallel Lifetime on Another World)

Rotah, like many of my *other-worldly* visitors and teachers, originally came to me in a dream. One morning some years ago at 3:00 a.m., I awoke with the image of this gigantic whale in my mind. I was especially drawn to his deep, sad, haunting eyes. Then something very strange happened.

I turned on the light and was drawn to look in the mirror. For a brief moment I saw the whale's image superimposed over mine. Chills and goose bumps made the hair on my neck stand up. I gasped, wondering what that was about. Had I imagined it? It looked so real. Could I still be dreaming? No, I was not longer dreaming. I rubbed my face and head. I was standing in front of the mirror, and I had seen the whale's image while completely awake.

I had the feeling that Rotah had come to me for some very special reason, one I was eager to find out about.

"*The way you will find out is to write the story,*" I heard in my mind.

That was just as well because I was too wide-awake to go back to bed. Sleep was a thousand miles away, so I got up. I had a cup of hot chocolate and then went to my desk. I took out a notebook and pen and wrote what came to me. The sun was starting to rise when I finished.

I was flabbergasted. I had written the entire story in less than three hours—or rather, the story had written itself through me. The words came very fast. It felt like automatic writing, which it probably was. The story had some interesting metaphysical spiritual teachings in it. But who would believe it? People would tell me I just made up a fantasy story.

I asked my guide Dresda what was going on. She said that through the story I was recalling another lifetime on a parallel world where I was the mighty whale Rotah, and she was the wizard boy Joran. *Geez, now I knew that I was ready for the psych ward—and maybe she was, too.*

I tried to stay calm and remain open-minded as I constantly encourage my clients to do. My mind and belief system had been stretched many times before. So what was one more time?

I asked Dresda why she didn't clue me in before I wrote the story. She said it was very simple: I would not have believed her. As open-minded and filled with an insatiable curiosity as I am, to tell me I have been a whale on a parallel world would have stretched my mind to its limits. I would have truly thought I had lost my last marble. I might even have some kind of mental breakdown. Dresda said that it was not yet time to learn about my lifetimes as animals and plants. When the time was right, I would learn. And that is exactly what happened.

Looking back, I see that Rotah's coming to me at first in a dream was no surprise and my writing the story while totally conscious was likewise no surprise either. It just shows that there are other realities that we can tap into while being fully conscious and awake. It also shows how real, vast, and valid the subconscious mind is and how it is filled with immeasurable knowledge and information.

After all, I had written my last book, *Morning Coffee with God*, from an altered dream-like state. My central character, Mr. Divine/God said that dreams are very real on other planes. What's more important is the information that comes through them. He said that many divine and profound teachings have come through dreams and that we ought not dismiss them so easily. Now I no longer feel surprised if ideas and teachings come to me in dreams, reveries, and half-awake states. I just give thanks to my muse, guides, and subconscious mind and write what comes to me. I might add that I never take notes or have any idea of what I am going to say, like a lot of writers do. I realize that one could say I am just tapping into my imagination. My question to this is "Just what is the imagination? What does it truly entail and what do we really know about it?"

Rotah was too close to my heart to be merely an imaginary character in a fantasy story. That I have a very strong attraction and affinity to whales also reinforces my belief about what Dresda said. Plus, metaphysical and spiritual teachings are not what one ordinarily finds in fantasy stories. This is something I have noted in my *other-worldly* visitor stories.

Rotah is one of my favorites. Before I share the story, I want to give a little background on my attraction to whales. My first emotional reaction to whales was when I read *Moby Dick* by Herman Melville in an English class in high school. Reputed to be one of the great American classics of literature, I found myself repulsed by the sailor Captain Ahab, who was obsessed with killing the mighty white sperm whale, Moby Dick. I only read the book because it was required, and I hated his quest to kill Moby Dick.

The Star Trek IV movie *The Voyage Home* about the humpbacked whales is my favorite among all the Star Trek movies. Many years ago I got a copy of Paul Winter's recording, "Calling: In Celebration of the Voices of the Sea." Whales and other sea creatures sing on the tape. That tape is so beautiful and haunting to me. I have played it so many times that I have backup copies because I wore out the original. I have read several metaphysical books that say whales and dolphins are among some of the most evolved beings of the universe.

Dresda told me that magic was prevalent in other civilizations and parallel worlds—and still is on others. She said that for me to have been a magical whale is not a fantasy experience fabricated by my imagination. She said the reason I am so drawn to whales and mermaids is because I have indeed had lifetimes among them as one of them, and my soul still feels that deep connection. She did not tell me who the other characters in the story were, but she did say that she was Joran Kobaz, the young wizard who befriended Rotah.

As farfetched and mind blowing as it may sound, I now know that our souls can experience lifetimes in other non-human forms, such as mineral, plant, and animal. I have sensed this for a long time. I have a passion and deep love for all life forms. I actually prefer the company of animals and plants to most humans, and I make it a point to have lots of plants and flowers around me. I talk to them and give them love and energy when I water them. I thank them for their beauty and bless and honor them. As a child I was always rescuing this or that little creature. I almost threw up when we had to dissect frogs as part of our lab experience in biology class. I could not finish, and I gagged and told my teacher he could flunk me, but I was not dissecting an innocent little critter even if it was dead.

I honor the life and death process. I know firsthand that plants and flowers are alive and respond to human love and emotion. So do animals. My thoughts on this were validated when I read some of the regressions recorded in *Convoluted Universe Book III* by Dolores Cannon. Reading those sessions filled my eyes with tears of joy and soul recognition. I am a part of the whales as they are a part of me. We truly are all connected, and we experience many different life forms on our way back to merge with our Creator Source. Now I invite you to meet Rotah and Joran! Enjoy this whale of a ride!

A long time ago deep in the Gorban Sea lived a giant golden whale named Rotah. He was the largest, fiercest creature anyone had ever laid eyes upon. To make matters worse, this whale was very angry. *Enraged* was the word to describe him and not without reason, but no one had bothered to find out what lay at the root of Rotah's anger. Had someone done so, the land of Kozan could have been spared many lost human lives.

Unfortunately, all the people wanted to do was destroy the giant whale Rotah. Now Rotah was no ordinary whale by any means. He was a whale who possessed much magic. He knew how to lure people to him, and he took delight in conversing with them before devouring them. Something else stood out about Rotah. He had lived other lifetimes as a human, and his soul memory was so keen that he completely understood humans. He could even speak their language and read their innermost thoughts.

Legend had spread near and far that this unusual whale could speak the human language and was more intelligent than the greatest wizards. Yet no one knew for sure since no one had survived an encounter with Rotah. He ate every human he came in contact with because every single one that pursued him was an unkind soul who did not possess purity of heart. This is what so infuriated Rotah. It was always impudent men and a few wizards who boasted that they would meet the giant whale and kill him. The women respected the tales and begged the men to leave the whale in peace, but being proud and stubborn, they did what they wanted.

A young wizard named Joran Kobaz had been dreaming about Rotah since he was an infant. He described the whale perfectly when he was three years old. The townspeople of Kozan concluded that the gods had blessed them with a new wizard when on his eighteenth birthday, Joran spoke ancient words that the wizards had not heard in years. "Huzar. Hokah bekab. Jetuh. Makei. Sustah!"

Someone called in the master wizards. A total of ten wizards were assembled, but only one wise one could translate this phrase.

"The words are very ancient," Mozor the wise one said. "I have dreamt those words, as well as their meaning. They speak of an ancient prophecy which dictates that one day the struggle will cease, and peace will once more reign between the land people and the sea creatures."

Upon hearing the words *sea creatures*, Joban Dok shook his staff high into the air and cried out, "Death to the golden whale."

"You only think of killing and destroying life!" Joran shouted. "When are you going to learn that taking life solves nothing? It only causes more death and destruction. Our creator gave us life, which is precious and meant to be valued and honored. Why should we take life when it is not necessary?"

"Silence, my son," Joran's mother said.

"I will not be silent," Joran retorted. "None dare upset the balance of life and death without paying dearly. We are paying dearly. Don't you people see? Rotah's wrath is so strong because of your useless killing of sea creatures. We have plenty of food, and yet you kill in vain."

"Because they kill us!" yelled Joban.

"I don't believe they would kill without a reason. I am going to find out how long this killing has been going on, and who started it."

"It began hundreds of years ago," roared Joban. "Maybe thousands. Such is our way. We call it tradition."

"Call it what you will. I call it senseless murder, and something must be done to end it all. I will go deep into the waters and find this awesome Rotah."

"Do that and you'll never return to speak another word," snapped Joban. "Who cares if your spirit can descend and remain in the water for hours."

"I think this Rotah can be reasoned with, and I'm going to see him tomorrow."

"Fool," replied Joban. "You are a fool like your father was. Once you have made up your mind there is no stopping you."

"I have heard enough," Joran said. "My mind is made up. It is destiny that leads me to Rotah. My heart tells me that I must face this Rotah whom I have seen in dreams all of my life. I am convinced that he is an adept who can see through deception. He can also probably read the heart. I do not believe that Rotah is an evil creature, and I am going to find out and verify what my intuition tells me."

Mozor stood up and spoke in a commanding tone. "Leave Joran be. He has told you that his mind is made up. Perhaps this *great test* is part of his coming into the fullness of his power. Who are we to say the contrary? The powers that be ask much from those brave and pure of heart. Joran has more courage than I shall ever have, and we all know that he is pure of heart which is more than I can say for any of you."

He placed his hand on Joran's shoulder. "I wish you godspeed, Joran. May the mighty Sea Dragon of the Great Gateway Isle watch over and protect you," he said, giving Joran a hearty embrace.

Hearing the words the Great Gateway Isle sent shivers down Joran's spine. He had dreamed about them but seldom could recall much of the dreams. He had been told that the Isle existed. How he wanted to go there, but he had no idea of how to find it.

Yet hearing those words from Mozor gave him hope that a way would be shown to him. *Oh, that this should come to be!* thought Joran, letting out a sigh. He had heard how a journey to the sacred Isle changed people and helped them come into the fullness of the Great Knowing. *I would gladly meet twenty giant whales for one day in the Great Gateway Isle*, his thoughts continued.

Joran thanked Mozor for his blessing and then left swiftly.

He spent the rest of the day in the forest. His mother knew he would not be home until late. She was accustomed to his solitary wanderings and preferred not knowing the details of his forest journeys. She would listen to Joran's tales of how the spirit of an oak tree would whisper secrets to him and then go about her work. It wasn't that she didn't believe spirits could talk to people; she simply had no interest in spirits.

"Let the dead find comfort among the dead," she had told Joran when his father had been devoured by the whale five years ago. Joran recalled that day often. He had dreamed about the event three nights in a roll and begged his father to stay away from the sea. He said that dreams meant nothing and insisted that death would be a fair price for one glimpse of the mighty sea creature. Like all the others, he never returned.

Joran woke up before dawn the next morning and quietly moved about so as not to awaken his mother who was a light sleeper. He knew she would only try to dissuade him from going.

He wrote her a note and left it on the table.

I have gone to make peace with Rotah. All will work out just as I have dreamt. I will be back before dark. I promise.

Love,

Joran

The sun was just beginning to rise when Joran arrived at the sea. He spread a blanket, arranged his things, and then spent a long time watching the rippling waves dance on the water. The sea always made him feel peaceful and nostalgic for something he couldn't explain, but he sensed it had to do with the Great Gateway Isle Mozor mentioned.

Watching the waves made him feel drowsy. He fell fast asleep, and his spirit form was soon swimming deep in the sea. He chanted the words he had chanted at his birthday party. "Huzar. Hokah Bekab. Jetuh. Makei. Sustah." He repeated them several times, more loudly each time.

He began to sense a powerful overwhelming presence approaching him. "Rotah," he whispered. The words are leading him to me. "Rotah," he whispered.

Moments later, an echo repeated the exact words he had just chanted. Then, the voice slowly transformed into a deep basso profundo, which rumbled so loudly that Joran thought the mountains were falling into the sea. Moments later in front of him, observing him carefully, attempting to delve deeply into his eyes, was the largest golden whale he had ever laid his eyes upon. He was just as Joran had seen him in dreams. The whale's eyes were filled with immense sorrow and pain. Rotah was surprised that Joran did not flinch or look away. For several minutes, both continued their silent gazing and checking one another out with growing curiosity.

Rotah had felt an instant connection to this young wizard, but the benevolent sentiment soon vanished. Had anyone asked him, he would have vehemently denied it. Old prejudices and hatred do not disappear so quickly. Yet he could not help but be bewildered. *No mortal had ever spoken this chant: the sacred chant which leads the way to the* Great Knowing. *Who could have taught this to a mortal? And how could a mortal be so adept at maneuvering his spirit body?* For a moment Rotah looked away, thinking that perhaps he was dreaming. When he looked back, Joran was still facing him and staring deeply into his eyes

Joran did not speak. His instincts told him out of respect, he should let the whale have the first words. He assumed Rotah could read his thoughts but wasn't sure if Rotah knew that he was aware of it.

Rotah continued staring at Joran without blinking. Joran remained as immobilized as a statue. Then Rotah began feeling somewhat anxious. He had never seen a mortal so calm—not even the wizards he spied on from time to time in his spirit form. For a moment he thought that this young man was neither mortal nor wizard but a star being who took mortal form. Just as Rotah had vivid recall of lives as a human, he also had recall of lifetimes on other worlds, planets, and universes.

All those lifetimes had not been in human form. Rotah had long ago learned that things are seldom as they appear. Perhaps this mortal was a star being from an advanced world where war and killing did not exist. He could tell by scanning Joran's aura that he was no ordinary mortal because his heart was pure. What puzzled him was how much *knowing* this young mortal possessed. For an instant, his emotional attraction to Joran was replaced by fear—something he seldom felt—anger and rage—but rarely fear. *I'm being silly*, he thought, *entertaining such notions.*

Rotah swam around in circles three times. Then opening his large mouth, he bellowed, "Who taught you that chant? I demand to know. Only a few adept wizards know this chant, and you don't look like a wizard, let alone an adept."

"You should know that looks can be deceiving, Lord Rotah," Joran said softly.

"I asked you a question, not for your opinion. I demand an answer," Rotah said, enjoying Joran's use of the word Lord. No mortal had ever called him Lord.

"The spirit of an oak tree deep in the forest taught me the chant."

"You talk to spirits in oak trees?" Rotah roared so loudly that his laughter formed waves that shook them both."

"To be honest, Lord Rotah, I find the spirit of the oak tree more agreeable and sensible to talk to than most people—if you know what I mean," Joran added, leaning closer to Rotah's face.

"Humh," snorted Rotah, becoming more fascinated by Joran but still unwilling to reveal his thoughts to Joran. If the young mortal was, indeed, an adept or star being, he would have to prove himself.

The truth was that Joran could read many of Rotah's thoughts and was becoming quite amused by the golden whale's inner struggle. Then he felt a tinge of sadness. So many bad experiences with mortals explained Rotah's rage.

Joran knew to tread lightly with the grief-stricken, enraged whale. He didn't want to upset or aggravate Rotah in any way. He was here to help and would not let Rotah's anger or deep hurt deter him from his goal of reaching the whale's heart. They looked at one another several more minutes in silence until Rotah could be quiet no more. He was surprised by his need to talk because no one had ever *out-silenced* him before. Most mortals' constant babbling about trivial things disgusted Rotah. Joran spoke with conviction and chose his words carefully. No, he was no ordinary mortal. Rotah couldn't help himself. His growing need to communicate with Joran overruled his reason.

"The words that you chanted are the password to enter the Great Gateway Isle. To hear you speak them, obliges me to take you there if you should wish to go."

"I have waited all my life to go there," Joran exclaimed. "I have dreamt of a special sacred place deep in the sea where great teachings and lost knowledge are held and where the pure of heart can go to learn great things."

"That is true, young mortal. Shall we depart?"

"I am ready," Joran replied, his eyes glowing with a radiance Rotah never saw in mortals.

The golden whale swung his tail high and then sped away like lightning.

"He's not the only one who can swim fast," Joran said, following him. Within seconds, Joran was beside Rotah and kept stride with the giant whale. No matter how fast Rotah swam or how many tricks he performed—bouncing about, doing giant flips, swerving to the left and then the right—Joran was able to repeat them. Rotah thought Joran would not be able to swim backwards. He did so with the grace of a swan.

He is extraordinary, Rotah's thoughts continued. *Few mortals exercise such control over their spirit bodies.*

When they passed the mermaid cavern, four beautiful mermaids, two with gold and two with silver hair, waved at Joran wishing him godspeed. The fishes and sea horses did likewise. As Rotah would do various tricks with movements, Joran simply admired and enjoyed the scene. Rotah was further impressed that Joran had no desire to compete with him. Furthermore, Joran made no effort to keep up with Rotah. He swam several feet behind him.

He began feeling respect for the young man. When he projected his soul vision, he saw a bright, white luminescence surrounding Joran.

"Oh," he gasped. "One of the pure ones."

Impossible, he thought, looking at Joran several minutes. The light did not fade. *How can this be? There are no pure mortals, unless, of course, he is not a mortal.*

The old anger returned. Rotah's thoughts continued. *Mortals have killed countless whales and constantly fight among themselves. No sea creature has ever harmed another one. Even the ones who die for food, die willingly, knowing they are fulfilling their destinies. Ruthless mortals appear to experience great pleasure when killing innocent land and sea creatures. I hate them and will kill them all.*

Joran looked his way, noticing the bright red light surrounding Rotah's massive body. He said nothing. He knew the whale was undergoing an inner struggle which he hoped would result in a change of heart. Joran prayed that the whale's anger would melt so Rotah could see him for who he truly was. He knew that Rotah could sense his purity; however, old hurts do not heal overnight. For this to occur, there must be the desire for healing. Joran knew he had been sent to influence the mighty whale. Would his mission succeed?

Rotah looked in Joran's direction again. The white light still shone brightly. Rotah began to soften. He slowed down his pace. The light around his body shifted colors.

Joran could tell that Rotah was relaxing. Soon he was a hundred feet from the whale. When he was less than ten feet away, Rotah stopped and extended his light until it encircled Joran, who took that as a sign of welcome. He slowly swam until he was beside Rotah. Their eyes met.

Rotah was still surprised that the mortal held his gaze. Another sign of an adept. They do not fear anything or anyone.

Joran looked back at the whale. He had never seen such soulful eyes, filled with such deep sadness and kindness. *This is a creature that carries a great burden in his heart. Joban is wrong. Rotah strikes out of rage and hurt. I must reach him,* Joran's thoughts continued. *I simply must.*

Several more minutes passed. Joran kept silent, hoping Rotah would initiate conversation.

Rotah was in a quandary. If only Joran would fight him— it was the only way he knew how to deal with mortals! He would feel on familiar territory in a battle. Fighting with mortals was a way of life for him. Suddenly, his deep rooted prejudice was being uprooted before his very eyes by a young man who was still an adolescent. He wasn't sure he had the strength to overpower Joran even if he wanted to.

Adepts do not make displays of power in an attempt to impress or win over. Joran seemed to possess several qualities of an adept: humility, patience, courage, and respect of others. Did Rotah want to challenge or do battle with Joran after what he had witnessed? He was overcome with anxiety and doubt. No mortal had ever had the audacity to befriend him. Feeling very confused, Rotah was at a loss at what to do.

Joran's restraint caused Rotah to believe that he possessed depth and integrity of character. Joran was well-aware of how much more powerful he was in his spirit body. Without the physical body to encumber him, he had greater access to the powers of the mind and spirit.

Rotah wondered if Joran could overpower him if he wished. He had never entertained such a thought before, and it was most unsettling to him. In a way he wished Joran would initiate a challenge. He would at least find out how much power the young one possessed. Not knowing bothered him; however, Rotah's heart reminded him that Joran was pure of heart and soul and must not be harmed. How could that be? This was an entirely new concept for Rotah—one almost impossible for him to believe. Rotah now faced the ultimate test—one he must not fail.

The thought occurred to Rotah that Joran was a powerful dark sorcerer who had temporarily taken on some other form and was befuddling him. He thought about other sorcerers in other lifetimes who had tried to win him over through trickery. But what about the white light surrounding Joran? That was no working of sorcery. Rotah could always read the auras of all life forms. No, he was not being fooled. If anything he was being tested. The Great Ones are at work here. I can feel this in my heart.

Rotah had a glimpse of the last meeting with the Great Sea Dragon behind the Gateway. He remembered the Lord's imposing presence and commanding voice, "Your final test will involve meeting and befriending a young mortal who is humble of heart, courageous, forthright, and kind."

The memory of this incident faded, as they always do—until now. It was nearly impossible to recall the time spent in the Great Gateway Isle. Rotah could never remember more than bits and pieces of phrases he heard while there. How could this young mortal recite the total password chant? Was he an initiate or star being? No one outside the Isle knows the chant, yet reality dictated that someone outside the Gateway must have taught it to him. Just who was this spirit of the oak tree? Another adept?

Rotah's musing continued as he swam. Joran paced nearby in silence. A half hour passed. Then a golden light began to surround the entire ocean. Soon they approached a wall. Bright red flames burned along the edges and corners. Two colossal golden doors appeared. The left door opened, and an imposing Sea Dragon appeared.

On his head was a crown with twelve golden stars. Around his neck was a huge ruby hanging on a silver chain. Joran had never seen a more regal-looking being. His presence was commanding and imposing. Even Rotah was gentle and meek in his presence. His head was bowed low as the Sea King examined the two very different visitors. Joran immediately knew that this Sea Dragon was a mighty adept.

Joran, who had never looked away in the presence of anyone, found himself unable to maintain eye contact with the mighty Sea Dragon. He feared to do so would cause his spirit to melt and fade into the Great Void. The Sea Lord looked them over a few more moments and then stepped closer. Joran wondered if the mighty dragon's luminescence would blind him. The Sea Dragon lowered his huge head and smiled.

"Welcome, Rotah and Joran, to the beautiful Great Gateway Isle, hidden deep within these ancient waters. Few beings of land, earth, or water know of these Isles. Here dwell only those initiates and students of the grand sacred mysteries. Only the pure of heart may come here."

Joran's face burst into a radiant smile. "I knew there was more to Rotah than an obsession to kill people."

"You are correct, young mortal," the Sea Dragon said, looking at Joran. "Behind the rage and pain which fill this whale's big heart is a magnanimous soul. He has simply forgotten some of the Great Knowing which he learned here a few lifetimes ago."

Joran looked at Rotah and sensed his embarrassment and awkwardness. The Sea Dragon smiled and then turned back to Joran. "Speak the password of entry. Then shall you be able to pass through the Gateway."

Joran looked away, hoping the Sea Dragon did not want him to speak the words. He glanced at Rotah thinking, *I really believe that you should speak the password of entry.*

Rotah's mighty fin tapped Joran on the shoulder. "The honor is yours, young mortal."

Joran burst into a smile. "If it pleases you, I will utter the password of entry."

"It will give me great pleasure, Joran. Please proceed."

"Thank you. I will happily oblige," Joran said, lifting his arms high in the air. Tilting his head upward, he cried out in a mighty voice which surprised Rotah as his voice had been so calm and gentle before.

"Huzar. Hokah. Bekab. Jetuh. Makei. Sustah." The words created a thunderous shaking. The wall crumbled. Two doors disappeared.

"Your intonation is perfect," said the Sea Dragon. "Well done. You are recalling much of the Great Knowing."

So he is an initiate or an initiate in training, thought Rotah. *That is as good as becoming a god.*

"All are gods and goddesses in the making," said the Sea Dragon, smiling at Rotah.

"Yes, Great and Mighty Lord Sea Dragon," said Rotah humbly, bowing his head.

"There is no need to bow before me," the Sea Dragon replied. "I am not your majesty. All are mighty here who have entered the Great Gateway, as are all who have not. The difference is those here are more awakened to the Great Knowing. Here *all* are powerful and more knowing. There are no secrets. How can secrets be kept from the all-knowing ones?" he asked, looking at Joran.

"I do not know, Great Sea Lord. My friend, the spirit of the oak tree, has taught me many things. He taught me the password of entry but not its purpose or meaning to me. He told me that one day I would learn its meaning and purpose."

"He is correct. Some truths must be remembered on one's own when the time is right. You are a pure soul. Your purity entitles you the privilege to enter the Great Gateway. Inside, you will see the Great Isle of purity permeated with beauty, goodness, and the *great love* which unites all. Have you learned your final lesson, Rotah?"

"I do not know, Great One. I have met a mortal whom I wish to allow to live, for he possesses much of the Great Knowing."

"This is good," the Sea Dragon replied. "Although you err to believe that you possess the right to determine life or death for anyone, you show much growth when your words reveal that your heart has opened to feel respect and affection for a mortal. The Great Ones have permitted you to kill many mortals. In a sense this is true and in a sense it is not. Those possessing more of the Great Knowing realize that no one can ever be killed—only the physical body can. The soul spark can never be annihilated. The initiates of the great mysteries know such truths. They practice them by honoring the spirit that animates all life forms and beings—sentient and non-sentient. You, Rotah, are one of the initiates, as are you, young mortal. What have you learned about this mortal, Rotah?"

"That he is humble, kind, and pure of heart. I have read his aura and his thoughts. He puts the well-being of his people before his own safety or life. His desire is to make peace with me and to see all beings and creatures co-exist in peace. He does not fear me. I feel respect and affection for him. Does this permit me the choice to remain here?"

"Yes, the choice is yours. A change of heart, such as you have demonstrated, merits a grand reward. If you wish, you may remain here where all possess much of the Great Knowing. Here, you are free to shift into concrete, abstract, or ethereal forms as you wish and to enjoy the fruits and pleasures of this beautiful Isle. If you stay, you will be assigned a mentor to complete your training. When you have acquired mastery over matter and spirit, you will then move on to deep waters of your choice on this or other worlds where you will reign as Sea King in any form you wish. If you wish, you may also return with this young mortal and spend your time helping to eradicate the fear and distrust of land people and sea creatures. Your friendship with Joran would demonstrate the *Great Example* that forgiveness *is* important, and all beings and life forms can co-exist peacefully. Many would follow your example. What is your choice?"

Rotah looked in Joran's direction. He had a big smile on his face. He wished for a moment that they both could stay. Now he felt closer to Joran than he had ever felt to any sea creature outside the Gateway. He knew that if he left the Gateway Isle, his knowing would diminish, and he would be faced with many challenges. He would also forget much of what transpired here today. Yet, if he stayed, he would have other things and more training to complete. True, there would be more camaraderie and fun things to do: shape-shifting and experiencing life in many different forms, blending and merging with light, and spiraling abstract designs of all sizes shapes and colors, and countless other experiences which he sometimes dreamed about.

There would be no hatred or rage. Yet there *would be* classes to attend in preparation for the next physical lifetime outside the Great Gateway Isle where one faces the challenge of manifesting and exemplifying more of the Great Knowing in a physical body. He knew how difficult it could be to achieve and that no creature or mortal is exempt from transferring the lessons from head to heart to everyday life. Retreats and reprieves are granted from time to time—such as the Sea King was offering to Rotah—but sooner or later all have to return outside the Gateways to apply their lessons in a physical body on a physical human world. It took many years and/or lifetimes before one awakened to the Great Knowing When individuals fail to learn from their mistakes, they have to return to similar circumstances to correct them. Rotah realized that he had not awakened to the fullness of the Great Knowing, such as the mighty Sea Dragon possessed. If he had, he would not feel any hatred or rage for mortals outside the Isle.

Rotah also knew that no one reaches perfection until he/she can manifest total unconditional love for all life. This is the Great Test—the hardest one to pass and one that everyone has to pass sooner or later. When he reached that point of soul mastery, then and only then, would Rotah be free to remain in the waters of paradise for an extended time or to move to other glorious waters, lands, or worlds whose incomprehensible splendor and beauty are unattainable to the unenlightened. Rotah mused a few more minutes and then made up his mind.

"Great Sea King, Lord Dragon, I have made my choice. I will return outside the Great Gateway Isle with the young mortal, Joran. No longer will I kill mortals. Having seen one who is kind-hearted has restored my faith and hope that others, too, can learn to treat the sea creatures kindly. It is my wish that Joran become my partner. Together we will work hard at creating peace. This is, if Joran agrees," said Rotah, looking at Joran intently.

"So be it," said the Sea King. "Feel free to spend some time inside the Gateway before you begin your journey back."

"Here all can shapeshift, my young friend. Want to see me turn into a merman, an octopus, and then a dolphin?" asked Rotah. "Here all is possible. You simply think what you want to become or manifest, and it immediately happens. I have been told that it was once that way with mortals on the land before the dark misuse of power caused such powers to be taken away from them."

"This is wonderful," exclaimed Joran. "I often feel like I am part of the oak tree when the spirit communicates with me, but that is nothing like this. You mean I can really become a cube, a spiraling flame, a musical note, or a geometric design?"

"That and much more. There are no words to describe what we are about to experience. We call it *the partaking of the Great Oneness and the Great All.*"

"I can hardly wait, Rotah, my new friend. You lead the way!"

They exited the Gateway Isle some time later.

"You were so magnificent, Rotah. I've never seen so many different types of fish, so many beautiful shapes and colors, and such bright lights or felt so much love. Nor have I ever been anywhere (not even in my dreams) where everyone smiles so much. Joy is everywhere. It is truly paradise here. Wouldn't it be great if life in the sea and on the land was like it is in the Great Gateway Isle?"

"It can be, my young mortal friend, and you and I are going to do our best to help bring this about. There is much of the Great Knowing that we have to share. Many will be anxious to hear and learn because the soul innately desires to evolve. This applies to every life form from the most minute to the mightiest Creator Lords. Eventually, everything and everyone returns to our beloved Creator Source as a fully actualized empowered being, and this helps Creator to know itself more fully. What do you say? Shall we begin our journey back now?

"Agreed," Joran replied. Soon they were swimming side by side. They were quiet awhile. Each had much to think about. A time later they arrived at the spot where Joran's physical body rested. Dusk was approaching.

"Life won't be beautiful like it was in the Great Gateway Isle, will it? Will I remember it?" Joran asked.

"No, and we won't remember much of what happened, but it will not be as difficult. Each time we enter the Great Gateway, we return with more of the Great Knowing, which means we can recall more and more teachings and experiences. We will remember some of what we experienced. We certainly will remember each other, and not as foe, but as friend."

"I've always felt that you were my friend, Rotah. I was just waiting for you to realize it."

"Yes. You possess much of the Great Knowing, Joran. We shall be friends for the rest of this life and for many thereafter. It is time for our bodies to awaken. Not a moment to lose. One last question for you—do you come from up there?" Rotah asked, pointing upward towards the sky.

"Yeah," said Joran with a big grin on his face. "And you have been with me up there before as well."

"I kind of figured that," Rotah said before he dashed away.

Joran slowly awakened a few moments later. He still saw Rotah's kind eyes, but the sadness had faded. He also retained memories of him turning into a dolphin, a blue bubble, and a green flame. He quickly jumped to his feet and looked out to sea. Soon Rotah appeared in his full magnanimous form. He looked at Joran without speaking. For a moment Joran feared he may have forgotten everything they had experienced and might attempt to devour him. He wondered if the Gateway Isle had been nothing more than a dream.

After several moments, he broke the silence. "Nice to see you again, Rotah."

"Nice to see you, Joran," replied the golden whale with a twinkle and glow in his eyes.

"So it was not a dream? We really did meet the mighty Sea Dragon king?"

"That we did, my new friend, and we certainly have our work cut out for us, but you need to head home now. You did promise your mother you would be back before dark."

"Goodbye, Rotah. When will we meet again?"

"Very soon. On that you can depend. We have so much to talk about," Rotah said as he swam away.

"We have so much to talk about," said Joran heading back home. "Mother will never believe this story. I won't tell her—at least not yet."

His stomach made a little growl. He gently tapped it. "I am famished. I wonder what is for dinner tonight?"

CHAPTER TWENTY-TWO

JOURNEYS THROUGH TIME

After the amazing experience with the whale adept, Rotah, I have never viewed whales, sea creatures, or any life-forms the same way again. Learning that I had been a mighty golden whale on a parallel world was rather mind stretching, to say the least. At first I was downright shocked and very taken aback at the possibility and the implications of such a concept. Now I see why Dresda waited so long to tell me about this lifetime that she and I shared on a parallel world. However, I can see why she eventually shared the truth with me when she knew the time was right. She and I both know that there are two qualities I possess which keep me from losing it or going off the deep end when such occurrences take place.

First, I constantly take steps to keep myself grounded. When I find my spirit going *out there* more and more, I pull back and ground myself on terra firma in different ways. Second, no matter how far-out or mind-blowing my experiences may be, I keep an open mind. My innate and insatiable curiosity gives me the courage, stamina, and ability to learn what I can from these unusual experiences, which I believe happen to me because some part of me attracts them on some level. My constant mind-expanding experiences remind me that I have only tapped the tip of the iceberg of who and all that we are and what we are capable of knowing and experiencing.

When I thought I had gone about as far as there was to go, I was to have yet another powerful mind-blowing experience in a hypnosis/past life regression. As frequently happens to us on the spiritual quest for hidden lost knowledge, things have a way of appearing or reappearing out of nowhere. I have found this to be true, for had my guides not prodded me to look through some old folders to locate a hypnosis session I had transcribed several years ago, this experience would have been left out of this book.

Actually, I was thinking to wind the book down when I was recently looking through a bookcase for a file that contained some jokes and humorous stories. I was scheduled to visit an assisted-living nursing home to sing, entertain, and read from my book of love poetry, *Dawn's Kiss*. I thought I'd refresh my mind on a few jokes. I found the jokes folder, but then I happened to stumble upon another folder that said "Hypnosis Session with Stephen Grant, August 16, 1992." I opened it, and there was an eight page transcript of a session that had occurred some eighteen years earlier.

"Stephen Grant," I said, as fond memories washed over me. Stephen had attended an ascended master channeling I did back in June of 1992. I recalled that he asked some very deep provocative questions for a young man who was only twenty-years old. Stephen was a musician but also had a strong interest and fascination for quantum physics, hypnosis, and metaphysics. He told me that he was impressed with the information that came through me in the channeling. He asked if I was interested in hypnosis because he dabbled in it. My eyes lit up. I said, yes, and told him that I witnessed a fascinating hypnosis demonstration in high school and dabbled in hypnosis a few times in college. I had also been put under by the renowned mentalist "The Amazing Kreskin" at a stage hypnosis demonstration in 1977. Kreskin had said I was very receptive to being hypnotized, and he encouraged me to pursue hypnosis.

Memories of the hypnosis session with Stephen came to me as I read the transcript. Tears filled my eyes. To my welcomed surprise (while lying on a couch with my closed eyes in a deep trance), my subconscious mind had talked with ease about our ancient beginnings and other topics. I've heard that nothing happens by chance. While looking for jokes, I came upon the hypnosis transcript that I had not thought about or seen in many years. I read the transcript three times and was flabbergasted at all the information those eight pages contained.

I skipped most of the induction where Stephen had me slowly step into a body of water and relax. The last part was relevant because it led into the regression so I will include that brief part.

Stephen (S) As you move into the water totally in peace, step into the water up to your neck. Turn and look back at the beach and see the sand. Dip your head under the water and become totally pure and totally fulfilled. Look around you and note that you can breathe under the water. Take the water into your body. Look around and see fish swimming, gliding magically through the water, living and being in their existence. Do you see?

Michael (M) I feel it. I become one with the water. My body disintegrates, and then it comes back when I will it to.

S: You are totally at peace. Is there anything you would like to see? Is there any time you'd like to go through? Anything you want to know?

M: What is it like to be formless before I stepped upon the shores of time?

S: (He makes a small chanting sound.) Can you take a look at our society—the way we do things? We have this idea that things are coming and moving through time—of past events happening leading to present events. I want you to look at that objectively. Imagine everything that makes up what you think you are. Trillions of particles. Each particle moves forward and backwards in time. These particles turn into existence from what appears to be nowhere. I want you to visualize this wall of nowhere—all the particles of existence shooting from the nowhere into the now. Everything that people think they are comes from the nowhere into the reality of matter. I want you to look at this wall. See the wall with these trillions of particles just coming through the wall—coming from nowhere, and they appear. Now, walk through the wall. Your shape is no longer real. You walk into the wall in truth. New forms. What do you feel?

M: I feel like a small ball of light energy. I bounce around, but I go through the void and move very fast since I'm very light and have no solid matter to wear.

S: Do you have emotions?

M: I'm not sure "emotions" is the word. I have sensations. I also feel other sparks—little balls of energy that sometimes traverse the direction I'm flowing in. Freedom of expansion. Freedom of movement. I jump in such lightness and revel in joyous existence.

S: What kind of understanding of diversity do you have?

M: We're like dancing flames from the central core, and we come from the Source. But the flames can intertwine and intermingle. There is no separation, no intrusion of space. There's no real feeling of me, but yet there is a sense of identity. It's hard to explain. There is much love, much joy, much playfulness. No hurt. No anger. No fear. We're simply sparks of energy that exist. We're the same, and yet we are somehow different. We have no need to control for we have access to everything. We can go anywhere that we want. We can dance with other flames. We're not offended if a flame wishes to move and merge with us, for we don't lose any sense of being when this happens. There is respect and a sense of oneness. Nothing is taken away. It is a wonderful sensation, but it is not an emotion. Emotions were created much later.

S: Much later. What do you mean by much later?

M: We don't experience time, so it's difficult to explain, but in a sense the sparks at some point began to move slower. We wanted to move slower. We were asked to move slower. We were challenged in a game, so we began to move slower. As we moved slower and slower, we began to take on form. It's kind of like a fan that moves faster and then slower when you push the slower button. Then you can push the fast button, and it moves faster again after it has experienced slowness. You don't see the fan's blades as they move faster, but as it slows down, it begins to show a form. As we began to move slower, we magnetized energy vibrations around us. We fused ourselves with these energies. In time we began to take form until at some point, we lost our freedom of movement—or so we thought. We created bodies if you will, but this was a very long cycle.

Emotions were not created until certain bodies were created. This is why we sometimes feel alone. We know that we are spirit sparks. We remember at the very deepest levels of our soul that we are not this body that we have created for various experiences. It is a mere creative toy that we have manipulated and created as one would create pottery from the clay and the sand. We simply wove the energies together and created forms. But we are the formless, and we can recapture that sense of freedom and movement. It is so wonderful, but it is beyond emotion. We have a slight experience of this at some of the deeper levels of sleep and dreaming, but even in the dreams, there are often attachments and memories that prevent us from moving through the timeless void where we began.

S: So you moved slower and slower, and in time you formed the dense matter. Is there a point to where you can stop lowering yourself? A point where you cease condensing the energy and matter? What happens when you keep lowering and condensing the energy?

M: Oh, my God, I am in the void. How I love it back in the void!

S: See yourself now as you are in the wall of the void. Imagine the vibration rising to the point where form is no longer real. Now you can move at will through the void. I wonder what is happening when you slow down even further past the point of our understanding of reality. What happens when you slow down further past that point? What type of reality is that?

M: You mean when the form is completely solidified?

S: Yes.

M: One can lower their energies until there is no sense of consciousness, but it's like covering the soul. It's like wearing a shroud or veil so we can create a veil of forgetfulness, but it is nothing more than a veil of illusion. Then if we wish to descend further, it is possible to actually experience oblivion and have no sense of conscious awareness. However, the soul and higher self are always aware. One can temporarily lose consciousness or the sense of what consciousness is. This would not be life in the form of a rock, a tree, or even a leaf. This would be descending even further down the evolutionary scale. I don't think that I have been there, but I sense that there are energies that have coalesced even more compactly than what would appear as solid matter.

There is awareness in the rocks, the trees, the flowers, and plants. I did not choose to descend to the point of oblivion although the choice is always there. It is always temporary because the soul force and spark never die. It innately seeks its way back to Source Creator whence it began. I chose to have memory and consciousness no matter how dense the matter and energy became. No matter how low the vibration, I could not bear to totally forget where I came from and who I was. Even when I was swaying with the wind as a reed on the waters and in the joyous dance of the movement, I experienced life, and I was stimulated by the touch of the wind. I could not speak words, but I had consciousness. This has been the case for me individually since time immemorial.

S: What do you understand of the magnetism of energy of all those trillions of particles that to most people it just appears to be chance that they stick together and form into solid matter? What do these particles do? What are they guided by? What is this consciousness? Is it made up of some sort of solidified particles also, and how does that interact with our solid matter?

M: It is will and desire that create these particles of which you speak, but in the absolute sense, these particles are mere floating energy waves. It is through the consciousness and through the will to experience energy condensation and compactness that you create what you call particles which can become compact and join and become solid matter. But they only exist according to the degree of your perceptions. In the absolute sense, there are no particles. There are only energy waves. The basis of reality corresponds to your level of perception in accord with your will and your desire to create and experience. Collective and personal free will create everything.

S: Michael, this is very interesting and fascinating information that you have shared. Thank you. Now I would like to change our pace. I want you to go backwards in time before this incarnation to something else other than Michael as he knows himself in this incarnation. Can you share a memory of some other form that you have experienced—something of interest to you? What comes to your mind? What form are you now taking?

M: I am the cat! I spring with quick movements. I am swift of step and movement. I jump about. I am strong and I am wise. I am still with Michael. That is why he fears me a little when he sees cats. He's somewhat disconcerted, for I am that part of him that he has not completely accepted and experienced. Still, he holds me in awe, but there is no reason for I am part of him. I am the cat! I spring to life. I follow my instincts without the encumbrance of thinking. This, Michael needs to remember!

S: Now let's look at your incarnations as though you're looking through a fog, and you pick out a human incarnation. You pick out one and now become that incarnation. Become it. Where are you?

M: I'm old. I'm in a cave. It's dark and secure, and I dare not go out to see the light for I'm afraid of the light.

S: What do you eat?

M: I eat what is brought from the clansmen. They bring forth meat, berries, and nuts. I will not venture into the light for the darkness is my abode, and I do not wish to see the light. So they bring me food.

S: Who are the clansmen?

M: They are the tribesmen who walk the lands with bent posture. Their lesser developed minds are composed somewhat of animal consciousness.

S: What is your relationship to them?

M: They don't quite understand me for I don't make the noises they do. The clanspeople growl and make strange raspy sounds. When I touch them on the forehead, I sense their primitive thoughts. I am an old wise being, playing with form. I see far beyond form even though part of me interacts with it.

S: Do the clanspeople understand this?

M: They do not understand me, but they hold me in reverence.

S: So they bring you food. Do they worship you?

M: Yes, and I cannot convey the idea that I am simply a symbol of a symbol. It is very frustrating for me at times, but this is a lesson I must learn in this particular lifetime— that some people need a tangible person and objects to behold and idolize, for they cannot grasp the infinite any other way. So I must play this role for them.

S: How does the light make you feel?

M: I have not seen the light in this life. It would blind me, for I see with inner vision. The darkness is my light. I do not ever leave the cave whence I was given birth. My mother died in the cave, and then the clansmen came and found me. When they tried to take me outside, I made a very high shrill sound which frightened them. It was a shrill sound they had never heard, and it caused pain to their ears. They put me down, and I didn't make the sound anymore. They automatically knew to leave me alone.

S: Look at your darkness now. See with your eyes closed. I want you to feel it shifting back into your perception of the darkness in the cave and your reality of that experience. Feel the consciousness shifting back. Can you see the clansmen bring you food? You said that to them you were a symbol of a symbol. Very interesting. It almost seems as though for the intangible to be conveyed, it would require the use of a symbol of a symbol, almost like going out into infinity. Perhaps the symbol could help their consciousness expand so they could grasp infinity more. I am wondering if it could be like taking two mirrors and facing them towards each other. A symbol of a symbol. Can you elaborate more on that?

M: They have a sense of a greater presence. They have a word that I cannot say to help them express their idea of the *greater* presence.

S: Feel your forehead relax and your third-eye open up. Your eyebrows become totally relaxed. Your third-eye opens more, and you become even more relaxed and receptive. What were you saying?

M: (in a softer tone) They have a certain word that represents their perception of a greater being. But just to conceptualize the greatness itself is a condensation of energy, for in the absolute sense to even perceive God is separation from that greater energy through a symbol of a symbol. I, to the clans people, am the symbol of their idea of God. God is not the right word. They had another word. I don't hear this word even though it was a symbol itself because all symbols are only fractions of the essence. Symbols can shatter very easily. When true essence is perceived, there are no symbols. Symbols are a vague mask to perceive, see, or sense something very dimly.

S: Now you are thoughtless. No thoughts. You are just in a *being* state, and you will hear the sound that comes through for the clans people's understanding of God. Be silent. The first sound that enters your mind will be that word.

M: Be Yah! Be Yah! Be Yah!

S: Interesting. I want you to move in time again to another incarnation. You are now in another incarnation. What do you see?

M: (Laughter) I am a very beautiful woman, but that isn't who I am at all. That's who I am perceived to be. Oh, how the men want me even though they don't know me at all. They are so unevolved in their consciousness that it lowers their perceptions of beauty and desires and creates lust to have sex with a physical body. I allow them this diversion as I constantly laugh. I don't take life seriously, for I am simply as a mannequin. My true form is light. I just play with form as a child plays with toys. (Laughter). They are lost children that are searching for something that is within their own heart and soul. For me to give them thrills is what they like. It makes them feel loved. Being a shape-shifter, I can take on the form of a different woman to each man I am with. They think I consider them special but the truth is that I am not even there when they have sex with me.

The telephone rang and interrupted the session. We felt we had done enough for one day. The phone ringing did give me a jerk and startled me a bit. Stephen placed his hand on my forehead, and I lay still a few moments. He told me to take my time coming back into my body. That was interesting because at that moment I felt lighter than a feather, and it seemed that I could just float in the air. For days I had images of the beautiful woman shape-shifting into many different female forms. Sometimes I would see a golden glow around her, and she would be entirely encased in a golden bubble. A few times her form disintegrated, and she transformed into a brilliant spark of light and sped away towards the sky.

I would also see the reed gently swaying on the waters while enjoying the touch of the wind and the water. This stirred up a childhood memory when I used to sit for hours at ponds and watch the cattails sway back and forth to the movements of the ripples on the pond. I loved to watch the movement of their reed-like leaves and touch their long brown fuzzy spikes. It gave me such comfort, and I felt a sense of belonging at the ponds. It was like the reeds and cattails were welcoming me. Perhaps they were.

CHAPTER TWENTY-THREE

JOINING

From the beginning, I knew that Izira was very powerful and that she was from faraway. She simultaneously attracted and scared me, especially when she told me that I possessed as much power, if not more, than she did. She said that coming into my power would involve partaking in a dangerous mission.

Izira was a mysterious and fascinating woman. I got lost in her eyes every time I looked into them. How I loved her piercing, black eyes. Sometimes their gaze was cold, primal, and intense; other times, it exuded warmth that made me feel giddy and dizzy. I knew that she was doing something to me when she gazed at me deeply, but I could never figure out what—nor did I care. We never spoke about it.

She had soft white skin and long fingers. Coal black hair fell down her shoulders to her waist. Her lips were full, round, and slightly red. I was inclined to think she might be part elf or faerie. Her ears were slightly pointed, and she walked so fast that I actually thought she glided at times. She also laughed a lot. I had heard that faerie folk laugh a lot. She would giggle every time I asked how faraway faraway was. She'd say that her power made words like time, space, and motion irrelevant and that when I tapped into my power, I would understand what she meant.

When Izira wasn't teasing or laughing, she'd often look dreamily into space. There was a deep yearning in her eyes during those times as though she were longing for something or someone. A few times I saw her tears but never said anything. I didn't want to intrude on her private reveries.

Izira could stare into space for the longest time.

When I'd call her back because my body was getting stiff sitting or from standing so long, she'd apologize and say, "I forget that time is real for you. I must learn to be more sensitive to you."

Sometimes, she'd gently touch my face as she said my name. That gesture sent me reeling. Her touch was magical. Everything about her was. No human had ever made me feel so much wonder, mystery, or love! She once told me that she came from a faraway place where magic was the norm. I often thought about that and tried to imagine living somewhere like that.

Izira said that we create magic when we align our soul with the positive forces of the universe. It is then that things begin to manifest for us. We discover that the universe is a loving place where our wishes truly can and do come true if we work with the universal law of attraction in these ways: 1) state our intentions; 2) be in the proper state of mind; and 3) maintain a positive flow.

Izira told me that everything and everyone is interconnected. The people on her world understand this. They can manifest what they wish because they can join themselves with all life.

"Manifesting is not a thinking matter," she told me one day. "Manifesting is a matter of knowing and joining."

One day I saw her crying beneath an oak tree in the park where we sometimes walked. I quietly watched her speak with the tree as though it was a real person. I even wondered if she had brought the tree to life. I could hear her words in my mind.

"Everything is alive. We can communicate with any form of life."

Then she sat beneath the branches of the oak tree. Moments later, two branches lowered and tapped her gently on the shoulders as though trying to console her. Startled, I jumped away from the tree where I was hiding and walked towards her. She was taken aback and jerked, letting out a cry when I tapped her on the shoulder. Then her head jerked, and she fainted in my arms. The tree limbs recoiled from her grasp. The entire tree seemed to shrink back.

"Good heavens," I cried out. "I've done something terribly wrong. I've probably killed her. How selfish to do such a thing just to justify my need for answers."

I had never felt worse in my life and vowed that from that moment on, I would never demand explanations.

"You can't be dead," I said softly. "You're too powerful."

A few minutes later Izira woke up. We were both sitting under the oak tree.

If I didn't know any better I'd say that the tree guided me to sit under it, I thought.

Izira looked deeply into my eyes, and my head began spinning. Then she patted the tree trunk and leaned her face against it. I actually felt jealous. She was quiet for several minutes and then moved closer to me. She took my hand in hers and spoke softly.

"The tree and I were almost in oneness. You disrupted our joining by startling me. It wasn't your fault. You didn't know what you were doing. I am sure that what you beheld was very strange and difficult to comprehend. It is time you learned more about me. I do come from faraway. I'm from another star or world as you call it. It's not really so different there as here. Magic exists there as it does here and everywhere else when you look for it, or shall I say create it? The tree and I were almost joined at the non-distinction level when you tapped me. Everything is possible at the non-distinction level.

"These ideas are too far-out, Izira. "People don't think like this in our world."

"There a few such people, Michael. Part of the reason I came to you a few months ago is because I need your help regarding my brother Lanar."

"Really? Izira, please tell me why you chose to come to me. How could you need me for anything?"

"Because you are far more powerful than you realize, and we have a very strong connection. I think that you are now ready to be told that you, Lanar, and I belong to the same soul family. You have been with us before, and your soul knows this. This is why I have come to you. You are my star brother, Michael. I need your help and so does my twin brother, Lanar, who is also your star brother. I need you to communicate with Lanar and free his soul from the big purple stone. An evil sorcerer named Rokar deceived, mesmerized, and imprisoned Lanar's soul in a stone. This happened one month ago up there on the star called Decily. This is where he lives and where I sometimes live. Lanar is growing weaker every day while Rokar absorbs and steals more of his lifeforce. At best he can hold out a few more days, probably less than a week."

"Izira, my heart goes out to you, but what makes you think I can help Lanar, even if he is my star brother?"

"Michael, after the scene with the tree, you know that communication is possible in ways you didn't believe in before. I know that you can free Lanar's soul. I have dreamt that you can. I know that this is not an idea that you would call crazy. I know that it sounds like a fairy tale or fantasy story. How I wish it was, but it is not. If Lanar's soul is not freed soon, his physical body will die."

"Izira, I've never heard anything like this before."

"Yes, you have, and you are not totally lacking in experience or knowledge of such matters. Michael, on your world there are some voodoo practices where certain evil sorcerers can steal souls. Zombies are believed to be victims of soul theft, and they wander the earth as the undead. Not alive. Not dead but undead. There is more truth to this than people believe."

"I've always wondered about such things. I have a voodoo horror movie called *The Serpent and the Rainbow*, which is about soul theft and zombies. I always get chills when I watch that movie, and I've seen it four times. The scene where the captured souls are released from the jars where the evil sorcerer had sealed them in especially affect me strongly. Part of me thought the story and premise were fiction, but as I thought more about it, I realized that I had never investigated voodoo or zombies. Then how can I be in a position to make an intelligent conclusion or judgment one way or the other? I try to keep an open-mind when it comes to spirit or demonic possession, voodoo, soul theft, black magic, and such things, but, to be honest, these are not areas I am drawn to explore."

"You do not have to research voodoo and black magic. You already have some experience with sorcery. I know about the experience you had where part of your soul entered into and merged with a rock."

"I have not thought about that strange experience with my friend Robert in a long time. I remember somehow manifesting a bright light to encase and protect the part of my soul that entered the rock. I also manifested another bright light to surround my friend and to help protect him. As farfetched and strange as it sounds, while I was in the rock, I held onto my friend's silver cord and guarded it. I somehow protected and kept his body safe while he went to the astral plane and did battle with a dark sorcerer who wanted to capture his soul. To be honest, I didn't know what I was doing, but somehow I did it anyhow."

"Michael, your soul knew just exactly what to do. Had your soul not known what to do, you could not have created a shield of protection, and the dark sorcerer could have come after you. I tell you, Michael, you are a very powerful sorcerer who works for the light. You do it on many planes that you are not conscious of just as your friend did battle on the astral plane with a dark sorcerer."

"There is not much that you have not done, my star brother. You have been a spiritual guide, mentor, and intergalactic, interstellar negotiator and ambassador of good will on many other worlds. I will tell you about some of them sometime. This is why you are a natural teacher. Now I beg you to help my brother. Please help," she pleaded.

I looked at her without saying anything for a long time. She took my hand and spoke softly a time later.

"You do believe me, don't you? You must. Michael, you know far more than you let on or even realize."

"I think about things, but I'm not sure I'd call it *knowing*."

"It is *knowing*, and it is time for your knowledge to be put to use. You don't have to understand everything to affect changes. You will help me, won't you?"

"I will try," I said softly. "I've always felt there was some deep power in me wanting out, but I was afraid, especially since I don't understand it."

"Part of the reason I have come to you is to help you understand and embrace your power, but first you must let it out."

"I'm not sure how. Sometimes I'm so energetic I have to shake my hands in the air to release energy."

Izira looked at my hands that were trembling slightly. "Don't be afraid," she said, gently rubbing my hands. "You are going to tap your power soon, and then you won't need to shake your hands in the air for release. What a waste of your intense powerful energy! So, will you come to Decily with me?"

"I will come with you although I'm not sure whether I can help Lanar."

Izira smiled and touched my cheek. "Michael, I'll be sure for you. Now, since time is not the same, once we leave here, you will not be gone for more than two earth hours."

"I suppose if I can merge part of my soul into a rock and protect a friend's silver cord while he battles a dark sorcerer on the astral plane and retrieves his soul pieces, perhaps I can help Lanar. I shall do my best, Izira, even though I am afraid."

"There is no dishonor in fear. If you admit and face your fear, it will give you power."

"I have heard that before. Do you think the sorcerer will be able to steal my soul and lock it in the stone?"

"No, and let me tell you a little secret. You possess more power than Rokar. After hearing your story about your friend Robert, I see that you bring power with you from many other lifetimes."

"I've heard that I have not always used my power for good and for the light."

"None of us have. This lifetime is your opportunity to pay off any old karma involved with the dark. Try and look at it that way."

I looked at her with fear in my eyes.

"I give you my promise. Rokar will not defeat you. He is a master at words and illusion, but if you pay him no attention, you will be immune to his power."

"Why did your brother fall under his spell?"

"I wasn't there to warn him, and he was foolish," she said, looking away sadly. "I never thought Rokar would come to Decily. I was gone when he arrived." Izira fell silent for several minutes.

"Come now," I said awhile later. "Shouldn't we be on our way?"

"Yes," she whispered. "Now I need you to lie down on your bed. I will help release the part of your soul that will make the spirit journey with me. You will feel lightheaded and dizzy for a few moments, and then it will pass. Your physical body will sleep peacefully until we return."

"Thank you. I always look forward to spirit journeys."

A few minutes later we were on the distant world of Decily. It was night. Every star twinkled brightly. They seemed to be smiling and even whispering to each other.

Izira burst into a smile. "The stars are happy that I am back, and they are happy that I have brought you. They sense that something wonderful is about to happen. Notice how they are aglow and are so much brighter than usual."

"I like their confidence and wish I had some."

"You shall soon have the confidence you presently lack."

I was in awe of all the beauty. The trees were so tall they seemed to reach the sky itself. Their leaves were lush and full. They seemed to somehow be more alive than the trees on the earth. A sweet scent permeated the air. I felt like I was in the Garden of Eden or some similar paradise.

"This place is magical," I said, "even though it is night, I can see everything. It's like nothing I have ever seen. The colors are exquisite, and everything is so beautiful."

"Yes, Decily is a world where both night and day are bright," Izira said.

"How could your brother be trapped in a stone here?"

"Sorcery. Lanar possesses much power, but he does not think so. As his star brother, you can help him unleash his power by joining with him. You will know how to do that when we arrive at the stone. As I said before, there is much deep knowing inside you waiting to come forth. Just as you knew what to do with Robert, you will know what to do with Lanar."

"I will take your word for it, and I sure hope you are right."

Izira led me through a dense forest. Several animals came out and observed us. Izira made different sounds as she petted and greeted them. Sometime later we approached a hill. A purple glow permeated the air. A sense of fear and dread gripped me.

"You are only sensing Lanar's fear and Rokar's anger. Rokar knows that we are here. A powerful sorcerer can always sense another one's presence. Try to calm yourself. Breathe in the fresh air. Take in the beauty. Let it fill you."

I took a few deep breaths and felt better. When we ascended the hill, the glow was so bright I had the feeling I was about to enter a dream. A few feet away stood a huge purple round stone. There were red flames darting back and forth on the top of the stone. I could see little faces on them and feel a burning rage emanating from each of them."

"Those nasty flames are creations and projections which are fed by Rokar's rage. They are no more than fabricated illusions, but even illusions can take on a certain life force when imbued with energy. As you know, rage is very powerful energy. One illusion can easily be substituted for another if you understand illusion, and I have the feeling that you do. The flames cannot harm you if you hold your power stance and follow your intuition."

"Okay," I said, not feeling as certain or confident as Izira.

"Your intuition will activate your knowledge and power. You must act on knowledge in very specific ways. Combine a strong will, knowing, and the right words, and there is no limit to your power. It is really a matter of naming what you wish to create, for thoughts are truly things. Unfortunately, many people have forgotten how to manifest their desires. They seem to think that things must be done the hard way via vigorous mental or physical labor."

"I want to awaken my power, Izira."

"Awaken is the word," she whispered, tapping my cheek. "I shall be glad to provide you with ample opportunities to awaken your powers."

"You are so confident. Why can't you free Lanar from the stone?"

"I have been shown that this is *your* task to help bring you into your power. It is also a soul promise and agreement that you and Lanar made long ago. Now let us proceed with our mission and approach the stone. I sense your fear. Let it gather power. You have plenty of power inside you to ward Rokar off. You just have not yet had the opportunities to tap some of your deeper powers. You shall soon have it."

"Should Rokar appear, he will sense your fear and will try to steal its power. As I said before, fear contains a lot of power. The key is to harness its power, not let someone else steal it. You do so by following your deepest instincts even in your greatest moments of fear. Rokar is an evil, greedy egotist. He's not even worth looking at, and you must not look at him. There are many ways to steal energy and power from eye contact. Your fear can shield you against his power, but you must not look at him, or he could steal your power. I regret not teaching this to my brother. He was overtaken by Rokar's power because instead of focusing on his own power, he became enchanted by Rokar's amazing feats and displays. He should have sensed the sorcerer's evil intentions behind his façade and refused to give him audience. Once the vile sorcerer got Lanar's attention and curiosity aroused, he knew that he had him under his control.

"Lanar could have blocked Rokar by looking away. Remember, if Rokar looks at you, look away—no matter how difficult it might be. His eyes are very compelling, but he cannot force you to gaze at him. He will tempt and try to enchant and hypnotize you. To hold eye contact with him for even a moment is risky and dangerous. Oh, how I wish I could have warned and prepared Lanar."

"How can you know everything in advance, Izira?"

"Unfortunately, I can't. Even power has its limitations. It is time for Lanar to be free of this evil power that binds him. Let us advance to the stone now."

When we approached the stone, dark ominous clouds covered the sky. The wind began to howl.

"That's Rokar up to no good," she said, waving her hand. A patch of white clouds superimposed themselves over the storm clouds, preventing them from reaching them.

"He can have his storm if he wishes, but we don't have to participate in it. There is always counter-power to destroy or neutralize negative power. Never forget this. I can't destroy Rokar's storm, but I can keep it from us. He has no right to impose his dark rage and hatred upon us. Tyrants must be stood up to!" Izira said as she shook her fist.

I stood amazed. Thunder clapped and lightning bolted— but only above the white clouds. All below was tranquil and serene. It was like seeing a movie super-imposed on another one.

"Yes," Izira said, reading my thoughts. "You need not view the storm. He is only trying to impress you with his power and instill fear in you. Give it no attention."

We slowly made our way to the stone. I immediately noticed a shadowy form inside. The flames hissed. A few darted towards me. Instinctively and quickly, I visualized a large cube of ice and blew it in their direction. The flames instantly melted. Then I visualized a bucket of water and poured it on the stone. There was a loud sizzling, and the flames disappeared.

"This truly is a world where thoughts are things," I said.

"This is a world where thoughts enhance power. The power came from inside you, Michael."

I shifted my perceptions and concentrated on seeing inside the stone. A loud hissing sound pierced my ears as a huge bird with sharp talons was rapidly descending from the sky in my direction. Izira shape-shifted into a fierce dragon and took on the huge bird. After a brief struggle, it fell to the ground. I was huffing and gasping for breath.

"Don't be fooled or frightened, Michael. That was only illusion. Rokar is only trying to scare you away. I will counter his illusions while you free Lanar."

I waited a few moments. No more creatures attacked.

"I think we are safe for the moment, Michael. Rokar senses that I have garnered a lot of power since I was last here, and he is right. I think I have enough strength and power to hold him off should he try anything else. Please continue, Michael."

I felt a strong urge to place both my palms on the surface and lean my body against the stone.

"Very good," Izira said. "You are joining with the stone. Power has its own way of instructing us when we're receptive."

I leaned tightly against the purple stone. My eyes closed. The shadowy form of Lanar maneuvered itself until he was in the same position as I was.

"Let him join with you. Release your power. Let it penetrate the stone and absorb your and Lanar's fears. Let your power awaken Lanar's, but do not enter the stone too quickly. Rokar's power will try to suck you in before you and Lanar have joined. Joining takes time. Do not rush."

I felt immense fear flood through me. A very powerful force was trying to suck me into the stone. It took all of my will-power to resist this force. Several times I almost pulled away to be free. My spirit body started shaking until I feared I would shatter into a thousand pieces and disappear.

"You are joining with Lanar's fear and power," Izira said. "Just a few more minutes." The shaking and jerking intensified. I was being yanked into the stone.

"Resist!" Izira cried out. "Don't let Rokar's energy pull you in! Resist! You have to resist! You are stronger than Rokar. Keep going! You are almost done. Fight him! Refuse to give in! Step into your power! You can do it, Michael."

My head throbbed til I felt it would burst. I sensed Rokar's evil presence and overwhelming stench nearby as he fiercely fought to pull me into the stone. Still I persisted. I could feel the stone weakening. I felt Lanar and I begin to meld. We began feeding each other power, which grew stronger by the moment. No words were spoken. I gritted my teeth and wondered if the veins in my neck would burst. Some force deep within me pushed me against the stone. It forced its way into the stone, penetrating its mass. Deeper and deeper it pushed until a small opening appeared. It was time for the complete joining.

I pushed forward, and my spirit body entered the stone. Lanar reached for me. We stood in a solid embrace. Our spirit bodies jerked and twisted. I could feel our souls merging. Soon a bright golden light appeared. Our combined energies created tremendous power and light. Moments later, the stone exploded.

"It is over," Izira shouted in glee. Lanar threw his arms around her.

"My sister," he cried out, tears streaming down his face. "I never thought I'd see you again." I noticed that Lanar resembled her except that he was a little taller. They both reached for my hands, and we walked away.

Strange shrill noises sounded from where the stone had been.

Each of our names was imitated by our mother's pleading voice, "Michael, Lanar, I beg you! Don't abandon me! Help! Save me!"

"That is Rokar's illusion—nothing more. Ignore it," Izira said, walking a little faster.

We slowly descended the hill. We spent the next few hours visiting different sites. There were beautiful white domed temples and gardens. There were crystal palaces and groves and orchards with all kinds of exotic fruits dangling from the trees. There were treats and delights that we do not have on the earth, and there was the beautiful star-filled sky with stars aglow so dazzlingly and radiant that the night was bright. I felt like I could spend the rest of my life exploring the beautiful star world that was bright both day and night. I felt so at home. Izira reminded me that we needed to return.

"This spirit journey has taken a lot of energy, and your physical body needs nourishment to be replenished. There will be time for further exploring in the future, Michael."

Lanar and I hugged and looked deeply into each other's eyes.

"Thank you for rescuing me, Michael." he said, tears streaming down his cheeks. He pulled me closer and held me more tightly, crying softly. I didn't think he'd ever let me go, but a few moments later, he gently released me. He kissed me on both cheeks.

"Michael, you are my star brother who has been gone a very long time. How I've missed you." He placed his hand on my heart. So much energy poured into me that I staggered.

"Thank you for everything, my star brother. Don't worry. You'll be seeing me again. We will have lots of tales to share. Goodbye for now," he said as he waved goodbye.

Moments later, Izira and I were back in my apartment.

"I don't get it," I said. "It happened so fast. Lanar and I didn't exchange a single word."

"That doesn't mean that you did not communicate. I cannot thank you enough," she said, hugging me tightly. "Michael, I knew that you had the power to free my brother. I always knew it."

"I think I had a little help from you," I said, smiling. "I could feel your strength."

"Yes, but most of it you did alone. You took Lanar's fear and power into yourself as he did yours as you merged with one another. That's what caused the jerking and twisting. You were mirrors for each other as each battling your deepest fears. Lanar's fear was that the stone would imprison him for eternity, and your fear was that your fear would keep your power locked inside you. In a sense, you freed each other. Your mutual strength empowered both of you, giving you access to deep inner reservoirs of power. In time you are going to learn to do things with energy that you could never imagine."

"I don't really feel that powerful."

"You don't need to. Feelings can be deceptive. Besides, power is something that you acquire and wield; it is not something that you necessarily have to feel."

"I sure could feel the power surging through me. Izira, you know there were moments when I didn't know whether it was Lanar's fears or my own that I was battling."

"This is common when you're joining with a kindred spirit. Your power is amplified, which means that your fears amplify as well. Your identity can feel quite nebulous during the experience."

"I feel different now, Izira. Somehow more complete."

"Yes, you are both more complete now. Lanar has helped you awaken your power as you have helped him awaken his. You will soon find out how simple it really is to manifest things. I don't mean necessarily out of thin air, although that is also possible for the adepts. You will find more and more that what you think and focus on with passion and strong feelings will be drawn to you. This is why you must watch your thoughts and the words that you speak."

"Does one have to meet one's fears to receive this power?"

"Yes, fear is one of our greatest and most difficult teachers. It offers more power than our other teachers. It is not our enemy, like most people think. It is our friend once we join with it. Each time we act and do what our heart tells us is right, we merge a little more with our fears."

"That somehow makes sense. I was never so frightened as when Rokar tried to suck me in, but at the same time I was never so challenged. I became willful and determined to save your brother. I had to. It meant more to me than life itself. Once I leaned against the stone, I knew we would win. I don't know how I knew. I felt a similar resolve as a child when my father would constantly put me down. It somehow gave me strength, and I knew that I would come out ahead no matter how difficult things were."

"Yes, your father was a great teacher for you. He used mental black magic and imposed intense suffering upon you. This type of thing happens far too often on your world and accounts for so much misery. People can and do get into other people's heads. The stronger the will, the easier it is to influence and manipulate others. Your father was very powerful but even at a young age, your will was very strong. He could not break it, plus you had some assistance from your *other-worldly* friends," she said, winking at me.

"Your instincts and intuition are very strong, and they told you what to do to save Lanar. Now I must take my leave, my star brother, so you can get some dinner."

"You will come back, won't you, Izira?"

"Certainly."

Izira hugged me, kissed me on the cheek, and then disappeared. I woke up feeling light-headed and hungry.

I thought about the experience with Izira and Lanar many times. I thought about Robert who had said that some of the greatest and most difficult battles are not fought on the earthly battlefields but on other planes and dimensions. Unlike Robert, who said he had many more battles on the astral planes to help other souls retrieve missing and stolen soul pieces, I hoped and prayed that freeing my star brother's soul was my last battle.

At heart, I am more of a poet, mystic, and lover than a warrior. I was grateful for my experiences on the star world. I will never forget that challenging, fascinating adventure on Decily—the world where day and night are bright. Time alone would tell what my next adventures would be.

CHAPTER TWENTY-FOUR

A GLIMPSE OF ME IN A FUTURE LIFETIME

The diva sang several encores and the audience gave loud bravos and shouted, "Viva la diva!" with standing ovations for an extended period of time. The applauding slowed down and finally died as people rose from their seats and began leaving the opera house.

A tall, well-dressed handsome man, sitting in the plush purple seat as the people left, thought about this remarkable singer. He had read her raving reviews. As a matter of fact, he had read everything he could about her. His bedroom wall was lined with various pictures of her in her opera costumes, as well as many of her modeling photos for magazines in Europe, the United States, Australia, and South America. He never missed her local opera performances and concerts. He had her tour schedule memorized along with all of the dates and places where she performed operas and concerts all over the world.

Journalist after journalist. Reporter after reporter. Photographer after photographer commented on the ethereal beauty of this amazing singer with the pristine, coloratura voice. Many reviews stated that hers was the most beautiful voice since Brooklyn, New York's prima donna, Beverly Sills, who had blessed the world with her exquisite vocal skills in some fifty operas in the second part of the twentieth century. One critic called her an angel and said that even God, himself, would take leave from his busy schedule to be enchanted by her magnificent presence and singing.

The lovely, strawberry blond diva wearing a smooth-fitting emerald green gown with glittering sequins and a sparkling diamond necklace with earrings to match, stood on the stage looking around as though she were searching for someone. Her eyes roamed each and every aisle until she came upon the man sitting crouched in the plush seat. *How could she spot him so far away?* I wondered when it looked like he was half under the seat, hidden from view.

As she looked in his direction in the quiet auditorium, she began to sing a very haunting song. It had a lot of runs, trills, and high notes. It was like every single note was making its way to the very seat of his soul. He had never heard such passionate singing. The language was not English. The man slowly rose and made his way towards the stage.

The diva ignored him, completely lost in her haunting song. Tears spilled down her cheeks. The man also began to weep as he, too, was lost in the music of this beautiful singer. He took a seat on the front row.

When the singer finished the song, she slowly made her way towards him. She seemed to glide off the stage. She reached out her arms to him. The man rose from his seat. When she embraced him, the man totally disappeared inside her; the two became as one.

I jerked my head and came out of my reverie. The empty snowy screen in front of me made me feel like I was in some type of twilight zone. Until then I was unaware of the scratchy noise. I turned the TV off then sat back down and closed my eyes.

"Who is that woman?" I asked. She looked so familiar, and why did the man just evaporate and fade into her? I tapped my head gently then pointed towards the TV screen. The documentary I was watching about the life of the famous seer Nostradamus was near the end.

"Nostradamus, are you playing tricks on me, ole seer?" I asked aloud. "Have you pulled me through time?" I asked, pretending and half hoping that I'd get an answer.

Who was that beautiful woman? I found myself asking yet another time.

The name Stella Marie Bergman popped in my head. In my mind I heard, *This is the year 2063, and you are making your grand operatic debut at the royal opera house in Stockholm, Sweden, singing Gaetano Donizetti's famous opera, 'Lucia Di Lammermoor.'*

You, I gasped. *Who are you?*

Why you, I heard, then a voice laughed. *This is your next life. You are a prima donna Swedish opera singer. Hasn't this been your dream for a long time?*

I coughed a few times and then came out of my reverie. It took a few minutes to acclimate myself to my surroundings again.

One of the teachers came in and greeted me. "What are you doing, Michael? You look you've just seen a ghost?"

"Worse," I wanted to say. "I've just seen me in a future life as a prima donna opera singer.

Instead I said, chuckling, "Yeah, I think I saw a ghost. I think I drifted off. I was previewing a video I want to show the students about the famous French seer, Nostradamus."

"Well, happy dreaming," my fellow teacher and friend Jenny said. "Be sure and don't drift off when you show the movie to the students. We must always set a good example." She then waved goodbye and left.

The memory of that day haunted me for a long time. It also brought up a lot of old yearnings and unanswered questions from my past. During my first two years of college, I was obsessed with the desire to become an opera singer. I took voice and piano lessons and learned everything I could about the operas. I read all the plots and every opera magazine I could get my hands on. I listened to as many recordings as I could find. I loved listening to different renditions of the arias and art songs and acquired quite a collection. I practiced every spare moment. To my great disappointment, I just could not get a grasp on the music. I had a mental block when it came to reading music. Emotional blocks and fear prevented my voice from opening up. I could not relax enough to allow the music to come out of me. That struggle continued for two years.

One weekend I was visiting my voice teacher and friend, Janette, who had become a second mother to me and my girlfriend Martina. I was in the back room singing and hitting some high notes.

Janette came back and said, "Who is that woman who was singing?"

"There's no woman in here, unless you are referring to the recording. I am listening to Leontyne Price sing the farewell aria from the opera 'Madama Butterfly.'"

"There was another voice," Janette insisted, "and it was a high soprano voice. I know that I heard two voices, but how can that be since there is no other woman here? I most certainly was not singing and even if I had been, I can no longer sing the high notes that I just heard."

"Oh, that was just me, singing along with the recording. I think I went into falsetto or something."

"Simply amazing," Janette said. "Michael, you have been struggling for over two years to sing in your natural tenor voice. Now you go into falsetto, and the voice is natural and lovely—but it's not a tenor voice. It's not even a counter-tenor voice, which is even higher. It's what is called a sopranist voice. You might be able to do something with that. You could actually develop quite an act. You could go on stage and sing the soprano arias and hit the high notes, then step aside or come back and turn around and sing the tenor arias. You could be a real big hit. Plus, there is a lot of baroque and early music that would suit that other voice perfectly. They had the castrati in the Renaissance. You've just still got all your equipment. Nothing snipped," she said, laughing.

"Yep," I laughed, "the last time I looked, the equipment was still working and all there."

After I relived many memories of my opera singing dream days in college, I thought about my vision in 1987 at the high school where I taught. As I read more about Nostradamus and other metaphysical books, it occurred to me that perhaps I had stepped through time and had a glimpse of a future life. This woman looked and felt so familiar to me. Perhaps she *was* me. Maybe that is why I saw the image of the man who disappeared and merged with her. Perhaps the past and the future were merging. After I gave up my dream of becoming a professional opera singer, I would still sing for myself and for friends. The women envied me saying I could sing higher than they could.

To this day, I can sometimes sing higher than many women. It really makes no sense unless something deeper and more far-reaching could be going on. I have heard recordings of boys who sang soprano arias around the age of twelve or younger, but once they entered puberty, they lost their soprano voice and become either a tenor, baritone, or bass. Why would I be able to retain my original tenor voice, as well as the soprano voice? And to make things even more clear as mud, as my friend Maxime used to say, I've also developed a baritone voice which enables me to belt out songs like "If I Were a Rich Man" from the musical *Fiddler on the Roof*, "If Ever I Would Leave You" from *Camelot*, and "Ole Man River" from *Showboat*. As a matter of fact, I sang "If I Were a Rich Man" at one of our talent shows in the high school where I was teaching in 1987. I even was given an initialized plaque with my name carved for my performance—which I cherish to this day.

I've never figured out what is really going on, but I have some ideas. First of all, I ask what if we can glimpse a future life—that is, if we do indeed have future lives? I claim to have no definitive answers or proof that this woman making her grand operatic debut in 2063, in Stockholm, Sweden, was me. However, I find it interesting that I saw myself making my debut singing Donizetti's opera, "The Bride of Lammermoor." I had a past life reading at the renowned spiritualist camp, Camp Chesterfield, in Chesterfield, Indiana, some years ago. The psychic told me that in a past life I knew the composer Donizetti in Italy. She also said that I was one of the few people who truly believed in his work. Is it not at all surprising that he is one of my favorite composers?

"From what I have read, we can carry our soul memories into future lives and sometimes activate past life memories, which we then incorporate into our present lifetime. But to physically manifest a type of soprano voice in this lifetime? Hmmmm. That seemed farfetched and strange to me.

I asked my friend Janet about it one day, and she said that there is a good chance that I will come back as Stella Bergman and be an opera singer in Sweden. Then again, I had asked my character Mr. Divine in my book *Morning Coffee with God* about that, and he said the choice was mine. I might even choose to sing opera on a parallel world or lifetime—it depends upon my free will. My final conclusion is anything is possible if we have an open mind and heart.

It reminded me that what we do and accomplish in this lifetime can help determine and influence our future lifetimes and even help decide where they will be. The Buddhism and some other spiritual teachings say that karma, desire and attachments are what bring us back to the earth in future lives.

To remind me that synchronicities and so-called coincidences occur frequently, I will share a little story. While I was working on this story about Stella, the opera singer, something interesting happened.

Recently I made some phone calls to the local Cincinnati bookstores to see about arranging some book signings for my book of love poems, *Dawn's Kiss*. When I called the Barnes and Noble in Florence, Kentucky, I was told that the manager was on a conference call; however, she would be in the office until 4:30 p.m., and I was welcome to call her before she left.

I waited until 4:15 p.m. Then I felt the urge to call her. I was put on hold while a clerk went to find the manager. The music playing on the other end of the phone was a tenor singing a song I had never heard before. His voice was very beautiful, and he was singing some high notes. I just snickered, and said, "Okay, spirit, somebody does not think I'm losing my marbles here." That made me feel better because I seldom hear opera when I'm put on hold. It could not have come at a more suitable moment.

To further demonstrate my conclusion that we might be able to look into the future and even glimpse our future life/lives, I'd like to share another story. It happened the summer of 1988, several months after the experience at the high school where I had the vision of me singing opera in a future life. I was staying at my sister's in Louisville, Kentucky, while on summer break. I was friends with one of the neighbor boys, Bobby. Sometimes I would play basketball and poker with him, his uncles, and some cousins. On occasion, Bobby and I would hang out and shoot the breeze. He was a member of some Masonic club. He called it "Demolay" or some such name that I could not spell. One evening we were sitting outside talking. I kept getting bit by mosquitoes. I noticed that Bobby was not once bitten.

"These damn insects," I blurted out, "they're just feasting on me."

"Not me," he said, confidently. "I just have a talk to them, and they don't bother me. They know to stay away from me."

I had no idea what he was talking about nor did I care to explore the subject matter any further. I just went and got a can of bug spray to take care of the problem, and yes, I was intrigued as to why not a single mosquito bit him. *Maybe I'm just hot blooded or something*, I concluded and am more appealing to the insects.

Actually, I wasn't that surprised as I had read that certain yogis and spiritually developed people could control their body functions or even reduce their breathing to the point they appeared to be clinically dead to anyone in a medical establishment. Some of the books I'd read said that Jesus' advanced yogic training allowed him to perform such a feat when he was in the tomb and supposedly dead. Maybe my friend had been an advanced yogi in a past life and knew how to ward off the bugs.

A few nights later, Bobby and I were outside chatting and stargazing. He told me that he could close his eyes and sometimes see things as clearly as if his eyes were opened.

"What do you mean?" I inquired.

"Like now for instance," he continued, "I see this image of a beautiful woman in costume on a stage somewhere very faraway. It feels like Europe somewhere. She is singing opera, I think it's called, as I have no experience with that kind of singing. I just know that she is singing very high notes and she is very passionate and beautiful."

"Interesting," I said, beginning to tremble slightly.

"If I ask, I can probably find out who this woman is."

"Don't bother," I replied. "I don't want to know who this woman is."

"Okay," he replied, nonchalantly. Then he began to talk about an old sports car he was working on.

Part of me believed that Bobby was seeing an image of that very same woman I had seen in my vision at the high school a few months ago. I was a little mad at myself for not asking him who she was. He could have come up with any name, but what if he came up with the same name that had popped into my head? That would have spooked me for sure. And what if he went further and said that she was me in the future? It doesn't matter, but the fact that he saw a woman singing opera on a stage in Europe caught my eye and attention, especially since she seemed like the singer of high notes that I had seen. What is interesting is that I had made no mention of this vision to Bobby. This experience made me think that some type of telepathic interplay might be going on between us. As I've stated many times, I believe that telepathy happens far more frequently than most people are consciously aware.

I never pursued the subject again with my young friend. Still, I wonder. To this day when I listen to those lovely soprano arias from the operas, there is a little voice in me that asks, "What if this woman is me out there singing somewhere in the future? Might she be me? Since I believe in reincarnation, I would definitely enjoy experiencing a life as an opera singer. I could handle being a woman because I have always preferred the female voice to the male voice. Most of my recordings are of women singers.

I discussed this unusual experience with my friend Janet on more than one occasion. One day she said she was picking up the fact that part of my soul was straddling two lives. Now that would explain why the future possible lifetime could somehow maneuver some of its essence into my present lifetime as Michael. This energy could have even helped create my sopranist voice or even my high natural tenor voice or falsetto. The implications here seem to be quite vast, but in my spiritual and metaphysical journeys, I have learned to keep an open mind and accept that anything is possible. I often listen to recordings of Beverly Sills and read through and look at the pictures from the books that she'd written. I get goosebumps when she sings those trills and hits those high E-flats she was so famous for. Sometimes I sing along with the recordings, and I wonder just how intriguing and fulfilling such a life could be!

I told Janet how I have always felt such a close connection to Beverly Sills. I have all of her opera aria recordings and several of her complete operas. I love lots of soprano voices, but she is my all-time favorite. I wondered if I might just be projecting my attraction to Beverly Sills upon this probable future me, who, like Beverly Sills, is a prima donna coloratura soprano opera star?

"I have an idea, Michael," Janet said. "You ought to do a little experiment. Why don't you write a letter to your future self?"

"How in the world would I even begin to know where to send it?"

"It's not that big of a deal. You said the name that came to you is Stella Marie Bergman and that you were making your debut at the Royal Opera House in Stockholm, Sweden, in 2063, didn't you?"

"Yes, but how do I know that could be her real name?"

"Lots of performers change names. I mean, come on, if Frances Ethel Gumm can become Judy Garland or Caryn Elaine Johnson can become Whoopie Goldberg, then anything is possible. Besides, I think the name Stella Marie Bergman is lovely. Just address it to Stella Bergman if you wish c/o the Stockholm Royal Opera House; Stockholm, Sweden."

"That makes no sense. Whoever might open such a letter would surely think I'm a nut case when this Stella Bergman is not yet even born."

"Maybe yes. Maybe no. You could say, 'To whom it may concern.' Regarding this letter, please place it in the archives and request NOT TO OPEN until 2063. Did you get the month of your opera debut by chance?"

"No, but I might be able to," I replied, getting excited about this strange adventure and new prospect. Janet excused herself to go to the restroom. I closed my eyes and saw the image of Stella Bergman again. This time she was sitting at her vanity table in her dressing room, putting on make-up. I somehow knew that she insisted on putting on her own makeup. For a moment she stopped what she was doing and looked dreamily out into space. There was a gentle knock on the door.

"Come in," she said. Inside stepped a tall, distinguished, handsome man, dressed in a light blue suit, a pink shirt, and a white tie. His eyes were sky blue, and his hair was honey blond and very curly.

Stella looked at him and said, "Hello, handsome, what do you have for me? And why that look on your face as though you have seen a ghost?"

The gentleman slowly approached Stella and reached out to hand her an envelope. He dropped it as his hands were shaking.

"Come, come, now, Frederek," Stella told him. "Please tell me you are not the bearer of bad news."

The gentleman nodded as he picked up the envelope.

"It's a letter, Stella, from a very long time ago. One of the boys found it in the archives yesterday."

"How very interesting!" Stella answered, her eyes getting bigger. "I have not seen a real letter for ages since my grandmother used to read me some that her beaus used to write her. How very unusual that I would receive a letter and a very old one at that."

"It's definitely an unusual letter, Stella," Frederek said, looking at the faded envelope.

"Let's have it. I requested that you open my emails to sort through the junk, all the declarations of love, and God knows what else my fans write to me about. If something bad has happened, please tell me. I can take it." Stella gave Frederek an intense look and said with a grin on her face, "Unless, of course, the letter might be good news. Could it be something to give me a little excitement? You never bring me fan letters unless they are important enough to merit my attention."

"Well, Love, I think this one deserves your attention."

Stella grins. "You just never know. Maybe some lost relative has left me a fortune."

"Not the case," Frederek replies. He takes the letter out and reads it to Stella. She is spellbound.

Finally Frederek says, "My darling, you have received many strange letters, but this one tops them all. The good news is that this Michael Dennis character is not asking to meet you like most fans do. He is not requesting any personal information or money. He does not even ask you to take this letter seriously, for he said he was not sure what to make of it. He simply wanted to share the vision he had of you and tell you how he loved your voice that he could hear in some of his visions. What do you think of that?"

Stella reached for the letter and held it next to her bosom. She looked dreamily into space for several minutes, remaining calm, poised, and lost in her thoughts.

A few minutes later she softly said, "This man was a very sweet and gentle soul. It is obvious how much he loved opera and the soprano voice. How strange that he says he had dreams as a young boy that he was a woman singing high notes on stage, and that when he studied opera, along with his tenor voice, he also developed a baritone as well as a sopranist voice that was higher than the voice of many sopranos. He also had a musical, artistic love affair with the American diva Beverly Sills whom he never met in person. I, too, have great respect and admiration for Beverly Sills. Although she sang long before my time, she was still talked about when I was a little girl, and she was also my favorite singer. I'd even tell my mother that when I grew up, I was going to be a diva like Miss Sills. To be compared to her always humbles me and fills my soul with love and the desire to sing even more trills," she said, chuckling. "Michael Dennis, I would like to have met him sometime."

"But Stella, he claims that you are him in a future life. You surely don't believe that, do you?"

"My darling Frederek, as Hamlet in our beloved Shakespeare's play says, 'There are more things in heaven and earth, Horatio, than are dreamt of in your philosophy.' Anything is possible. Be off now. I have a performance in less than an hour."

I told Janet about the vision I had. "You have to write that letter, Michael, that is all there is to it. For now you have seen it delivered to the future you. If you don't write it, you will prevent it from happening."

As of today, January of 2010, I have not yet written the letter. I sometimes think about what I will say. When will I write it? You just never know!"

CHAPTER TWENTY-FIVE

WISDOM FROM THE DELARIANS

As this book was coming to an end, I decided to include a telepathic experience I had on July 23, 1996, with a collective group of souls who said they come from another solar system but had an affinity with certain souls on the earth. My friend Elizabeth was doing energy and Reiki healing on me at the time. This somehow opened me up more and made me receptive to new energies and beings. In the course of three months, I went into a trance several times, and different extraterrestrial beings came through and spoke. Most said they were part of a group collective soul. One group referred to themselves as the serpent people. My voice became a dark baritone, and they spoke in a chant instead of ordinary normal conversation. Other beings presented their messages through singing. I misplaced or lost most of the tapes during one of my many moves, but I did manage to save this one.

Elizabeth and I meditated for a few minutes before I went into trance and channeled. I never knew who was going to come through. We just went with the flow. My guides assured me that I was encased in the protective white light so only benevolent ET's could speak through me. I would do some chanting, singing, or toning before channeling. This opened a portal and helped make me more receptive to their energies. Before the Delarians came through, I chanted longer and louder than usual, and I was chanting words and phrases I had never heard before. A few minutes later, my chanting became more subdued, and then I stopped. I took a few deep breaths, and then they began speaking in a very monotone chant. That was to change as the Delarians became quite emotional at one point in the channeling. Let us now hear from the Delarians! "We are happy to be here with you. We have not spoken on this planet for a very long time. A few of your Native Elders speak with us in dreamtime, but most have forgotten who we are. We are an ancient people. For people is the word we must use. In truth, we are not limited to such an expression of energy. We live faraway on a world called Delarius. This is not to be confused with the word delirious even though there is some similarity in the sounds of both words."

"Sound is also utilized to move energy by many troubled souls on your world who enter various delirious states where their energy becomes erratic and imbalanced. Such persons can become prone to outbursts of hysteria. To be delirious is to be in an excited state. It is an agitated movement of spirit and energy. There is so much dissension on your world at this time because of the improper use of sound. Proper toning and use of sound could help neutralize much of the dissonance and dissension on your world and help bring relief to souls who suffer from mental and emotional imbalance."

"In reality, the throat chakra is not properly activated and used to the point such as we did when we were there. The people were not ready to take in our higher vibrations. We were here long before your Native American peoples and some others. We taught the people the ancient tones and the singing of the celebration of the cosmological order and the All Who Be. You, we, and everyone are part of the All Who Be!"

"It is important for people to learn to make proper use of sound. Sister Elizabeth, one of the things that you will do in your sacred healings is to work with sound. Please prepare to make the necessary adjustments in your vocal apparatus. You will need much physical strength, for you are going to be working with sound healing and tones. It was the movement and maneuvering of light and sound which brought forth life and creation on terra.

Your holy book says, "Let there be light." Light is the origin of all matter, and there must also be sound for creation to occur. Sound can break down the cellular and molecular structures at the quantum levels. At some point, your astrophysicists are going to realize it is through sound and pitch vibrations that they will be able to split the atoms and molecules at whatever levels they wish. It is not going to be with simple scientific instruments. It is going to be through the manipulation and the use of light and sound."

"The ancients knew these things and this is why sound is so important in many rituals and ceremonies of your indigenous and native peoples. We are very happy to speak with you at this time. It is very healing to move the energy, and we do wish that more people studied the vocal arts. This should be— what is the word—encouraged, in your educational facilities because when the lungs are strong, then the soul is able to resound the cosmic sacred tones through the physical apparatus. There are so many blocked energies that could be released through sound, resulting in much needed healing on your world."

"Is there anything you would wish for us to discourse upon? We do not wish to sound like talking boards, but we do enjoy making that vibrational connection with those of you who are ready to receive the summoning of our call—for we are your family. Far past the light and sound barriers where the sacred sounds permeate everything everywhere and where soft gentle humming tones abound, this is where we meet. This is where we teach you in some of our ancient retreats. It is important to be at a certain vibration of energy before we can make this connection. There will be a point in the future where both of you will be in a position to be a channel for more of these types of energies. What is the correct wording in your language? We cannot begin to convey complete messages because we must rely upon the channel's limited vocabulary. There is so much information which we cannot transfer to you because many concepts lie beyond mortal human comprehension. However, we come forth in an effort to convey as much information as we can to remind you of your true nature and your infinite possibilities. However small our success may be, we are still joyous to be able to make a connection with you. Is there anything that you would wish to ask? We are a group soul. We are at least twenty or more, and we keep growing as our individual consciousness units expand to include more of the collective consciousness of those souls who inhabit our world."

"Both of you are expanding. You are uniting with your soul. This soul union is not quite soul retrieval, as you would experience in your shamanic practices and healings. Your shamanic teachings and practices only can retrieve a slim portion of the essence of the actual soul. Fortunately, true connecting with the soul is taking place more upon your world as more humans are beginning to ascend in consciousness and connect with the light of their higher being. We would like to issue forth the term *soul claiming*. Soul retrieval is similar, and as you know, there is the soul spark within each and every one. The size and radiance of this soul spark varies from individual to individual, based on soul evolvement. More people are making progress merging with their souls."

"You will play a part in helping souls accomplish this monumental task. There is so much light and so much peace coming into this world. We are here to say that there will be a grand golden age once more after much purification and cleansing. You will fully claim and embrace love, power, each other, and all life as you arrive at the understanding that everything is connected, and all life originates from beloved Creator Source. This will bring you peace and happiness. You have barely begun to touch the tip of the iceberg of the expansion of your soul star, your soul flame. How are you, friend, Elizabeth?"

"I am fine. Thank you. Can you say something about Michael's voice and the use of sound?"

"Michael is a friend of yours who knows about the power of sound. He is a bard, a poet who used to be a messenger from what you would call village to village. This is why he carries a very strong force of vocal activity. He needs to move and merge with more sound, such as the small demonstration he gave you in the car. We would encourage you to step into an environment where he can release the sound. One way he can move sound is through music and the singing of the many songs he knows."

"There will be some chanting, such as he let us chant some of the ancient tones earlier. As Michael works more with sound, he will release many dispersions of energy and experience tremendous healings. He will be able to move the energy via soft, as well as sometimes booming loud sound. In singing it is the pianissimo notes that are the hardest to sustain, for it takes much vocal and breath control. The softer tones can be the most challenging vocally. They stimulate the chakras and energy centers in ways the louder deeper tones cannot."

"Activating and stimulating the throat chakra via sound is very healing. The chanting that Michael is doing is very good. He is going to make more connections with other star family and beings. His hearing is going to be opening up much more. This is a time for him to use his voice. This is why even speaking a foreign language (as he is being drawn to his beloved French once more) is healing. It is not so much that he will be simply sharing one of the languages which he loves but that he can enjoy his past life memories when he speaks French. It is the maneuvering of sounds by different vocal intonations that brings the energies more into balance and alignment with the soul and higher self."

"It is difficult to convey some of these concepts in this English language. We do not ordinarily express our thoughts and ideas with human words, so we must access the vocabulary of the channel. This is an interesting and educational experience for us."

"Yes, Michael is a friend of sound. This is why he loves music so much. Please, when the opportunity avails itself, do allow this unrestricted flow of sound to pass through the vocal chords. Sound can help you to move beyond your sphere and through the planes. There are many beings from other worlds who do wish to communicate with Terra at this time. And please remind Michael that he does not need to take off his weight. He is so worried over petty trifles, such as having an attractive physical body. He is making efforts to move the body energies to strengthen the muscles through exercise. He is going to need the bulk and to be very grounded in order for the new sounds to come through him."

"Is there a reason in terms of sound healing why I have such a low register. I can't sing in the high register like Michael does."

(In a darker richer tone) "You plunge the depths. We cannot reach these tones, for Michael does not have the voice to reach the lower register, such as a bass or basso profundo would be able to do. If you wish to join in, go ahead."

"You have been a spiritual leader and teacher in many of your incarnations. Several were on Atlantis. On another world you were one of the special keepers of the ancient songs. You were an adept sound healer. You knew the importance of singing and intoning. You understood the healing effects of hearing the sounds of the lower and higher register of the musical scale. Through deep, dark sounds you moved the kundalini energy lower and lower. The kundalini energy must move down before it moves up to cleanse and activate the chakras or energy centers. It begins its serpent movement at the base of the spine and works its way upward through your body and etheric body. We cannot begin to sing as low as you did. The low toning helps to ground the energies and move them at the proper speed, so the chakras are not opened and stimulated too quickly. To force, rush, or move the energy too quickly can do damage to the neural and nervous system. This is known as kundalini or chakra burnout."

"The lower toning helps to slowly move the energy. It moves from the spine to the solar plexus. Then it makes its way to the heart and then on to the third-eye and finally the crown chakra at the top of the head. This process helps to align the etheric body with the physical body. It helps matter and spirit come more in alignment, let us say. It also aligns the light body of the higher self and stimulates hormones in the pituitary gland. This opens up the psychic and soul senses and will be a means by which people will make direct contact with their soul and discover its infinite possibilities and powers."

"Some of your monks in monasteries and religious orders have a certain grasp of these concepts, and this why they sing or chant or pray while holding beads in some instances. They chant in this or that language. But on civilizations before this present one, you moved these sounds through a much deeper, vaster stream of pure light. The lowest note would basically correspond to your color black. Your very highest note would correspond basically to the color white. So you are of the *black ray*, which unfortunately has been unduly distorted in your world of third-dimensional understanding. There were people who did not understand the mystery, magic, and power of your toning. They perceived these sounds to be the roaring of Dark Lords in chambers of evil. But such is not at all true. There is power in the lower, deep, dark sounds."

"Is this helpful?"

"Very."

"Is sound one of the ways that I am going to help people connect to their higher self?"

"Yes, it is, and we would recommend that you undertake a bit of vocal coaching so that you strengthen your diaphragm. You are going to need to exercise more breath control. The free movement that comes through unrestricted breathing and the movement of the throat chakra will allow you to bring forth many healing sounds. You will begin to rumble and tumble the energies, and this will help to break down blocks in the auras and energy emotional fields of those you will be working with. It will be the deeper, darker tones that will be affective, appropriate, and needed here. The darker tones go deeper. Do you not you feel this?"

"Yes."

"To connect with the higher self, it is first necessary and important to make the journey into the deep, dark caverns, shall we say, of your being where many old hurts, memories, and blocked energies are located. You have been doing this as a part of your self-healing for many years. To get to the light, the people must make the descent into the depths of their own souls and meet their dark shadow selves. As people move through their inner darkness, clear out old energies and inner baggage, take in more light, and attain more enlightenment, there will be a greater demand and need for the toning of the higher lighter notes. Then they can move through the more ethereal, lighter energies and bring in more light from their souls and higher selves. But first the old subconscious baggage, to use one of your words, needs to be cleared. Most everyone has a certain amount even though some of your more New Age type people might be the first to deny it."

"Once you have gone deeper into yourself and explored the terrains of your psyche, you will lighten up and be ready to take in the light, higher notes. Your friend Michael can do this as his voice has quite a high range, but he has also developed a darker baritone sound as well. This is natural, for he equally explores the depths as well as heights. The vocal toning reinforces and helps to assimilate and integrate the energies. There will be the creating of some seminars on sound healing called Heart Vibrational Openings or some similar title or other terms you would come up with. There will be syncopated pitch toning because there is so much darkness that must be moved through. The valley of the shadow of darkness must be trodden. Most people have not made this journey to the sufficient point needed for soul realization, actualization, and liberation."

"It is time to go down. Down. Down. This is why you have such a special voice. It is a wonderful unique gift. We wish we could let you hear some of our sounds. You do hear them in your dreams and meditations."

"Will working with sound be an important part of Michael's healing?"

"Yes it will, although he resists because he has seen and witnessed abuse of sound. This happened when a great crystal was split and moved through the maneuvering of sound. This abuse led to major explosions and reverberations, which had negative impacts on the environment and land and accounts for partial and total destruction of some civilizations. There were many abuses that he witnessed but he will balance this lack of wholeness."

"Is your group going to be available to people like me and Michael?"

"Yes, we from Delarius have a special love for you earth people. There was a time long ago when we were part spirit and part person. We had loving rapport with nature and trees. We were able to join with the essence of all matter, and we could take on different forms. This enabled us to move about on our pathways of exploration and to have many adventures, to quote one of your favorite words and past times. We came to your world to play. Unfortunately, many of our (voice becomes emotional and tearful) brothers and sisters forgot who they truly were and many have suffered so much."

"We have to move the voice up a little, for this channel needs to work on his vocal control. Some of our brothers, sisters, and families got lost and forgot their starry origins, not remembering who they really are. It is very important to us, and we have a strong special heartfelt wish to find and reconnect with our soul family. We all have a special connection as all soul families do. There are not so many on your planet, but you and Michael have known us before. This is why we are able to make this connection and speak through Michael."

"We have been magic wielders and magical explorers as we understand the workings of what you refer to as universal laws. We know how to use our mental powers to maneuver energy to create lots of beautiful things. We are also time walkers and explorers and know how to shift our awareness and maneuver our spirit body so that we can go to many places and visit our ET friends across the starry vast cosmos. One day earth people shall be able to do this again as well. We are very drawn to you. We will share our love and our light, for we have walked the lands of your world in many times past. In the changing times, you will be able to walk with us hand in hand as well."

"Could you say something about the importance of the sinus cavity?"

"The prana essence must move through the sinus cavity. They are very sensitive, and some people have so many problems because there is a blockage of flowing of this pranic energy. People do not know how to breathe in the air correctly, and the throat blocked energies affects the sinus movement. Certain sound exercises can help to free people from these sinus allergies and drainage problems and help heal infections. It is partly due to an improper use of blocked sound and movement of chords and tones. This is one reason why Michael's throat has bothered him and has been somewhat red and slightly irritated for many years."

"He does not have cancer or any disease, but there are energy blockages he has carried for many years and many life times, which need to be released. Michael has not sounded many of the sounds that he needs to sound. It would behoove many people of your world to have a *few screaming fits* to move the energies. This will be an area that you will be at liberty to work with. As you perform your sound healings, you are going to become immune to the dust and the pollen that would move around in the air about and around you. You are going to create a sound barrier to these negative energies that would block and constrict the movement."

"Is this helpful?"

"Yes. Thank you."

"Please let us know when it is time to stop. We do not wish to take up too much time. We are so very happy to come into your field of energy and vibration. At future discourses we will be able to perhaps elucidate upon the topic of *delirium states*. Many of your so-called insane crazies are very enlightened souls. Why do you think some of them scream and holler? (Her voice becomes stronger.) They are moving the sounds. They need (tearful) to be heard. (Her voice now is so emotional that the words seem stuck in her throat—each word struggling to present itself.) Our hearts hurt for our children—some who are locked away in solitary confinement. Many are misunderstood and have simply been abandoned. This is why Michael hurts at times and weeps for the misunderstood, abandoned ones. He often says that he will go to the local loony hospital and join his family."

"There are floors upon which the criminally insane dwell. If they had qualified healers and shamans to work with them with sound therapy, many of their inner woes and the voices that torture them could be silenced. We are getting emotional. This is not something that we do often. We know there is so much power in the voice and sound. Some of these unfortunate beloved children and family suffer so much. We must weep for our family. This is quite a display. Now your friend has had two cries in one month. What will he do when he hears this tape?"

"He has always been sensitive and compassionate to so-called crazy people. It was not by mistake that his mother spent time in mental hospitals. Michael was very attuned to sound even as a child. He was a sound healer even then. This is why he would sing with some of the patients when he visited his mother on the ward. He would also listen to them talk and to their songs. Some were remembering their lineage with us and would find themselves singing strange notes, words, and tones they had never heard before. This can happen when two familiar souls reunite. They feel like kindred souls to each other because they are. Their souls recognize each other, and they communicate with each other upon many planes."

"We imparted some of our energy and gave some of the tones and songs to Michael and his soul companions in the mental hospitals. Michael helped give them relief by listening to them talk and singing to them although he was not consciously aware of what he was doing. He did not need to be. His soul, which is connected to us, knew exactly what it was doing. That was partly why he was the only child out of five who would visit his mother and the other patients the most frequently in the mental hospitals. Just being in the presence of these soul companions was healing to all parties. All communication is not verbal nor is all energy exchange and healing conscious. Even your own Jesus the Christ had to periodically take leave of the people and go to the mountains for solitude to rejuvenate and replenish his energies."

"You can call Michael's hospital visits part of a soul mission he had agreed to fulfill before he was even born. And let us say that he is not done working with mental patients either. As he works through and heals more of his internal emotional pain, he will have so much more compassion and love to extend to others. There are many affective methods to move blocked energies and to gain access to the subconscious mind in order to locate the origins and roots of emotional pain, anger, and unresolved issues. Primal screaming therapy is one very useful, effective method."

"Many of your healers, teachers, therapists, and psychologists do not have the understanding needed to be able to bring about the healing that primal screaming therapy offers. It is so important to retrieve the soul pieces that have split off and fragmented due to trauma. Music and sound can help bring them back home to the person where parts of the soul have shattered. Is there anything you would wish to add or ask before we take leave?"

"No. I hope I will be able to tune into your energies. This feels like a very old connection and a very wonderful one, I might add."

"Yes, we are the ancient ones, and you feel our love and our depth, for you are a very deep soul dear to our hearts. This is why you have moved away from the conventional third-dimensional way of living that occupied your time for a number of years. You are moving past your role as psychotherapist into the role of spiritual therapist and healer. Our friends who are the lonely, forgotten ones touch your and Michael's hearts most profoundly. You both know on a soul level that you have been, how do we say, put away before, and it was because you were simply misunderstood."

"You did not share the ideas of what constituted correct and rightful behavior and living of the particular culture, and so you were banished and ostracized. Both of you share an interest in madness and the diverse mental states from neurosis to extreme psychosis, multiple personality syndrome, and schizophrenia. We could do an entire discourse upon the topic of schizophrenia and perhaps will at another time."

"We will be coming again to share with you. There is much work we could do together in a group type of setting. If you should wish to have a weekend workshop or what have you, we would be more than delighted to work with sound and to help people to learn to resonate to the various pitches and soul vibrations to heal their emotional, etheric, and spirit bodies. There are general sounds which provide healing energies and can help remove blockages, but there are also personal sounds that are in alignment with the soul and the throat chakra and voice of each individual. We could help the group discover these tones, which their soul will be more than delighted to have them discover and intone."

"In parting, we give you our blessings and our love as we sound and sign-off. Until we meet again. Lar a li ta. Lara lo. Lar a li ta. Lara lo. Lar a li ta. Lara lo. May these gentle sounds sway you into remembrance. We welcome you into our hearts, loving soul friends."

CLOSING THOUGHTS

The energy of the Delarians stayed with me for several days. It was as though part of my soul had merged with them, and I could feel them inside me. I found myself spontaneously singing and chanting to ground and balance my energies. I listened to the tape many times. The chanting style of communicating their messages particularly appealed to me. I received an in-pouring of healing energy each time I listened to the Delarians. As I pondered their concepts and ideas, I became even more bound and determined to heal my old hurts from childhood and past lives. I felt less alone when I remembered my new star friends, and sometimes I dreamt about them and went on spirit journeys with them.

The Delarians reminded me of our ancient roots from other planets, multiverses, or star systems. I believe that explains why some of us can feel so depressed and lonely to the point of despair. We miss our homes and often long to return there.

It is highly possible that Elizabeth, I, and others like us shall never be completely free of depression until our souls soar back to our starry homes. In the meantime, we shall seek out our star families. We shall share meals, stories, hopes, dreams, knowledge, information, and memories and derive much joy, satisfaction, and comfort from their love and company.

About the Author

Michael Dennis has both local and national Media Exposure. He has been featured on FOX and CBS TV. He was featured on the Jerry Springer Show in 1991, and has appeared on numerous Radio Shows. In April 2000 he completed a six month Psychic Radio Show for MOJO 94.9 F.M. in Cincinnati. He has also been featured on WAIF 88.3 a.m. and on WSAI 1530 a.m. where he makes guest radio appearances. He was interviewed in the 2000 Millennium Edition of The Cincinnati Enquirer, The Pittsburgh Tribune, March 2003 the Columbus Dispatch, April 2005 and the Dayton Daily News in May 2008 for his Mother Teresa Channeling. He has been working Psychic Festivals and Fairs since 1986 in the mid-west as well as in Toronto and Ottowa Canada. Michael is also a writer and his first book Halfway to Heaven was published in 2003. His book of love poetry Dawn's Kiss, will be coming out in the summer or Fall of 2009.

One of Michael's earliest PSYCHIC EXPERIENCES is when he was a subject of the renowned Mentalist, "The Amazing Kreskin" at an oudoor Hypnosis Demonstration in Chautauqua, NY in 1977. Kreskin told Michael that he was unusually sensitive and he encouraged him to develop his psychic abilities.

Over the next several years after college Michael trained extensively and apprenticed with various Metaphysical Teachers. **In 1985, Michael became a professional Psychic.** In 1995 he gave up a foreign language teaching career to pursue his writing dream, and Psychic work full time.

In 1992 Michael began to expand his psychic work by publicly channeling Ascended Masters, Angels, Native American Ancestors and Shamans (Voices Of Our Ancestors), Benevolent Extraterrestrials and well-known beloved celebrities. He has publicly channeled The Blessed Mother Mary, Kuan Yin, Mary Magdalene, Archangel Michael, Nostradamus, Ascended Masters St. Germain and Hilarion, St. Francis, Helen Keller, Montezuma II Aztec Emperor, Sun Bear, Native American Medicine Shamans (Voices Of Our Ancestors), Fun and Frolic with the Faeries and a Past Life Exploration channeling with Vilura of Venus. He channeled Mother Teresa in Dayton in May 2008. Michael has tapes of all his channelings and sells them for $5 plus postage. He has begun to transcribe the tapes for a book called Wisdom From Beyond.

Michael is based in Cincinnati, OH, but has a world-wide clientele for Telephone and Email Readings.

To reach Michael please call:

513-281-5696

email: paxomnis@aol.com or mike@mikethepsychic.com

website: www.mikethepsychic.com